2003

Handbook for the
Beginning Teacher

Handbook for the Beginning Teacher

An Educator's Companion

Courtney W. Moffatt
Edgewood College

Thomas L. Moffatt

Boston ■ New York ■ San Francisco
Mexico City ■ Montreal ■ Toronto ■ London ■ Madrid ■ Munich ■ Paris
Hong Kong ■ Singapore ■ Tokyo ■ Cape Town ■ Sydney

Executive Editor and Publisher: *Stephen D. Dragin*
Editorial Assistant: *Barbara Strickland*
Marketing Manager: *Tara Whorf*
Editorial-Production Service: *Omegatype Typography, Inc.*
Manufacturing Buyer: *Chris Marson*
Composition and Prepress Buyer: *Linda Cox*
Cover Administrator: *Kristina Mose-Libon*
Electronic Composition: *Omegatype Typography, Inc.*

For related titles and support materials, visit our online catalog at www.ablongman.com.

Between the time Website information is gathered and then published, some sites may have closed. Also, the transcription of URLs can result in unintentional typographical errors. The publisher would appreciate notification where these errors occur so that they may be corrected in subsequent editions. Thank you.

Library of Congress Cataloging-in-Publication Data

Moffatt, Courtney W.
    Handbook for the beginning teacher : an educator's companion / Courtney W. Moffatt, Thomas L. Moffatt.
        p.   cm.
    Includes bibliographical references (p.) and index.
    ISBN 0-205-34372-4 (alk. paper)
      1. First year teachers—Handbooks, manuals, etc. 2. Teaching—Handbooks, manuals, etc. I. Moffatt, Thomas L. II. Title.
LB2844.1.N4 M64 2003
371.1—dc21

                                                                        2002022753

Printed in the United States of America
10 9 8 7 6 5 4 3 2 1   07 06 05 04 03 02

Photos: pp. 3 and 11, Will Faller; p. 17, Michael Newman/PhotoEdit, Inc.: pp. 28, 55, 71, 79, and 86, Will Hart; and p. 42, Will Hart/PhotoEdit, Inc.

For Fred Brightbill, Trevor Helmick, and Ashley Helmick—
may they know the joy that they bring me.

Contents

Preface

In a 2001 interview with writer Lyric Wallwork Winik, Laura Bush remarked on the importance of teaching: "All of us remember a teacher who changed our lives. I think teaching is like a calling because it is very hard. The people who complain about giving teachers the summer off ought to spend a couple of hours in a school trying to teach 30 kids. Really good teachers are the ones who accept the challenge that teaching offers" (Winik, 2001, p. 4). We have met hundreds of dedicated individuals who are up to that challenge and we applaud them. Bush, in another interview, recalled her difficulties as a new teacher starting in the classroom decades ago. She proceeded to degrade her college preparation for the everyday task of teaching reading at the second- and third-grade level. She continued to say that she hoped to work with college and university education departments to "really beef up" their teacher training programs.[1]

She further suggested that teachers who find themselves unprepared should let their former professors know: "I want to encourage teachers to write back to their teacher preparation programs and say, 'These things were really valuable and these things weren't.'"[2]

It is not our purpose to degrade departments of education and their preparation of future teachers. Teachers in schools across the United States are better educated and informed than ever before. However, in the many interviews we conducted with both experienced teachers and teachers just entering the profession, we found that teachers are frustrated with the difficult task of trying to set up their own classrooms and meet the extremely varied needs of their students. The challenges facing educators today are greater than ever. Therefore, teachers need as much information, training, and support as possible to face the growing diversity of cultures, academic needs, and student abilities in the classroom. We have addressed those needs in *Handbook for the Beginning Teacher* by providing practical recommendations, theoretical information, and useful resources. Chapter One discusses preparing for the start of school by using the Countdown Calendar, which provides a detailed schedule for planning for a successful year. Chapters Two and Three address classroom techniques for developing effective methodology and establishing good communication with students. Chapters Four and Five provide strategies for creating a safe classroom environment and dealing with typical behavior problems. Chapter Six discusses inclusion and offers techniques for handling students with distinct abilities and special needs. Chapter Seven discusses grading and assessment, and Chapter

---

[1]G. Toppo, "Laura Bush to Help Train Teachers," *Detroit News*, July 27, 2001, available at detnews.com/2001/schools/0107/29/schools-255931.htm.

[2]Ibid.

Eight offers tips on dealing with school administrators and other political concerns. Chapter Nine contains reviews of numerous software and book-form teaching aids, providing valuable information that will help you assess and choose materials that will be best suited for your students.

More practical help can be found in the two appendixes. Appendix A provides several classroom activities and games for enhancing communication, building students' self-esteem, increasing concentration skills, and other important teaching goals. Appendix B provides 100 Teacher Resources such as forms, letters, checklists, and so on. These resources are an invaluable aid to new teachers. To strengthen the pedagogical aspect of this text, the Teacher Resources are linked to the discussion throughout the text. Whenever a topic relating to one of the Teacher Resources is discussed, an icon like the one here appears in the margin directing the reader to the location of the accompanying Teacher Resource.

With the support and encouragement of our editor and publisher we have attempted to fill the gap between the formal education future teachers receive in teacher preparation programs and the everyday problems that the new classroom teacher will experience. We hope we have, to some degree, accomplished our purpose in this workbook.

ACKNOWLEDGMENTS

Because this book was designed to help teachers in their first year, we are indebted to all the teachers who shared with us their experiences and frustrations in their beginning teaching experiences as well as their entire careers in the classroom. Many, many teachers were willing to give up their time to help us understand the needs they see in schools today. Many thanks to all of them.

We also thank our families for the hours they did without us as we researched, wrote, and collaborated on this material. Their understanding and patience is very much appreciated.

Many others earned our gratitude, especially those individuals who helped us by reviewing the material and giving us suggestions in so many areas. Special thanks are due to Mary Paynter, O.P., Ph.D., for her guidance in the areas of English and education. She was so very generous with her time and her encouragement. We thank reviewer Ellen Browning of Edgewood College for reading, evaluating, and improving the text with her helpful and positive suggestions. She has been a constant source of support and kindness for the past 7 years. We also thank Andrea Kenny, Edgewood College Reference Librarian, for her persistent assistance with our references.

Steve Dragin, Executive Editor and Publisher, also deserves special thanks for his contribution. He developed the idea for the book and encouraged us with a gentle hand and much humor throughout the endeavor. The professionals at Allyn and Bacon also are much appreciated, especially Barbara Strickland, Editorial Assistant, for her help and continual vigilance. Our appreciation goes to Dona Biederman of Omegatype Typography, Inc., for the knowledge, time, and energy she put toward improving our manuscript.

Last but not least, our continued amazement and appreciation for all the children in our lives who make education such a wonderful career and life a continually exciting mystery.

Introduction

It was the first day of school and nothing was ready. The class list was sketchy as was everything else about the job except the gossip. The secretary was very helpful in this area, but no other. She could not resist spreading the gory details about all the students and their families. One student assigned to me had been skipped up a grade because the middle school did not want him. One boy brought bullets to school last year, without a gun, and the school was ready and eager to kick him out of school again this year, before he even entered the door of the school. Another was said to have a great fondness for explosives. I had a list of students provided to me by the district, but it was not clear where they would be when school began, whether in regular classes or in my special education room all day.

I was the new teacher for students at the high school level who had learning disabilities and emotional disturbances. My list of 18 students contained 17 males. As a 5-foot, 2-inch female, I was viewed by some of the staff as the one who needed her head examined. My one female was newly referred, had never been tested, but had been failing in school for the past 2 years, since she had moved into the district, though no one had any idea why.

As a new and inexperienced teacher, working with students only 4–8 years my junior, I was unprepared and had no idea where to start. I was unsure of the role I would play in the school and confused about how I could effect a positive influence on the lives of my students and the other teachers in the school. At the time I was too naive and timid to ask for or even demand the information I needed to make effective plans for my students' education. Fortunately, as time went on I would learn and eventually develop programs and curricula to meet each student's intense and varied needs.

Unfortunately, I wasted valuable time figuring out how to get started and how the school system worked. Looking back, I now see that there was a better way to begin. First of all, I could have gotten a much earlier start. Long before school began, I could have evaluated the students' files and interviewed the students' past and present teachers, guidance counselors, principals, and parents. I could have initiated contact with the students themselves before they came to school so that I would have a better understanding of their needs. Preparation before the students entered the school building on the first day of school could have saved them and me so much time and energy. I wish you much greater success.

Preparing Your Classroom for a Successful Year:
The Teacher's Countdown Calendar

- Twelve Months before School Starts
- Eight Months before School Starts
- Six Months before School Starts
- Four Months before School Starts
- Three Months before School Starts
- Two Months before School Starts
- One Month before School Starts

- Two Weeks before School Starts
- Two Days before School Starts
- One Day before School Starts
- Day 1!
- Day 2
- Day 3
- The Second Week of School

■ *What Matters*

*One hundred years from now,
It will not matter what kind of
car I drove, what kind of house
I lived in, how much I had in my
bank account, nor what my
clothes looked like. But the
world may be a little better
Because I was important in the
life of a child.*

—Author Unknown

The key to developing a successful classroom is trusting your students and being very well prepared. If having your own classroom is a new venture for you or if you have taught before but are beginning to teach in a new area, this chapter can make your task easier by jogging your memory and perhaps helping you think about some things you have forgotten to do.

TWELVE MONTHS BEFORE SCHOOL STARTS (AUGUST)

If you are a college student or an individual who wants to return to teaching who is not presently employed in teaching, you need to begin developing your résumé and gathering information that will help you as a teacher and help sell you as a teacher to a school district or private school.

Start thinking about where you might enjoy working and then research the schools and areas of your interest. You might decide to do a practicum or volunteer work in the schools you like best and where you feel your skills will be the best match. If you are in education classes, talk to the people you meet in class about the different schools and school systems they have information about and learn all you can.

EIGHT MONTHS BEFORE SCHOOL STARTS (JANUARY)

At this time you should have a résumé developed and you should be applying for jobs in the areas you researched. Remember that you will be very busy if you are in your student teaching semester, so have your job file completed now at your college, university, or wherever you choose to keep it. Be sure you have letters of recommendation in this file. To get good letters of recommendation, you need to ask the college professors and teachers you have worked with whether they would feel comfortable recommending you. If they agree, send them a copy of your résumé or an outline of some of your achievements in teaching to use as a guide for their letter and to remind them about your skills and interests. Include a stamped, addressed envelope in which to send the letter to your placement office or wherever you need it sent. A sample request letter is provided to give you ideas. Professors at teacher training institutions get many requests of this sort and may not be able to return letters immediately. Therefore, send them early enough that you do not have to ask them to rush on top of the favor of writing you a letter. Many professors do not work in the summer, and just as many teachers don't, so do not wait until the summer to make this request.

1.1, p. 125

SIX MONTHS BEFORE SCHOOL STARTS (MARCH)

Hopefully by this time you are writing to different school districts asking for the opportunity to interview for a job. As you are interviewing, you can further research the schools where you will be interviewing. You can also start developing your classroom management system, even if you do not know the exact school or even area in which you will teach. This will help you in the interview process and will give you a head start in preparing for the upcoming year of teaching in your own classroom. You can begin by writing down the answers to these classroom management questions: What behavior do I want? What behavior must I have from every student? What behavior can I *not* accept?

1.2, p. 126

Begin by mapping out what rules you will have for your classroom; how you will teach students to behave appropriately in your classroom, during lecture, during independent work time, during group work, during free time; and how you will teach students to treat adults and each other with respect. (Your classroom management system can be firmed up once you are hired and you know more specifics about your school and your students.)

The key to good teaching is good organization. I strongly recommend having a special file cabinet, organized alphabetically by topic, to keep materials you are gathering for your own classroom. This is an excellent way to organize the ideas you are learning from your classroom experiences and from watching others teach. Save lesson plans and unit plans as well as other students' material and notes about ways to improve them. If you find interesting materials in catalogues remember to save these catalogues with the pages flagged as you may need them in the future for ordering.

FOUR MONTHS BEFORE SCHOOL STARTS (MAY)

By this time you have probably been hired or are about to be hired. Contact the school office and get a copy of the school or district handbook as soon as you accept a job. Read this cover to cover and learn all you can about district policies and procedures. Then contact the school guidance counselor to discuss the school schedule, politics, parent support, and school support services such as ESL (English as a Second Language) and special education services. If you teach at a grade school or middle school, you also need to find out when your students are in their special classes, art, music, and PE. If you teach at a high school, you need to check your schedule for flow. Are your classes paced well, do you have many students who need extra help all in one class with no assistance and very few in another class where you would have time to give students extra help? Think about what would be ideal for the students, keeping in mind your human limitations, and go from there.

See whether the principal can spare some time to help guide you in your planning. If you are new in the district, inquire about obtaining a mentor on staff to help direct you and answer your questions. You may also find an individual willing to give you the names and home telephone numbers of teachers you will be working with in the fall. After meeting with a mentor and contacting your associates, you are ready to map out your curriculum. Remember you need to think about your curriculum in terms not only of the average students but also of the students who are moving faster and those moving slower through the curriculum. As you are studying the curriculum, check what skills are taught in the grades or classes students take before and after you teach your students. Every district should have a curriculum guide in each school as well as in the district office.

THREE MONTHS BEFORE SCHOOL STARTS (JUNE)

Visit the classroom in which you will be teaching. Carefully review the space and the materials that already exist in the room. When teachers leave a classroom, it is not unusual for other teachers to borrow coveted furniture and materials from the exiting teacher. It is helpful to make a list of furniture, supplies, and teaching materials to claim as your own and to discern what needs to be ordered. If this is too difficult, you can always bring in name tags or address labels and put them on the materials you want to keep in your room. Introduce yourself to the custodians if you have not yet met them, and obtain equipment repair request forms. This is a good time to check all desks, chairs, tables, cupboards, bookshelves, clocks, pencil sharpeners, and so on, and request any repairs that may be needed.

Consider requesting carpeting for your classroom if it does not already exist. This will make your room more comfortable and quieter. However, some students are allergic to the glue often used to tack down commercial carpet, so it must be installed at least 2 or 3 weeks before school starts.

Evaluate classroom lighting. If you have fluorescent lighting, does it flicker? This can interfere with students' concentration and has been reported to increase episodes of epilepsy in individuals who have this condition. Ask your custodians to change the tube. Evidence has shown that fluorescent lighting also adversely affects individuals with attention deficit disorder. Some teachers unscrew every other fluorescent light in their classroom to cut down on any adverse affects.

Find out how to control the classroom's heat and air. It is nice to know now whether either of the systems is deficient so you can have it fixed. It may be impossible for you to check the heat in your classroom in the summer, but perhaps you can ask the teacher who had your classroom last year so that you can get a jump on doing something to solve any problems.

Order supplies for your classroom. Be sure you have enough books and supplies for the number of students on your class lists plus two or three extras. When ordering materials, you need to know the following details of the product: the company, the address and phone number, the purchase order number (which you can probably get from the school secretary), the quantity needed, and the cost.

If you will be buying any materials independently, it is important to find out the school's reimbursement policy and to get your school's tax-exempt number. Businesses are usually happy to sell educational materials without tax, but you will first need to supply them with your district's tax-exempt number.

Check computer equipment and AV equipment. You may not be able to order more computers for your classroom, but you can get what you have in good working order and begin foraging for more among businesses and friends if you feel you need them. Don't forget to check and order any necessary software and teaching programs for your computers. If you are like most individuals, you might need to brush up on the use of computers in the classroom. Many districts offer computer courses or are willing to pay for professional computer courses for their teachers. Ask your principal for information about availability and reimbursement.

If you teach at a grade school, you may still be able to talk to the special teachers you have not yet met. Introduce yourself and find out when your students are in their rooms.

TWO MONTHS BEFORE SCHOOL STARTS (JULY)

By now you may have access to your class lists. If so, check the permanent files on all your students, gathering information that may help you understand them and their individual needs. These files should be available through your school office. You will probably be required to sign for each file that you take out of the office. Gather information on each student and store in a separate folder in your home. Some of the information you hear or read may be misleading or even untrue, so beware of believing everything. However, you can better serve your students by having some prior information about them.

Don't forget to check each student's medical information. Look for anything that might interfere with a child's ability to learn and anything that could be a medical problem, such as allergies and chronic illnesses. Check records of the children's vision and hearing test results to determine whether they need to be placed in a special location in your room during instruction, or whether they have difficulties hearing you among the background noises of a typical classroom. Also check whether they are on any medications you should know about and whether these medications are typically delivered at school. You need information on the individuals who have prescribed the child's medication and how you can reach them. You also need release forms so that you can talk to these individuals.

As soon as you have the names, addresses, and phone numbers of your students you can make address labels on the computer for all of them. Run multiple copies of theses labels and send out a parent/child newsletter introducing yourself, announcing your excitement at getting to know them, and describing some of the highpoints of what you want to do in the upcoming school year.

At this time, perhaps with the help of the guidance counselor or your mentor teacher, develop your classroom schedule. Schedules give students a sense of security and help you plan and cover information and skills in a smooth and academically sound manner. Without careful planning of how to achieve your goals, you are very unlikely to reach them. Give this plan to any volunteers or educational assistants that will be working in your room, as well as to any special education teachers with whom you have students in common. If you have students with special needs, especially students who have difficulty with change, they may benefit from reviewing the schedule before they begin school.

ONE MONTH BEFORE SCHOOL STARTS (AUGUST)

After your introductory newsletter has been received, it is very helpful to you and to your students for you to contact the students and their families to begin to develop a bond. You can reassure students about the upcoming school year and discuss with parents any concerns they may have about their children, the school, and/or your curriculum.

Visit the custodians to ensure that your classroom has had all major repairs completed, including any painting, floor waxing, or carpet cleaning or installation so that you can begin arranging your classroom for the upcoming school year. Politely inform them that you would like to set up your room. Remember you will need their help and cooperation throughout the school year. They may help you rearrange furniture or direct you to dollies so you can move things around without damaging the floor or hurting your back.

The classroom you teach in is your environment for the year, so make it enjoyable to be in. It will also be the students' environment or home away from home, so make it a room students feel a part of. Do not decorate every part of the room the minute school begins because that will diminish students' feeling of ownership of the space. It is best to use space for educational material and leave other discretionary space for the students in your class to decorate. This is more difficult in a high school or even middle school where you or the students may need to move from room to room, but if you are in a classroom for the entire day, you can give different spaces in the room to different classes.

Begin by placing desks or tables around the room for student seating. It is not advisable to place students' desks in groups because you do not yet know the dynamics of the classroom, such as which students need to be placed by themselves for optimum productivity. Give each student a permanent desk or table of his or her own. Students seem to feel most comfortable when they have their own space. Even in adult meetings or repetitive gatherings where seating is not assigned, individuals usually choose a space and return to it each time they enter the space. If you want to group students' desks in pairs or fours, you may do this later in the year when you know students better. (Students who are older usually like to be given the autonomy to choose their own seating. You can assure concerned students that, once you learn their names, they can earn the privilege of choosing their own places.)

Organize different areas in your classroom. You need spaces for detailed work, for independent reading, and for group work, as well as a place for your desk where you can observe all students with easy access back and forth. (Your desk should not be placed in front of the door.) Movement is very important in the classroom. The area for quiet work should be away from the traffic pattern and away from the distractions of the classroom door and the hall. It is also important that each student have a cubbyhole or in-class box in which to keep personal classroom materials. This helps eliminate confusion and students coming to class without class materials.

The class schedule and classroom rules should be posted in a prominent place where all students can see them. Post classroom procedures such as emergency evacuation, medical emergency procedures, attendance, absence and tardy procedures, and classroom jobs. Also important are procedures for leaving the room for the bathroom, library research, or for special help. Save a space in your room for student work to be displayed. Show students that you value and admire all their work and let them choose which work to display. Double-check books, supplies, audiovisual equipment, and computers, and assure yourself that all outlets are in good working order.

The room number should be plainly visible on your classroom door. Your name and/or your class name should also be easy to see. Distinguish your door with some visual element that can be recognized from a distance. Some students many not find your room as easily as others; consider those that have poor vision or have problems with reading, spatial perception, or directions.

TWO WEEKS BEFORE SCHOOL STARTS (AND COUNTING)

Try to meet with classroom aides or teacher assistants assigned to you, perhaps with an offer to take them to lunch. Once you have told them how much you look forward to working with them and appreciate their help, you can begin discussing classroom duties. It is helpful to find out what their perceptions of their tasks are before assigning them to any responsibilities. More information about effective communication is discussed in Chapter 3.

Develop a classroom clipboard with a list of students' names on it and any important information you need to teach them better. Keep your soon-to-be-developed seating chart on the clipboard so that you can easily see who is where and begin to learn students' names. Keeping a copy of your class list on this clipboard can also help you tally students' responses. It is helpful to have an easy system for collecting data on student participation, such as which students are asking and answering questions in class and which are not. Review this daily. Your clipboard should also have a section on classroom modifications for regular students and students with exceptional educational needs (EEN) so that you can double-check that you are doing things correctly and meeting each student's needs as you are teaching. Finally, make a list of things you need to do and keep it on the clipboard as well. The list can be prioritized with these categories: do today, do this week, do this year, and do next year.

TWO DAYS BEFORE SCHOOL STARTS

Check with school support staff and discuss students' special needs with appropriate personnel. If students have exceptional educational needs (EEN), ask to see their individualized education program (IEP). Make note of their individual goals and classroom modifications. Find out when they are and are not in your classroom. Develop a classroom seating chart. This will help you learn student names and keep track of their attendance. Keep this chart on your classroom clipboard.

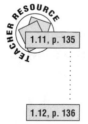

Begin introducing yourself to every individual in the school, including lunchroom personnel and secretarial/office personnel. As the school year continues, try to get to know every teacher and staff member in the school. Their support is essential to your success. Be prepared with a detailed outline of your first day of class. See the checklist in Teacher Resource 1.12 in Appendix B.

ONE DAY BEFORE SCHOOL STARTS

Don't leave anything important until the day before school starts. Leave this day open for all the last-minute things you may find to do. This is the day when other teachers are running around in a panic, and this will probably affect you, making it difficult for you to get anything done.

Visualize how you want your first day to go. Then, look at your first day of school checklist (Teacher Resource 1.12), and check off each item that is adequately prepared.

DAY 1!

Plan to come to school at least 15–30 minutes early. Be ready to delight with your students and their parents in this new beginning. Welcome each student personally and then as a group into your classroom. Let students know that your classroom exists for all of them and that together you need to make it a comfortable and welcoming space for all.

Discuss classroom rules and procedures. Review procedures each time a procedure needs to be implemented during the first week of school. Review rules daily as well. Point out the area of the room where students can go if they need to readjust their mood.

Also describe to students how to get from your classroom to the office, their lockers, the nurse's office, the library, the lunchroom, the bathroom, and the parking lot. If lunch is after your class, you can tell students that you will be going to the lunchroom and you are happy to show them the way. Some students learn much better by doing than by hearing directions. It is very helpful for some students if you arrange for them to walk with someone else to all the places they need to be during the first week of school. However, this should be done discreetly and tactfully, without blatantly singling out anyone, or it should be done for the whole class.

DAY 2

A good way to start off the second day is to ask students how their first day went. Although some students are afraid to speak up in a large group, some students will answer. Their participation lessens the strain and lightens the mood for everyone.

Today is a good day to help students get to know you and each other. This is the time to use your ice-breaking activities. Students need to begin interacting with each other so they can feel comfortable working and learning together. While facilitating these ice-breaking activities, a good teacher can also remind students of the rules of cooperative learning and review social skills that will serve them in all aspects of their life.

Remember to review important procedures and ask students what other information they may need to make their school day easier. Do not forget to explain to your students the school's hidden curriculum—the information about the school social environment that is not usually explained to them. This information concerns how to negotiate nonacademic school social time, such as what to do when you arrive at school before the bell and where to go after you finish your lunch. Some kids learn how to conduct themselves by doing, but other students, especially those children who have a difficult time making friends, seem to have to learn these school social behaviors the hard way, by the mistakes they make. As a teacher you can find the answers to these questions of social behavior and review them with your class so that everyone knows where to go and what to do during nonacademic school social time.

DAY 3

Now that school has been in session for 3 days, you can assign a short and fun homework project, preferably one that can somehow involve significant others in the student's life—be that a parent, grandparent, boss, or family friend. Be sure you give students the opportunity to use anyone for this project, not just their parents, as not all students have parents, or the luxury of daily access to parents. Before assigning homework, discuss your homework procedures: when homework is due, where it should be turned in, how it will be graded, where and how the work will be recorded, how and when it will be returned to students, what happens to corrected work that contains mistakes, and how late homework is treated. Students need to know all these procedures. (See the form in Teacher Resource 1.15 in Appendix B.)

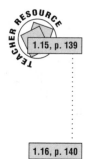

Give a copy of this information to students and have them take it to their parents or guardians to sign it. Let students know that they will receive extra points when the form is returned. Make note of any homework information sheets that do not get returned. Call the student's parents or guardians to find out what the home situation is in case the student is having family problems and needs community assistance. This would be a good time to send out a Family/Community Resource Form (see Teacher Resource 1.16 in Appendix B). Parents are a very important part of a child's academic life. Their support and the support of the community are crucial to the child's success. Getting their cooperation and information can help you extend learning resources to the homes and communities in which your students live.

THE SECOND WEEK OF SCHOOL

In the second week of school you will need to have an understanding of the basic skills of all your students. No matter what age or grade level you teach, having knowledge of each student's basic reading and writing level is helpful. Therefore, whether your task is to teach reading or writing, you will be able to judge the appropriateness of giving any reading assignment, writing assignment, or test to any student in your class. Chances are excellent that your textbook will be too easy for some students and too difficult for others. If you have students who are in special education, you will probably have a documented reading and writing level for the child. But often, other students have academic challenges not yet discovered. Even one student who slips between the cracks is too many.

An especially good way to gauge your students' abilities is to have each student develop an individual portfolio. This portfolio may include a tape of a student reading, an essay to demonstrate writing progress, or perhaps a short research paper to use as a baseline for future progress. This is also a nice way to grade students and help them to begin to evaluate their own work. (See Chapter 7 for more information about portfolios.) It is very important to pretest students on the material you will be introducing in the next few weeks. After pretesting students, you can arrange skill groups for teaching students the specific skill they will need in each area of your curriculum. (See Chapter 2 for more information about methodology.)

If you have been able to come this far, you have accomplished a great deal and are on your way to a wonderful and fulfilling school year. Students should be getting comfortable with you and with each other now, and their academic skills, seemingly forgotten over the summer, are now returning. The most important things you can do now are to remain well organized and stay positive. Hopefully, the Teacher's Countdown Calendar has made you feel more secure in getting ready. Enjoy your students, and they will appreciate your efforts in the months to come.

2

Where to Start to Develop My Own Methodology

The aim of education should be to teach us rather how to think, than what to think.

—*James Beattie*

■ Pretesting Student Skills

■ Getting Help

■ Facilitating Learning through Effective Instruction

■ Motivating Students

■ Self-Evaluation

Dear Mr. Duren,

Thank you for such a wonderful year in Environmental Studies. I have learned a lot and think it has changed me as a person for the better. Very few teachers have had this great an impact on me. I would like to thank you for being one of them.

Sincerely,

Trevor

PRETESTING STUDENT SKILLS

As the children entering our classrooms become increasingly diverse, we as teachers need to become increasingly able facilitators of learning. Not only are teachers expected to teach to a wider range of student abilities, but they are also given an increasingly large quantity of topics to cover. The days of teaching only reading, writing, and arithmetic are long gone.

It might be profitable to realize when teaching large groups that everyone's skills are not equal. Therefore, you might be a more effective teacher if you divide the group by skills and teach only those skills that are needed. Groups are only effective if they are constantly fluctuating. Once students master the skills you want them to learn from the chapter or unit, they should be free to move into different skill groups. This is not a grouping like the old reading groups many of us are familiar with, but rather a flowing group of skill sets developed with the needs of the students in mind.

The only way teachers will be able to teach such a wide range of class abilities is by increasingly individualizing learning. We can no longer assume that a one-size-fits-all curriculum will fit our diverse experience, ability, and skill classrooms. It seems the very phenomena that make our classrooms increasingly rich environments also make our jobs more difficult.

So how do we start the process of individualizing instruction? By finding out in greater detail than ever before exactly what each of our students needs to learn. The only way to do this is through a system of constant assessment. Before you get frustrated and give up on this idea, let me say that by assessment I do not mean for you to be giving students formal tests all the time. Instead I mean that you need to find more efficient and easier ways to keep track of each student's progress.

Fortunately the tests are already available. Most curricula provide tests that accompany materials and these are a good place to start. Therefore, teachers can get in the habit of giving pretests, or posttests if no pretest exists, before teaching a chapter or unit. You may think that students do not like the extra testing, but most students prefer having the opportunity to avoid monotonous work in areas in which they already have skill and understanding. Tests are not the only way to assess present skill level. Competency can also be gauged through homework or work samples. Having students save their work in a portfolio may make assessment even easier. If a student in English Composition is being evaluated on her ability to write a good paragraph, one look at her latest composition would probably show the English teacher that she does know how to write a good paragraph. It would also give this teacher a good idea of what the student does not know.

So now what? You divide your students into groups by their needs, for example, one group for which your unit is too easy, one group for which the unit is too hard, and one group for which the unit fits fairly well. First consider the group of students who already know what you are about to teach. Can you imagine the agony of having to spend 2 or 3 weeks hearing all about something you already know? No wonder students fall asleep in class. (That's if the teacher is lucky. If he or she isn't lucky, the student may find other, more creative things to do with themselves that may not fit in with the lesson plans at all.) Usually more than one student in the class fits this circumstance. These students do not want or need to spend time on skills they've already mastered. Instead of giving these students an opportunity to entertain themselves in a negative way, thus disrupting other students and not learning anything of value to them because they are bored and unmotivated, a wiser course is to work with them to find material that challenges them.

Now consider the students who come very close to demonstrating they know the material. In 2 to 3 days they could be in the passed-on group. It makes sense to give them the chance to learn the entire chapter or unit or topic now that they are motivated to join the students doing something else. For other students this chapter or topic is just about right, given they receive special attention for the parts of the material that are extra difficult for them. These students will profit from the traditional teaching most of us were taught to give them.

Unfortunately some students in your class probably are not yet ready for this information because they have not yet mastered the prerequisite skills. Consider moving back to more appropriate work for these students, and you will save yourself hours of discipline and behavior problems that result as students become overwhelmed and give up in sadness, frustration, and anger.

Simply grouping students by skills and interests can go a long way to helping you better meet students' needs and better manage the classroom, but at this point you can see that having more than one teacher would be really helpful. What options might you have for additional assistance?

GETTING HELP

How can you go about getting assistance that isn't already assigned to you? One way is to work with other teachers who teach the same subjects you teach. By evaluating all students before teaching, you can divide the task of preparing and presenting different levels of material. Another way is to inquire whether special education staff have materials or time to help teach students who are having trouble. All schools should have in their employ individuals who are directed to work with gifted and talented children. If not, you could call the parents of these children and discuss ways of finding individuals who might help oversee and challenge the group. In either case, you might find some individuals interested in working with or helping you design materials for your most skilled students.

Your next task is keeping straight who has mastered which skill and who has not. By having students keep track of their own learning, students become more motivated. What better time to teach students responsibility for their own learning than right now? (Student management techniques are discussed later in this book.)

FACILITATING LEARNING THROUGH EFFECTIVE INSTRUCTION

2.2, p. 144

2.3, p. 145

Once children are assigned to their skill group, they need effective instruction. No lesson should begin until the instructor has gained the students' attention. Signal the children when you are about to begin. Present information clearly and in the simplest way possible. Teach information in short sessions of no more than 5–10 minutes. Then stop and allow children to apply what you have taught them to make it their own. Give students opportunities to use what they learn and evaluate their understanding for themselves. Practice does no good if a student is practicing doing something incorrectly, so check for understanding to ensure that children are correctly practicing what you have just presented. Encourage students to elaborate their answers to help them see where else the new learning could go. Teach and reteach students until the information or skill is firmly implanted before moving on to something new. Review skills often, emphasizing what is most important for their life and why.

When you finish a lesson or topic and want students to switch activities, use a signal to let students know that you have new instructions. For example, some teachers turn off the lights when students need to stop what they are doing and listen to instructions about the next activity. Some teachers raise one finger to their mouth, the symbol for quiet, when they want to give instructions. As students see the symbol, they become quiet and put a finger in front of their mouth. Soon the entire class is quiet without the teacher having to say a word, and the class is ready to hear instructions for the next activity. The whole class can easily be prepared to receive important information this way. Remember, some students have trouble transitioning from one activity to another, so they may find it especially helpful to be notified ahead of time that important information and a transition are coming.

According to the research good teachers routinely use many procedures that make their teaching highly effective. Good teachers have a signal for their class when they are about to begin. They begin only after gaining the students' attention. They present information clearly and in the simplest way possible, teach in short sessions, and allow students to apply what they have been taught to make it their own.

Effective teachers also provide children with constant feedback, check constantly for student understanding, and acknowledge and elaborate students' responses. They teach and reteach until the information or skill is implanted. Using new methods, various examples, or alternate procedures, effective teachers give all students the opportunity to learn many worthwhile skills. Students who do not understand are not pushed through the material. Instead, good teachers find ways to make the topic interesting and valuable for the student. The best teachers review skills often, emphasizing what is most important. They know their students well and prepare their students for times of transition by informing them of upcoming changes in routine.

MOTIVATING STUDENTS

One of the greatest complaints of teachers today is students lacking the motivation to learn. However, this need not be an overwhelming barrier to learning. Teachers can do many things to help increase their students' motivation to learn, such as giving students work that is at the appropriate level, that relates to their real life, or that touches their imagination. You can also motivate students by building on past information and bringing parents and community into the school.

The greatest motivation a student can have to do academic work is knowing the assigned work is something they can accomplish. If the assignments you give students are at the appropriate level, they will be more willing and eager to attempt them. Therefore, you must maintain students' trust by thoroughly understanding their skills and abilities. This can only be accomplished through continual assessment of students' present level of functioning in all areas (as discussed earlier). (Remember, assessment does not necessarily mean administering a standardized test. It can mean observing which skills each student needs to learn and listening to what each student tells you about his or her needs.)

Students are also more motivated to attempt academic work that is meaningful to their life. To make students' coursework more valuable to them, it is most important to choose activities that relate to real-life skills. Every time you ask students to learn something new you should ask yourself, How can I adapt the learning of this skill to my students' previous knowledge? Ask whether this skill will be useful to students 5, 10, and 20 years down the road. Only if you have positive answers to these questions can you feel confident that what you are teaching is meaningful.

Teachers have reported that using imaginative activities with their students can be especially motivating. Children especially like activities that relate to a fantasy world where extraordinary things take place. Through this world children can experience life's ups and downs vicariously. They can also work through frustrations and desires safely without upsetting their normal routines. By giving children a fun arena to explore, their schoolwork can become much less routine and boring for them.

Any arena that draws on class interests can be used to develop a setting in which learning skills makes sense to children. By finding a topic your class enjoys studying, such as dinosaurs, you can guide them to learn skills they need throughout their lives. Students who are allowed to choose the topic will feel that what they study is relevant to them and will not be so unhappy and bored with school. In most cases, personally picking a topic also makes learning more concrete for children, and, therefore, skills are easier to learn.

2.10, p. 153

Students seem to be more motivated to complete academic tasks when their curiosity is piqued. By giving the learner surprising or interesting facts or by presenting material with an unexpected outcome, students may become interested in an area they would not normally find appealing. Teachers who take the time to make their subject interesting are more likely to catch the attention of their students, thereby teaching their students more effectively. (Also, when teachers themselves find a topic interesting, it is much easier to share that interest and enthusiasm with their students.)

Another way to increase student motivation is to empower their own efforts to learn. Students like to feel they have some control over themselves, their environment, and their learning. By giving students some choices in their education, such as the time, broad topics, order, and assessment of their learning, we can increase their motivation and improve their learning outcomes.

Students are often motivated to learn something when they see the relationships between old information and new. Information is much easier to process when it can be linked with something already understood. Children learn with much less effort when connections are made between the concepts presented and past information covered.

One barrier to learning for some students is the lack of parental involvement in their education. Parents all have unique skills and they can contribute to the educational system in many different ways. Parents can serve as assistants in the classroom. They can help prepare materials for the class. They can help students with their academics by tutoring and assisting children that need extra help or further explanation. They can share with the class their areas of expertise or arrange for people they know to come in and share their expertise. (One little boy brought his great-grandfather to class during a history lesson on World War II because his great-grandfather had been a pilot in the war. The children were very interested in this man's perspective, and the little boy was proud to have his great-grandfather involved with his class.) Parents can also be involved in the school through advisory boards.

If parents cannot come to school, perhaps students can go into the community and see what their parents do on the job. Parents could facilitate work internships for students who are looking for job-skill development. Or they could chaperone or help develop a field trip to a community site that would be valuable for the class. Field trips require good organization but when done well can be highly enjoyable for all involved—teachers, parents, and children. (Use the checklist provided in Teacher Resource 2.11 in Appendix B to help you organize the trip.)

2.11, p. 154

With school budgets tightening, many school districts no longer provide free bus transportation for field trips. Increased concern about liability and lawsuits makes many teachers fear the risks involved in taking students away from the school. Scheduling a field trip for individual classrooms is usually fairly simple because only one teacher is involved. However, arranging trips in secondary schools is far more difficult due to the short class periods. Sometimes students' other teachers are uncooperative and impose stiff penalties on students for missing their class for another teacher's field trip. If this is the case, you may need assistance in helping students make choices about the trip or find substitute work to present to the teacher concerned. Students should not find themselves caught between two teachers' wills. As adults, teachers need to leave power struggles outside the school building.

SELF-EVALUATION

We all need to be setting goals for ourselves and evaluating our progress toward those goals. As a new teacher you will want to have specific and general goals for yourself against which you can measure your progress. By participating in ongoing assessment of your teaching, you can keep a record of your progress to encourage yourself and to provide to those in your administration who also are evaluating you. It is wise to set up a specific conference time for midterm and year-end evaluation of your teaching experience before you even start your first day. Keep a record of all your evaluations. Invite the principal to come to your classroom and observe you, as well as teachers whom you respect who teach with you and know your subject area.

2.12, p. 155

2.13, p. 157

The factors listed in Teacher Resource 2.9 (in Appendix B) have been judged by university faculty and practicing teachers to be important to the success of teachers. Grade yourself on how well you do in each area. After evaluating yourself on the Effective Teaching Checklist (Teacher Resource 2.9), consider what goals you can set for improving your teaching in the next month, semester, and year. Set your goals to be evaluated at the end of the month and paste them in your calendar or teacher's planning book. Any weaknesses you have can be conquered if you have a plan for correcting them.

Good Communication: The Hallmark of All Effective Teachers

I have never let my schooling interfere with my education.

—*Mark Twain*

- Establishing a Climate Conducive to Learning
- Avoiding Problems through Effective Communication with Your Students
- Grouping Students
- Reducing the Threat—Teachers as Authority Figures

- Communicating with Other Educators
- Communicating with Parents
- Communicating with Traditional Families from Other Cultures
- Communicating with Principals and Other Supervisors

Dear Teachers,

My name is Lauren. My favorite teachers are Amy B. and Amy T. When I was in their class, I did gardening, which was fun because we planted zucchini, carrots, and tomatoes.

We also had lots of room outside in the fields to play and have gym outside. In gym we played hide-and-go-seek, relay races, and other fun things. We had a small playground and a hill to roll down that had flowers and soft grass on it.

Almost every afternoon some kids would go to Spanish class. We learned the words for fruits, vegetables, and family members.

Outside we could play and talk to our friends. When I talked to my friends I wanted to see how they were doing. When we talked in class or when kids didn't listen, Amy B. or Amy T. would gently tell us to listen or stop talking. That is how teachers should talk to their students so they won't hate their teachers.

Other good things we did in our class was have our parents come in school and tell about themselves. I liked that because it gave us kids a chance to learn about each other.

Also every week we almost always had a clean room. It gave us lots of space to do stuff and made the room smell fresh.

Thanks for being good teachers,

Lauren

ESTABLISHING A CLIMATE CONDUCIVE TO LEARNING

Good communication begins with trust. Let your students know that you are their advocate and that you will listen to them. Establishing a favorable, friendly, nonthreatening climate is imperative if you want your classroom to be a comfortable place in which to learn. If you are sincere when you ask students how they feel or what they want, you will encourage feedback rather than discourage it. To further convey interest, use body language that matches your words: make eye contact with students and stop what you are doing to attend to them. Show them you are interested enough in them and what they have to say that you are willing to take the time to listen to them. Encourage the speaker to elaborate for you what they mean so that you can gain greater insight into the point he or she is trying to make. Hold off all interruptions until the speaker is finished. If your attention is scattered, the student will know you are not truly listening.

When you listen, be attentive to what the speaker is saying and refrain from negative remarks or criticisms. This will send to the student and the rest of the class the positive message that you take students' opinions seriously, welcome their input, and value them. Spending time treating children as individuals of worth helps them learn to value themselves. Using a tool such as the Student Inquiry can help you get to know your students better (see Teacher Resource 3.1 in Appendix B). Such a tool can provide valuable insight into how students view themselves and useful information about students' learning styles.

If a student is upset and becoming defensive and hostile, try to defuse his or her anger with positive comments that reflect your concern for his or her feelings. Move on

TEACHER RESOURCE 3.1, p. 158

to a subject that is less emotional or threatening. If the student tries to return to the subject of his or her anger, kindly reassure the student that you intend to return to the subject at a future time. However, be sure that you don't ever brush off a student. Always reassure students that you care about their feelings and that you find them important enough to give your valuable time to. Remain approachable to students no matter how trivial their problems may seem. When students recount their problems to you they need to think about them in some meaningful way. This simple act of telling helps them gain perspective and understanding, which bring them closer to solving their problems.

AVOIDING PROBLEMS THROUGH EFFECTIVE COMMUNICATION WITH YOUR STUDENTS

Two-way communication must be worked on continuously. Sometimes students don't listen to adults because they feel adults are not listening to them. Often they are right. Not only do parents not listen to them, but some teachers spend so much time talking that they have little of it left to hear what their students have to say. Without this feedback teachers are not teaching as effectively as they could. It is difficult, if not impossible, to teach someone to do something if you don't know much about that person. Knowledge about students' likes and dislikes, skills and weaknesses, and preferred learning styles makes the difference between lecturing and facilitating learning.

Another factor that affects communication and student learning is appropriately pacing a lesson. Speaking slowly facilitates learning for some children who cannot process information at the fast speed at which some teachers speak. Being as concrete as possible and giving information in as many modalities as possible are two more ways to facilitate learning. If you want students to follow multitask instructions, make the instructions as short and to the point as possible. Numbering specific tasks, writing down each step of the directions, and teaching children to cover up all but the particular direction on which they are working are all helpful strategies.

3.2, p. 159

Don't assume that students know the rules of good communication. They may need to be taught to be polite to each other, to listen to each other, to look at the person who is speaking, and to respond when they are spoken to.

Be clear with students on how to respond to questions in the classroom. As a group, students may decide that they want everyone to raise their hands. If so, explain the procedure for deciding who calls on the students. (That person can also tell students when to put down their hands.) If it is decided that students are to answer in unison, tell them to do so at a specific cue. If your procedure is to call on students going down a list of their names, you may want to give the list to one of your students and allow him or her to choose who will answer the questions. Students will develop sense of ownership of the class, and they can help you ensure that each student gets a turn to answer a question. Many teachers find using a list an excellent idea because all students know they are expected to respond and no one is off the hook. (Students can settle back in their chairs and relax knowing they each will get a chance to respond. In the meantime, they are freed up to listen to each other instead of thinking about what they want to say or how to get the teacher to notice and call on them.)

3.3, p. 160

In addition to these, many students also need to learn about personal proximity. Having students participate in STOP, a body-positioning exercise, will help them visualize proximity from the eyes of other students (see Teacher Resource 3.3). The STOP acronym helps students remember to *s*tay *t*hree feet *o*utside of other *p*eople's space— the arm's-length distance our culture uses as a norm for personal proximity. It might also be helpful to point out that the comfort distance between opposite sexes is farther apart than with same-sex relationships.

Closely related to personal proximity is the issue of teachers touching their students. Touching children on the head or shoulder can convey empathy, reassurance, or encouragement, all of which can be positive experiences for children. However, some individuals find being touched, even in gentle ways, uncomfortable. Therefore, ask students whether they mind before you pat them, tap them, or hug them. You may not need to ask every time; watch carefully to see whether they seem to shy away from or enjoy being touched.

The classroom is a good place to teach and reinforce good communication skills. Remember to teach students that one person talks at a time; that they should look at the person who is talking; and that they should watch people for nonverbal cues, such as smiles, frowns, and questioning looks, which may not match their words.

GROUPING STUDENTS

Teachers often have students work in groups so they can learn from their peers. In groups, students have opportunities to hear about each other's experiences and hopefully to feel better about their own. We all need time to talk to others because through discussion we clarify our thoughts and opinions, learn about others' points of view, and develop trust and acceptance from peers. This process of enlightenment is even more essential for children.

For good things to happen when we group students, we must facilitate the development of an esprit de corps by which students' relationships with peers unlike themselves can slowly grow as they work toward common goals and share common purposes. To develop this atmosphere start with a motivator. Give the group a joint purpose to improve involvement. Involvement can be fostered to a greater degree by allowing the group some sharing time and/or fun time (not a time to lecture). Try organizing a group meeting or group project they can all enjoy.

Next, consider whether your room and its circumstances feel safe and secure. Students can work together effectively only when they feel really safe. Have you ever asked your students how safe they feel in your classroom? You might be surprised to find that students fear each other. Children and adolescents are often insensitive to each other and to adults. If students are uncomfortable together in class, you need a Things Stay Here rule and a No Put Down rule. Gather together to discuss the classroom rules you set at the beginning of the school year.

Students need to cooperate with each other and listen to each other. These are excellent work and life skills for students to develop. A class meeting is an opportunity for students to set up their own classroom rules. It might be useful to teach your class Robert's Rules of Order because many organizations in their adult life will use this format (see Teacher Resource 3.4). Exercising classroom democracy helps students learn to set reasonable limits for themselves and to listen to each other and communicate their needs. After students' rules are formulated, the teacher can add any rules that are important but were not addressed by the students.

REDUCING THE THREAT—TEACHERS AS AUTHORITY FIGURES

Most successful teachers are friendly and approachable in the classroom. They are not sarcastic or negative; however, some may be considered strict. Successful teachers handle sensitive and confrontational episodes with care and understanding while keeping them manageable. Because minor problems are identified quickly and managed carefully, more difficult problems are usually avoided. Most situations escalate because of a lack of understanding among the participants. The good teacher can act as a clarifier to enhance understanding which sets the stage for an amicably controlled solution. Simple problem-solving techniques can help deflate the controversy. When teachers lose their tempers over students' behaviors, which happens to us all on occasion, it is best to step back from the situation and handle the problem at a later time when you no longer are fatigued or upset.

Classroom rules are very important to both students and teachers. If all decisions about classroom operating procedures and discipline are established and handed down from the teacher to the students, students will feel unimportant, uninvolved, and unempowered. To increase each student's sense of personal worth and to give students practice in developing self-determination, give students more responsibility and greater opportunities to work together toward establishing classroom policies and rewards. Remember that autocratic adults (which describes many adults) give students something to rebel against.

Mr. Smith, the science teacher at one of the schools where I taught, was an ineffective teacher. He loudly and constantly demanded respect, yet he refused to respect his students. As you can imagine, his demand was never satisfied. He did not realize that respect is earned, not demanded. Nor did he set a good example of what respecting someone would look like.

Students, particularly adolescents, respect people they feel are honest, informed, and fair. As we socialize students to live in the world, we need to remember that one of the most effective ways learning occurs is through modeling and observational learning. Are we giving our students multiple opportunities to earn our respect and to show respect for each other as well as for us? Currently many common practices in our schools are disrespectful of teachers and students alike. For example, it is common for school office personnel to interrupt the classroom many times a day to handle minor details. Faculty regularly step in front of students to get their lunches but insist that students not step in front of each other. Many more examples of inconsistencies are acted out among students, administration, and faculty.

So whom do our students model themselves after? Not always their parents at this stage, although recent studies reveal that parents have a much greater impact on adolescents than we had suspected. Students mainly look to their peers for acceptance because this is their entry into society. As peers influence each other, which peers do you suspect influence students the most? The popular peers, people they find attractive and competent, are a great influence, but even more influential are people they see as similar to themselves or who share characteristics with them. It is useful to find out whom your students emulate: a rock star, an athlete, a popular student in your class, or a trusted friend. If any of these influential people make good role models, use them to help students learn to mature and become more responsible. Students need as many positive examples as possible to preview how to act.

COMMUNICATING WITH OTHER EDUCATORS

Communicating with other educators is extremely important to your success as a teacher. At a time when educational practices are constantly under fire and budget cuts are reducing resources, the problems arriving at your door are escalating. Teachers, now more than ever, are competing for limited resources. This tends to interfere with the cooperation necessary to establish schools that can make all our students successful, contributing citizens of the twenty-first century.

How can we be successful against such difficult odds? We cannot change our class sizes or ensure that all students are emotionally and academically ready for our classes. It takes the work of all teachers, administrators, parents, and communities to make a difference for our children. To increase our chances of being successful, we must all pull together. Collegial support is imperative if we are to solve the tough problems that face us as educators in the twenty-first century.

How do we begin? First, get to know as many of your fellow teachers as you can. Meet with them in the teachers' lounge, in the break room, or during lunch period. Sit with as many different people as you can so that you all get to know each other. Try to converse with other teachers about something other than teaching. Don't launch into school business every time you see them. They will soon tire of seeing you if you do.

Another way to get to know the people you work with and teachers in general is through teacher association meetings. Educational conferences and workshops can be used effectively to establish contacts throughout your district and in neighboring districts. Strategies and ideas can be learned and shared at these conferences, both in formal sessions and in informal conversations.

Many different models exist to help teachers in their struggle to work together and serve difficult populations of students. Let's consider three of the most popular service models: consultants, teacher consultation teams, and collaborative teaching. When teachers are faced with difficult classroom problems and need suggestions on how to solve them, a consultant can be called to come and visit the classroom and help the teacher solve the problems. Usually the consultant begins by observing in the classroom. Later, the classroom teacher attempts to restate the problem until it is clear to both the classroom teacher and the consultant. Next, the teacher and consultant brainstorm and plan possible interventions. After implementing the intervention, the effectiveness of the intervention is monitored, and the consultant and the teacher can modify the intervention as needed.

The second service model is the teacher consultation team, also called prereferral teams or child study teams. Teacher consultation teams are teams of teachers who support teachers and are concerned with all students and teachers in the school. A team of teachers collaborate to solve classroom and student problems. (These teams are distinct from special education teams, whose purpose is to evaluate and serve students with exceptional educational needs.) To develop a teacher consultation team, volunteers who have the time and interest are enlisted to serve. Once the team members are chosen, a coordinator for the teacher consultation team is identified. This person can facilitate meetings, take notes, complete the paperwork, and serves as the contact person for other teachers in the school who need assistance. Next, a regular meeting time is set. These teams are only effective when they meet regularly. The team, or coordinator, then sets an agenda for each meeting and uses a team problem-solving process.

3.6, p. 163

Consultation teams exist because teachers in our schools today rarely have the time or opportunity to share with one another. Teams of teachers, sometimes with guidance counselors and social workers, can help teachers develop alternative ways of handling academic and behavioral problems and develop and implement innovative strategies. Teachers can work together to solve problems; they do not always have to seek the advice of outside "experts."

Collaborative teaching is the third service model. Collaborating teachers usually are two teachers who work together in the same class. This team of two teachers begins collaborative efforts by brainstorming all responsibilities that need to be met in the classroom. Next, the teachers divide classroom responsibilities according to strengths and weaknesses of the individual teachers. Having more than one teacher increases the chance that each student's unique individual needs are met because it is easier for each teacher to plan and facilitate optimal programming for all the different ability levels in the classroom.

3.7, p. 164

For collaboration to be successful, the process must be voluntary. Each teacher must want to work with the other and feel they have styles of teaching that mesh and are complementary. In addition, the teachers and the administration must be open to new ideas and ways of doing things. Without flexibility joint teaching cannot work. Both teachers should begin by describing to each other their present operating procedures, teaching styles, and educational values and philosophies. Then they both can compare the student needs to their varying teaching styles. Together they continue to develop a plan, using consensus decision making, delineating who does what, and choosing an approach with which they both can live. After implementing the plan, they evaluate it regularly.

Whether you are trying to establish a teacher consultation team, a school discipline committee, or a collaborative teaching arrangement, it is nice to first get to know the other teacher on safe ground. To do so, it is recommended that you begin with an icebreaking activity such as Why I Chose to Be a Teacher. Such an activity can give all leaders common ground as they share their individual histories recounting how in their own way they each got to this point in their careers.

COMMUNICATING WITH PARENTS

Meet as many parents as you can. Not only will they benefit by knowing you, but you will benefit by knowing them and being able to see your students in the context of their families. It is always easier to communicate with people when you have something in common. Fortunately for teachers, they have much in common with their students' parents. To begin with, both are interested in the best for the child. This gives parents and teachers something to build on.

Whenever talking to parents, start with the bond you have with their child. You know a lot about their child and have the ability to affect their child in a positive way. Your position as an adult who can influence the child gives you immediate access to each child's family and the chance to relate to each family because all parents want good things for their children. (Even the least-able parents want their children to be happy.) An added bonus for you both is that a content child is much easier to spend time with. If things are not going well for their child in your classroom, the parent probably will hear about it. Wouldn't it be better if they heard about it from you, as well as from their child?

You must learn to see parents as allies. They can help you in your quest to educate their children. Not only can they encourage their children to study, behave, and succeed in school, but they can help their children do all those things more effectively when they have a positive relationship with you, the teacher.

What can parents do for you? Perhaps you need to ask them. They have information about their children that could help you motivate and teach them better. You can have parents fill out an information sheet about their child (see Teacher Resource 3.9 in Appendix B). When meeting with parents, have everyone describe what positive things the child has going for him or her. Have each person, including the parent, begin by describing the attributes of the child that might help you teach him or her better. Write down these positive attributes. Hopefully they will be useful, but even if you don't have an opportunity to use them, it is always nice to see and say positive things about the child. These kind words also are important because they set a positive tone for the meeting. (They also give you something to report to the child as a gift from the team that met.)

Having parents as part of a team that is working toward the good of the child can be a very powerful asset. If parents are working in conjunction with you, they can back you up through their special relationship with their child. Whether families are healthy or dysfunctional, they affect their children in many ways. Often parents are able to influence even the most reluctant learner, perhaps with a discussion of earning privileges such as borrowing the family car, the timing or length of TV viewing, or some future release from chores. Parents usually have a better understanding of their child's needs outside school. They may be able to bring together the child's school life and home life. Having their support can make a big difference in the management of their children.

If you have students whose parents had a bad attitude toward school when they were students the parents' attitude could work against the relationship you are trying to build with your students. By meeting with parents and getting to know them, you can learn about their opinions and gain insight into the child. Let's examine two different student scenarios, Sean and Hannah.

Mrs. McKenzie had a high school junior, Sean, who was failing her English class. He came to school every day but never did any assignments. He never did his homework, even when he was given time in class to do it, and she suspected he had not cracked open his book all year. However, he was always polite to her and was often able to answer questions when he was called on. This was encouraging because she could see that he was not necessarily unable to participate. When she called in the student's parents, she was not too surprised that Sean's dad was reluctant to enter the classroom. After coaxing him in with a few kind words about his son and the upcoming deer season, she found out that he had always hated school himself and had never graduated. He had continually instructed his son that he had to attend school every day, but grades were unimportant and he did not expect his son to graduate. He insisted only on attendance. The child in this case was doing exactly what his father asked of him. He went to school but was aware that he was not to graduate because that would imply that school was important, a circumstance that seemed to threaten his father. Knowing the factors involved in the student's problem gave Mrs. McKenzie greater insight to deal with it.

Hannah was a student in Mr. Lima's sixth-grade math class. Hannah did not once turn in homework during the first 2 weeks of class. Mr. Lima met her parents at Go to School Night and set up an appointment. They came in and discussed her progress, or lack thereof, and were able to discern that Hannah was unable to see the board. She could neither see the examples of how to do the math problems, nor the assignments on the board. She was actually very happy in the back of the room because she was sitting near a boy she liked, so she never admitted to the teacher that she could not see the blackboard. Furthermore, she did not like how her glasses looked because some kids called her four-eyes when she wore them. Her parents agreed to get her contacts at the end of the first 9-week grading period if she moved to the front of the room, turned in every homework assignment, and pulled up her grade to a B at least. Her grades improved to a B average by the end of the 9 weeks (and to an A by Christmas break), and she was able to move to the back of the room, wearing her new contacts. Everyone in that situation was happier in the end.

Not only do most parents have a special effect on their children, because of what they can give them, but they also have the advantage of dealing with their child over the course of many years. In addition, the parent/child ratio is much smaller and more manageable than the teacher/child ratio in schools. All these factors need to be used to the teacher's and student's advantage, so a good teacher would be wise to do whatever possible to gain parents' confidence.

Once parents have confidence in us as teachers, we need to keep them in the loop of their child's school life. A quick way to maintain contact with parents is to send them information in the mail or over the Internet. Always start a written letter with something positive that is happening in your classroom. It is especially effective if you can tell parents that their child did something good or helpful. Ask parents to tell you about the positive things in their child's life and the things that their child particularly enjoys. This will help you better relate to the child and give the parent something positive to think about. It can be very useful to send a parent newsletter home regularly. Write the letter in an informal, nontechnical way. Include student work, such as artwork or well-written stories, and parents will be more likely to read it. Avoid addressing letters to parents as *Mr. and Mrs.* because they may not be married, they may not both be living at that address, or they may not have the same last name. Find out from the child's parents or guardians how they would like to be addressed and what address to use for each adult.

Before contacting parents, ask yourself a few important questions: What can I say that is positive? Am I attuned to cultural differences and what I can do to respect them? How can I be accepting of the family's values, even if they differ from my own? Included here are some historical norms of families of traditional cultures. It is most important to remember that none of these traits fits all families or perhaps even most families aligned with a certain culture. This information is added here only to give teachers a cultural framework and it may differ from the culture they experienced themselves. Being aware of different cultural perspectives may enable us to understand many students' families.

Be sure you highlight the child's progress regularly and help them stay abreast of their child's progress in school. Many teachers find it very helpful to develop a home note program for communication about students' social and academic progress. Teachers can also send home assignment sheets to involve parents in their child's schoolwork (see Teacher Resource 3.10). Parents can be your best allies in motivating children to complete assignments and to strive for excellence in school.

If you call parents the evening of the first day of school, you send a strong message to them and to the child that you are going to communicate with parents and that you hope to be accessible to them. Unfortunately, many parents are not available during the day, and it is difficult to reach them on the phone. However, the extra effort of calling them in the evening or sending them a note is well worth the trouble. Studies show that when parents are involved in their child's education, the student is much more likely to do well in school.

However, some parents may not want to be involved in their child's education. Respect their wishes and do not take this personally. Some parents work many hours and have little free time, or some may have been burned by the school system in the past and need to avoid the pain. Although such a situation does not make your job any easier, you must not view these parents as an insurmountable obstacle and give up on their child. The parents may not have the time, resources, or energy to deal with the school right now. But if you do not burn your bridges, they may get involved at a later time. Part of your job as a professional is to be patient.

If you are having difficulty with a child's behavior, chances are so are his or her parents. Most children misbehave because they don't know the appropriate behaviors others want from them or they are afraid they will be unable to produce the appropriate behaviors. Children usually are not difficult on purpose, and responding to a child's difficult behavior with anger and harsh punishment may not work. When discipline does not work for parents, they often become even more emotional because they feel helpless, which may cause them to discipline erratically. Erratic discipline makes the situation worse and can confuse the child and destroy the parent's authority and the child's respect. If the pattern of unsuccessful discipline continues, parents are likely to feel inadequate. (Society often sends a message that parents are bad, which is very counterproductive.) Unfortunately, some children have more trouble fitting into environments than others. If the messages these children receive concerning appropriate behavior are inconsistent, or if they are not able to read those messages correctly, the family may find coping with this child extremely difficult.

Parenting is a difficult job and differs with each child that is raised. Children teach parents how to parent through experience. Most parents are able to handle their children sufficiently to raise them to adulthood with only minor periods of difficulty along the way. However, these same parents may not be able to cope with the extra understanding and patience that a difficult child needs.

Not all children pick up information about behavior casually. Some kids need to be taught even the most basic rules of getting along with others. Other children learn slowly and ineffectively. The frustration of dealing with these children produces ineffective parental discipline. This makes the problem worse because parents have fewer and fewer successes in teaching the child how to behave. At a time when a child needs consistency and clear guidelines more than ever, parents are unable to satisfy these needs because they have lost confidence in handling their child. This can escalate into constant power struggles throughout the day.

Parents can feel bewildered, angry, guilty, embarrassed, and inadequate. They often feel isolated and trapped. They need information about their child, what works with the child (e.g., touching, warnings before changing activities), and specific management techniques. You can help parents find the resources they need by hooking them up with people in the area who provide these services and by supporting them as they work

through problems. You will already be helping them simply by letting them know that they are not alone and that someone else understands and cares about their child.

COMMUNICATING WITH TRADITIONAL FAMILIES FROM OTHER CULTURES

As educators we are aware that dealing with individuals or families in stereotypical ways is insulting and ineffective. That being said, different styles of communication and behavior have been promoted as appropriate for different groups of peoples. Therefore, our respect and understanding of these cultural nuances can help us communicate with individuals who may have been raised in traditional families from other cultures. We can learn to be more polite, and to avoid judging others using the standards of our own culturally limited forms of communication. With this in mind, we list some traditional communication styles that have been attributed to other cultures.

Cultural Considerations for Working with Children from Traditional Hmong Families

Parents of children from traditional Hmong families may have had little or no formal education in their home country. However, this is now changing. These families often place great respect and trust in professionals, assuming they know what is best for their child. As a result, the family head, traditionally the father, is very likely, when asked to participate, to hand over responsibility of the child to the professionals. When individuals from this culture come to the school and meet school officials and teachers, they may incline or bend over to signify respect for an individual they perceive as possessing higher status.

Many individuals in this culture believe that direct eye contact indicates disrespect, distrust, anger, or confrontation. They may also feel that a display of negative emotion or aggression is bad, and they will not argue with anyone they perceive as having higher social status than they have themselves. To people in the United States many Hmong individuals appear to be nonassertive and overly polite. They may automatically say yes to questions or give socially desirable or expected answers just to be polite or to avoid embarrassment. They believe their opinion is not as important as living in harmony. Time as we perceive it in the United States is not part of the traditional Hmong way of life. Watches, appointment books, and even calendars are not routine possessions. It is not uncommon for a traditional Hmong person to miss or be late for appointments without any thought of inconvenience or frustration on the part of others.

Cultural Considerations for Working with Children from Native American Families

It is difficult to describe the traditional Native American family because as much diversity can be found across tribes as across all other cultures. Often in Native American cultures the clan or family comes first in importance and the individual's needs come second. Some Native American languages have no word for *I*. Traditionally, the good of the whole or the clan has been important to Native American culture. Individual wants and desires are expected not to overcome the good of the entire group. However, each person is viewed as unique.

Elders are respected in almost all these cultures. Extended kinship also is usually very important. Children are taught to listen without asking questions. In many tribes asking questions of an elder may be considered rude, and the offending individual is ignored as punishment for the question. Children are expected to learn by example rather than by verbal directions on how to accomplish a task. Directions may also be considered rude because they are viewed as too forceful and bossy.

Cultural Considerations for Working with Children from Hispanic Families

Many traditional Hispanic families have a very diverse, yet closely tied, extended family network. In this framework children are often viewed as family members first and as individuals second. The closeness of the family unit creates a common hesitancy to use "outsiders" for help. Typically, the father is the head of the household and the mother is expected to be devoted to him and to the children, placing her needs last. Older children, especially females, are expected to care for younger children and older grandparents and eventually parents when the need arises. Children are often given a lot of love and affection and are taught good manners and acceptable "public" behavior at an early age.

Cultural Considerations for Working with Children from African American Families

African American families' long experience of institutional racism, prejudice, and economic oppression has resulted in their distrust for many public systems, including the public school system. Fathers in African American culture often have a peripheral place in their children's lives. Although they are not necessarily completely absent from their children's lives, they tend to remain unmarried to their children's mothers. Children often grow up in multifamily, multigenerational households. Strong family/kinship bonds are one particularly positive aspect of many African American families. Also positive is the unique learning style many children from this culture develop, which is based on emotions, body language, and social nuance. Individuals in this culture seem especially adept at understanding social situations and reading the emotions and moods of the individuals around them. In many of these families religion plays an important role.

Cultural Considerations for Working with Children from Traditional Asian Families

Although Asian culture is diverse, some aspects of traditional Asian culture are predominant. In traditional Asian culture, cultural roles are based on values that have existed for more than 5,000 years. Often Asians consider it important to value the larger social good over individual needs. Often, hierarchical roles and status govern behavior and subordination. Rules are very important and need to be followed. Children may be strictly controlled, and parents often have high expectations for them. Education is often highly valued. Teachers are highly regarded and are not questioned or contradicted. The interdependence of individuals is valued, especially in the family. Many traditional Asian families are extended and multigenerational.

COMMUNICATING WITH PRINCIPALS AND OTHER SUPERVISORS

To become an integral part of the school, attend all faculty meetings and try to take an active and positive role in the school. Supervisors are more willing to address your needs if they feel they can count on your support. Volunteer for extra assignments on occasion so that you are doing your part to ensure the school is running smoothly. If you have suggestions for improving the school, be sure to state them in a positive and constructive manner. Avoid disrupting your supervisors; do not argue with them for the sake of arguing. When you need to disagree or voice an opposing point of view, do so in a nonthreatening manner when the timing is right. Both administrators and fellow teachers get tired of people constantly questioning, arguing, or complaining at faculty meetings. Most teachers are tired at the end of the day; their patience may be seriously tried by anyone who makes the meeting longer than necessary.

CHAPTER

Planning for Student Safety

- Preventive Discipline
- Reducing Conflict and Confrontation
- Power Struggles
- Emergency Planning for Crisis Situations and Natural Disasters
- Protective Behaviors in the Classroom and in the School
- Helping Children Deal with Separation and Loss

4

PREVENTIVE DISCIPLINE

4.1, p. 175

4.2, p. 176

Preventing problems in the classroom is much easier than handling them after they occur. Good preparation helps alleviate the strains that can create problems. Most students would much rather behave than act out, and they appreciate a classroom in which they feel secure. The school curriculum should include anger management, crisis management, and conflict resolution. If your school does not, bring this up at the first faculty meeting.

As soon as your students enter your classroom, they are telling you about themselves. Watch your students. Who comes to class early and roams around scoping out the place? Which students seem to group together and which seem to fear being alone? Who sits down when they enter, and who moves right to the back of the room as far away from you as they can get? You will notice the students who help other students and those who lash out. Your students may not be saying aloud, "I hate school," "I am here to learn," or "I care deeply about my friends and need them around me to feel secure in this big, scary school." But if you look and listen carefully, you will discover what they do not tell you in words. Amazingly enough, many students are frightened the first day of school. It is human nature to be afraid of the unknown. You are a part of that unknown, as are the academic and behavioral expectations of the classroom.

The best thing you can do to alleviate your students' fear is make your classroom a *comfortable, safe,* and *secure* space for them to learn! They need to know as soon as possible that you are fair, kind, and dependable. They will feel secure in your classroom once they know the parameters for appropriate behavior. Recall the list of classroom behaviors in Teacher Resource 1.2: What behavior do I want? What behavior must I have from every student? What behavior can I *not* accept? Don't let your expectations for classroom behavior become a guessing game because some students are very poor at guessing what you expect and their failure will hurt you and the other students. Instead of being ambiguous, be forthright. Let students know what behavior you expect during lectures, group time, assignments, lessons on skill development, and skill practice time.

Clear expectations may take some time to establish, but they are of the utmost importance because students can learn more when class time is not taken up with discipline and behavior problems. The more on-task time, the more learning will occur. It is your responsibility to inform students about how to behave. They can then choose to behave accordingly (or not). Once informed, the students' behavior is the responsibility of the students. Teachers who structure their classrooms for learning spend much less time interrupting learning to discipline students.

REDUCING CONFLICT AND CONFRONTATION

4.3, p. 177

Having to stop lessons to take time to discipline students is a deterrent to learning for all students in your class. Therefore, it is important for you to know how you will deal with infractions when they occur. A good rule of thumb is to ignore minor behavior problems when your reprimand will cause more distraction than the behavior you want to change. It is also possible to discuss the offending behavior with the student at some other time or even to give the student a note requesting a change in behavior in the future. This is an excellent nonconfrontational way to inform the student of what you expect. (Also remember to give students positive notes as well.)

If you find yourself in a situation in which you must reprimand one or more students, try not to disrupt the rest of the class. How can you do this? Part of your preparation for the school year should include establishing a predetermined space for addressing problems. Choose a place that is not in the middle of instruction areas so that the student's disruption is as minimal as possible. Good teachers are multitask persons *always* monitoring the class, no matter what else they are doing. Students soon realize this. The teacher with "eyes in back of her head" is a well-known phenomenon. Be sure you are one of this breed. Be prepared with multiple, appropriate self-run activities, such as having games that help students review information previously learned, so that each student can have more individual time with the teacher. Students who choose to misbehave, taking time away from other students, should not be allowed to participate in fun activities.

If misbehavior is *not* minor, step in immediately and insist that your student (or students) take *responsibility* for behavior. Begin by describing the offending behavior. It is possible that the student does not know what he or she did wrong. After describing the behavior you do not like and what behavior you prefer, give the student a warning. Next, give the student a choice of two options. (If it is too difficult to come up with any options at this time, you can defer and instead require the student to sit in the quiet area. You can discuss alternatives later.) It is extremely important that you follow through at this point. Students need to know that you will do what you say you will do. If you have trouble remembering what you say, have the student write your requirement on the board so both you and the student can clearly see what you require.

Consider the story Susan Thomas relayed of an extremely disruptive student who balked at her every request. Lonny was an eighth-grade boy in her history class. She described the day he was talking loudly in the back of her classroom about his weekend exploits. His stories were getting louder and more graphic as the period went on. First she walked to the back of the room, as she continued talking, and placed herself between Lonny and the students he was talking to. When he continued despite her proximity, she placed a warning finger in front of her mouth and said to Lonny, "Could you discuss that later please? I need you to turn to page 14 right now, question 4." Unfortunately, Lonny ignored her and continued to talk and entertain his friends.

Mrs. Thomas tried again, this time giving him a choice. "Lonny please stop talking or I need you to sit in the quiet area." When Lonny continued to ignore her, she ended the confrontation by saying, "OK Lonny, you need to sit over here or you will be given an in-school detention." When he again ignored her, she asked the other students to move away from him and continued with her history discussion. The last-resort punishment of an in-school detention did not disrupt the other students but did show both Lonny and his classmates that she would not tolerate his defiant behavior.

Mrs. Thomas was successful because she did not lose her temper or try to win a battle with a very difficult student whom she knew she could not force to move or to be quiet. She did know that Lonny was too disruptive to ignore. By moving the other students Mrs. Thomas gained control of the class. The other students were back on track, and they knew that Lonny would be punished. They were easily persuaded to move to other seats and attend to the lesson because they did not want the same for themselves. Following these simple steps got Mrs. Thomas what she wanted—the ability to teach her class. Review how you might handle disruptive behavior:

1. *Describe behavior.* "Could you discuss that later please? I need you to turn to page 14 right now, question 4."
2. *Warning.* Standing near Lonny, the teacher placed a warning finger in front of her mouth.
3. *Choice.* "Lonny please stop talking or I need you to sit in the quiet area."
4. *Follow through.* "OK Lonny, you need to sit over here or you will be given an in-school detention."
5. *Final result.* Mrs. Thomas wins back her class by moving the other students away; Lonny is given a punishment to be carried out later in the day, about which he can do nothing right now.

Another story involved Mr. Jacobs and a child he had in his fourth-grade class 3 years ago. He fondly remembered the class and how one girl had a real chip on her shoulder that he was finally able to chisel down. LaSandra was very large for her age and seemed always to be using her size to push everyone around. She easily became angry when she felt she was being slighted. Most of the students were afraid of her. Girls feared her because she was physical with them, which was unusual in their age group. Whereas most of the girls tended to gossip about each other or verbally dress down each other when they were mad, LaSandra would haul off and hit them before they realized what they had done. Boys feared her because even though they were used to pushing and shoving, they did not expect it from a female. They had all been taught not to hit girls and did not know how to fend off her aggressions.

One day after lunch when students were coming in from recess, some teasing was going on and LaSandra came barreling across the room and grabbed Andrew, one of the tallest and toughest boys in the room. Mr. Jacobs was right behind her and quietly stepped in between her and Andrew. Very quietly he said to her, "LaSandra, I see you are very upset with Andrew. I am sorry to see this. Please go over to the back table and you can tell me what happened that upset you as soon as I put the math pages on the board." He then directed the class to their desks to work on their mathematics. This gave Andrew a face-saving excuse to get out of the area and kept the class occupied while he talked to LaSandra.

Mr. Jacobs returned to LaSandra, walking slowly and calmly, giving her a little time to collect herself. LaSandra complained that Andrew would not let her play squish ball with him and his friends, saying she should play with her own friends, too bad she didn't have any. Instead of saying much, Mr. Jacobs, mainly nodding his head and listening, let LaSandra boil on for a while until her anger burned out. He then asked her whether she would do him a favor and show him how to play the game tomorrow at recess.

He met LaSandra and brought along Anne, another of his students, and both he and Anne learned how to play the game. (Anne was extremely shy and usually spent recess watching other students play.) LaSandra and Anne continued the game for the rest of recess and almost every recess for the rest of the year. An unusual friendship formed between the two very different girls, and both seemed to profit from the relationship.

LaSandra had exhibited a normal reaction to emotional pain—anger. When people are angry, it is easier to understand if you can find out what hurt them in the first place. Once this is discovered, it is easier to avoid the hurt in the future. LaSandra felt rejected and left out because she had no one to play with. She needed a place to belong. Once she was paired up with a child who would not reject or hurt her, she was a much happier child.

When a student is angry, immediately separate him or her from the confrontation or hurt and provide a slowing-down, cooling-down activity. The student's high level of emotionality interferes with your ability to reason with him or her. Assure the student that you are willing to listen, but not at this time. (Be sure to set another time when you will talk to the student about the problem.) As you deal with them always stay calm and detached from the situation so that you are not pulled into the turmoil. Use only descriptive, not judgmental, words. Save your own anger or frustration for important times, and try to listen to the hurt under the student's anger. If you can do this, you will accomplish two things: becoming more sensitive and effective and calming yourself down if you also are angry. At all costs you must avoid a power struggle because power struggles rarely produce a resolution, especially in the long run.

POWER STRUGGLES

Teachers sometimes find themselves engaging in power struggles with their students; unfortunately, they may also find that they are losing the struggle. Power struggles are unhealthy for the class. They set a poor precedent for the students, who may now feel they know what buttons to push to control you. The key to avoiding a power struggle with a student is to know the student. Teachers need to know whom and what they are dealing with to make good decisions about how to proceed with difficult situations. Basically, one of two scenarios describe these situations. You will either face a child who is angry and motivated to fight or one whose explicit desire is to gain control of your classroom and make you look bad, thereby making him- or herself look good. If you know which scenario you are dealing with, and the intentions of the child before you engage in a struggle, you have a much better chance of avoiding the struggle entirely and finding a positive solution for yourself and perhaps for the child as well.

Every teacher's nightmare is losing a power struggle with a student. Unfortunately, students feel even more strongly about these outcomes than you do. Consider dealing with a troubled student, especially a middle or high school student for whom saving face and avoiding embarrassment is of primary concern. To put this in perspective, imagine a power struggle occurring in a room where the principal of your school is observing you and your spouse or significant other is visiting. You also know that your parents will hear about the outcome almost immediately. Your feelings about losing the power struggle under these circumstances are certainly equal to how a student would feel.

To middle school and high school students especially, the most important people in their world are their peers at school. They know that the outcome of a major power struggle with a teacher, or another student for that matter, will soon be the talk of the school. They also are aware that if they back down, they will be the brunt of incessant gossip, teasing, and perhaps even physical challenges resulting from their loss in status. Under these circumstances it is no wonder that students get trapped into power struggles they are unable to resolve.

If you look at a student's belligerence and defiance in this way, it is easier to understand why a negative outcome can easily occur. Few students in our classes walk in the door thinking, "I think I will ruin this teacher's day today by disrupting the classroom." Some students may have difficulty reading their teachers' messages when their teachers warn them with a stern look to behave in a more appropriate manner. Studies show that teachers are often unaware of students' inability to read nonverbal cues. Before misjudging a student, check that your meaning is clear to them.

Students probably do not come to school intending to ruin your day. However, before they arrive at school, something may have happened at home, on the bus, or outside the school to ruin their day. Personally saying hello to every student who comes into your classroom and having preplanned activities ready for students entering your classroom could save you from experiencing a difficult class period or day.

A student vying with the teacher for power over his or her class must be recognized immediately. The sooner you figure out what the student is about, the better your chance is for avoiding trouble. Teachers usually assume that when students ask a question, they are looking for a reasonable answer, and usually this is true. Unfortunately, the child who is trying to win power for him- or herself is not playing by the same rules. This child is not trying to find a reasonable explanation; this child only wants things to go in his or her favor. If such children do not win right away, often they will continue to push you even harder. If they do win, they will play this game whenever possible.

Once pulled into a struggle such as this, many teachers find themselves in no-win situations. As soon as you find yourself giving one explanation on top of another, and you begin to get frustrated, step back and analyze whether you are being tricked into arguing with the child. Your frustration may be your first clue. Usually the issue of the argument is moot. The point is that the child will not give up trying to engage you and hopes you will get frustrated and give up first. Many beginning teachers naively play right into this game.

In our society we admire persistence, but in the classroom no one student has the right to take up an inordinate amount of your time and energy. If you allow a student continually to use up your time and energy in such a negative way, you are probably elevating the child to the status of an adult. Attaining this status is important to a child playing power games because it helps establish a level playing field, wrongly putting teacher and student on equal ground with equal power. Remember that in the classroom the student has no business taking class time away from the other students. You and your students have the right to a peaceful space in which to learn, and unreasonable mind and power games are unacceptable.

Therefore, when you find yourself arguing with a student, first ask yourself why the problem occurred. Perhaps you sent inconsistent messages to the child, or family problems cause the child to try to gain control of all situations? Sometimes you might find yourself losing sight of what various students are doing in the classroom. Left to themselves, without the attention they require, some students get bored and disrupt the class.

Some teachers find it very helpful to have a system for managing students' behavior whereby the class earns points, privileges, grades, or coveted activities. Consequences must be clear and consistent so that you can act swiftly and effectively when students choose to misbehave. If you are prepared for the worst, it probably won't happen, but you will be ready with a well-thought-out response if it does. Give students opportunities to learn *internal* not *external,* control. Teach them that what they do matters. Then help them understand the concept of play and pay: one chooses what one does and then earns the positive or negative consequences. (This is only effective if the student is mentally capable of seeing the relationships between what they do and the consequence for that behavior.) Try to make it simple for your students by teaching them that classroom and school rules are not debatable. For students who enjoy the attention of debating rules, remind them that many rules are actually societal, as well as districtwide, schoolwide, or at the classroom level, and that they and their classmates developed some of them.

4.6, p. 180

4.7, p. 181

When a classroom begins to get out of control, the first thing an effective teacher needs to do is gain "think time." No matter what the student does, you must always remain in control of yourself. Don't let yourself blow. If one or more students have pushed your buttons and upset you, give yourself time. You may need "cooling-off time." What can you do to give yourself this time?

Thinking about what you will do is a great help during emergencies. One teacher we knew painted her nails when she was really upset. Another teacher sat at her desk and graded papers. Others choose to read a novel. It is usually helpful to have a designated time-off area and a time-off activity. You really don't need to dole out punishment immediately. It is often better initially to remove the child and at a later date to follow a course of restitution for the behavior. It is usually easier to face the student after some cooling-off time and after you have found a reasonable option.

For your sake, for the students, and for future reference, you need to make a record of the incident. Some schools require students' files to contain written incident reports for any disciplinary action that is taken. But even if this is not required by your administration, you will save yourself countless time and energy later when a record of the behaviors the child exhibits is needed.

Remember that the key to effective discipline is being prepared. You must be clear about your expectations, and clear about your responses to infractions. If you do not yet know exactly what you will accept, try the following exercise. Develop a list of acceptable student behaviors, a list of unacceptable student behaviors, and a list of your possible responses to these misbehaviors. It may be helpful to ask other teachers actions they have taken and what they find acceptable and unacceptable. Then try putting the information in columns, lining it up. Keep this list in your desk or in your cooling-off spot, adding to it as the year unfolds. When something goes wrong in the classroom, you can pull out the list, which is right next to your emergency cooling-off novel.

When an angry student appears ready to fight (or hit someone), the best thing for you to do is to stay calm and consider who can assist you. Try to stay near your source of help, be it a phone, intercom/office button, or the teacher in the class next door. Your first responsibility is to yourself: make sure you are safe. If you are unsafe, you cannot help the rest of your class. One teacher likened this rule to the directions on an airplane to place the oxygen mask on yourself first and then help your children and others. Like the airplane's emergency instructions, your next consideration is to those around you, your students. To keep everyone safe, you might have to have everyone leave the room. Never touch an angry student, because when uptight, students are often overly sensitive to tactile sensation. Nor should you talk about punishment, make threats, or argue with the student. An angry individual is highly emotional and cannot process information rationally.

Instead, reflect the student's feelings in a calming way, for example, saying something like, "It seems like you are feeling frustrated and angry." Then offer to help talk out problems. You need to gain some cooperation at this point and to distract the angry individual from his or her violent purpose, so ask for a *little* request, such as "Can you sit down for a minute?" Hopefully you have made up a package for yourself containing something for students to do. First students should be asked to sit. Then they should be distracted from their anger. Next they should be given something to help them work through their problem and to help them analyze it from another perspective. Your prepackaged plan should contain a work sheet such as the one in Teacher Resource 4.9. Follow the entire plan with as little deviation as possible depending on the situation. After this cooling-off period, talk about the incident with the student.

EMERGENCY PLANNING FOR CRISIS SITUATIONS AND NATIONAL DISASTERS

All schools must have emergency plans for crisis situations and for natural disasters such as tornados, floods, and fires. Teachers can be more effective in helping students when they are prepared emotionally for these situations. During times of disaster and of crisis, adults need their strength to help children and adolescents manage their uncertainty, fear, and grief. Most adults do not know how they might react in a crisis situation. This is scary enough, but teachers are also responsible for the children put in their care.

Children and adolescents are often especially inexperienced in dealing with emergency and with crisis situations. Therefore, as they look to us for reassurance, we must be prepared to calm their nerves, assuage their fears, comfort them, and return the classroom to some sense of normalcy. Unfortunately, during emergencies usually none of us is at our best as a result of the damaging effects a crisis situation has on our own life. However, just as we are instructed on airplanes to place the oxygen mask over our own face first, so must we also deal with our own fears and uncertainties before we can help our students.

Normal reactions to abnormal events vary. They may include, but are not limited to, disbelief, shock, loneliness, distractability, sadness, denial, anger, tearfulness, irritability, fear, feeling vulnerable, depression, emotional numbing, sleep disturbance, and/or loss of appetite. Each individual's reactions to highly emotional situations vary. Individuals may also experience multiple reactions over time.

As teachers we have the difficult position of supporting students' reactions at the same time that we are experiencing them ourselves. We might also observe some students exhibiting more extraordinary or harmful reactions, including fascination with guns, explosives, or other weapons that represent power and self-defense. Obviously this is not a productive way for children to react to a crisis situation. Such an unhealthy reaction might point to problems within the child or with the family's overall reaction to the crisis and its negative effect on them. If you observe these or other unusual reactions, notifying the school social worker to find support services for the child and his or her family is advisable.

If no immanent risk presents itself to the students in your classroom, the best thing that a teacher can do for the students is to maintain or return to as normal an atmosphere as possible. Although it is helpful to maintain one's routine, it may be difficult for students in traumatic situations to concentrate or complete tasks within that routine. Teachers must be understanding and pay attention to what each student needs. They should also maintain a calm atmosphere in the classroom and eliminate any additional stressors in the children's lives. Take work breaks whenever necessary, and give students extra time to process their experiences. Introducing new or difficult information is not advisable at a time when children are reacting to traumatic situations.

It is also normal during a crisis for both students and teachers to become fatigued and need additional rest and sleep. Try to give students ample access to recreational activities, and limit their access to television coverage of the crisis because this usually overstimulates the senses in the children and adults alike. Besides limiting media coverage in your classroom, advise students to take a break from the media outside school as well. Talk to students about their thoughts and feelings concerning the crisis. Brainstorm alternative recreational activities with your class, reminding them that they can go for a walk, enjoy nature, play a game, read a book, or watch a video. Encourage students to take part in other activities that they find refreshing and to eat regularly and get sufficient sleep.

It may be helpful for students to gather with their own community faith group or to become involved in a volunteer program such as a food or clothing drive (to gather things for people affected by the disaster or crisis) or a car wash (to raise money for a relief fund). Students, like adults, need productive activities to help them feel involved and useful, which, in turn, helps them feel empowered.

PROTECTIVE BEHAVIORS IN THE CLASSROOM AND IN THE SCHOOL

Schools also need plans to deal with students who are disruptive and need to be contained to avoid interfering with other students' safety or ability to learn. If one student is being disruptive but is not endangering anyone, giving that student a prepackaged set of instructions may be all you need do. The student stops whatever he or she is doing, retreats to a specified area of your classroom, and follows the prescribed set of activities. The student may begin with a situational self-assessment activity. What happened? What did you do? What did the other student(s) do? What could you have done differently? What would you have liked the other student(s) to have done differently to avoid this conflict? This assessment is completed privately by the student. It is usually in written format whereby the student is guided through a series of self-assessments (see Teacher Resource 4.9). However, if the student cannot read, an audiotape and earphones can be supplied and the student can be asked to think through the self-assessment, pausing when told to think about each issue.

This activity is designed to help students think about what happened that got them into the predicament in the first place. Students need to process the situation and then contemplate alternative behaviors in which they can engage in the future. First the student tries to generate these by him- or herself. At a later time the student continues with the help of an adult. (Once the events that set off the problem are understood, a plan can be developed to monitor and evaluate future progress on avoiding the same traps.) It may be helpful for the teacher and other students to role-play the chosen alternative behaviors. A social skills class might be a good place to model decision-making skills, appropriate behavior, monitoring behavior, anger and other feelings that cause loss of control, and ways to get emotions out in the open in a socially acceptable manner. None of these is an easy feat for children and adolescents to accomplish.

Our classrooms and schools as a whole need to be safe places for everyone to learn. How much could you learn if you were preoccupied with thinking about what and when another student was going to do something to you? Teachers need to protect children from bullies throughout the entire school. They need to protect the entire school from violent individuals. Such students may want to hurt others because of their own pain and unhappiness and may unleash their misery on students they do not even know. Students are especially vulnerable because they are put in schools filled with children of all ages and sizes, many of whom they do not know, and are then instructed not to fight. A student interfering with other students' learning is usually easily dealt with (described above). A child bullying other children is more difficult to handle.

To deal with bullying and harassment, classroom teachers need to arm their entire class with behaviors that will keep every student safe. The bully uses two weapons to gain power and to harass individuals. First, they wield the fear of intimidation: anyone who interferes with their bullying will be the next target. Second, they wield the shame of losing face that children experience when they break the unspoken code that a child who tells an adult is a "nark" or "stool pigeon." Both of these tactics award the bully with power he or she should not have.

Therefore, the first step in the process of taking power away from the bully is teaching students that they have their own power in numbers. If students stand with each other, face up to what is right, and refuse to accept the bully's harassing behavior, the bully will soon back down. Bullies are really cowards; that is why they are most likely to choose the most vulnerable victims to pick on—children who are smaller than they are or are loners who appear to have no support. By having students stand together, and by practicing with them what to do in a harassment situation, the bully most likely will promptly discontinue his or her problem behavior. A class unit on how to be good citizens and protect and support each other will teach students to protect themselves from bullies.

The second step in disempowering a bully is to teach students that the code of not telling an adult can be broken without shame because this code only serves to protect the bully's ability to harass other children. Moreover, not only should the code be broken, but it must be broken if students are to garner the support of open and understanding adults who can help when a bullying situation occurs. If teachers are informed of the problem, they can help students solve it and reinforce the advocacy powers that each child possesses. Teachers can also enlist the help of parents to eliminate retributions in the community for students who stand up to a harassing child. Ideally, these children should be praised in honor of their courage.

A much more complicated and disturbing issue is the presence of unknown students who threaten the safety of their classmates and educators. Recently in schools across the country it has become obvious that both teachers and children can be sitting ducks for frustrated, angry individuals whom they may never have even met. Many reasons explain the increase in dangerous behavior. In the past, individuals who were unhappy or unsuccessful in school were allowed to drop out and follow other pursuits. Today, students are not only expected to complete high school, no matter what their academic, emotional, or cognitive ability, but often are also expected to attend technical school or college. This phenomenon leaves to our middle school and high school educators a much larger population of disgruntled students. These students may feel that their situation is quite hopeless, which it may be, and they can be driven to desperate measures. (Desperate measures have been taken by seriously unhappy individuals in the past.) Teachers need to be more aware than ever that they are the first line of defense their classroom has against the angry, destructive person.

Although this problem is much less frequent than bullying, it is much more difficult to control. The key to a safe classroom is a prepared classroom. Often, so much is happening during an emergency, that it is impossible to stop and think about the safest course of action. Therefore, develop a clear set of procedures to follow, and no one will have to suffer any regret for actions not taken. You can eliminate many possible problems by spending a little time thinking through procedures with your students that will work best for your classroom. The first thing to consider when evaluating emergency situations is how quickly everyone can exit the room. Teachers need to design and arrange their classrooms to allow for easy escape when a problem arises.

4.13, p. 187

If you had an emergency in your classroom that required evacuation, how fast could you get your students out the door? Look around your room. Can the children in your class pass through the doorway quickly and at least two at a time from any place in the room? Discuss with your class the easiest way to exit the classroom and practice exiting the room with your students. Is your desk near enough to the door that you can block, lock, or barricade the door to keep out the danger of potential violence in the hall? Does your school have a warning system to warn you of impending destruction or violence? Emergency systems need to be discussed by the entire school body so that they can be put in place before danger presents itself.

Not only do teachers need to be able to evacuate children from the classroom or school building when necessary, but they also need to be able to isolate and remove a student who is out of control. To ensure safety teachers must recognize a student at risk for violence. Forewarned is forearmed. Certain behaviors are tip-offs that a student may have a tendency toward violence. Recognizing these behaviors, which may indicate possible upcoming violence, is a very important defense against violence. If teachers are aware of these behaviors, they are forewarned and may be able to protect the student and his or her classmates more effectively.

The various behaviors often exhibited by students with violent tendencies may not necessarily mean in and of themselves that a student is going to become violent, but all of them, at best, are problematic and deserve your increased attention. One of these behaviors is substance abuse. Teachers might notice increased use of alcohol and/or drug use. Students using drugs often discuss drugs and drug paraphernalia to the exclusion of most other subjects. Students who seemed before to drink alcohol moderately may begin abusing this substance, drinking too much at one time and/or drinking at inappropriate times.

Students may also display behaviors associated with increased sadness, negativism, and depression, sometimes accompanied by suicidal comments. Teachers may also notice that students' emotionality is heightened, often triggering verbal outbursts and increased arguing. Students may be articulating unstable emotional responses, perhaps continually complaining about being picked on, disliked, or plotted against by their classmates. Students who are emotionally troubled may display increased mood swings.

Fascination with violence is another characteristic of individuals at risk for violence. Students may talk about violence constantly, describing in detail gruesome images in violent movies, songs, and TV shows. They may also brag about their own violence toward other people or animals. Whether these stories are true is somewhat irrelevant. What is telling is that these students are preoccupying their thoughts with acts of violence. Teachers who are aware of a student engaging in this behavior should seek help for the student in need.

4.14, p. 188

For some students an outward display of a propensity for violence might consist of increased isolation or an unexplained increase in absences. For other students the withdrawal of large amounts of money and/or the possession of valuable jewelry or expensive apparel may signal trouble. For yet other students the display of any combination of one or more of these behaviors is worth investigating because they are all signs that a student needs help. Unfortunately, even when teachers are aware of impending problems, they are not always able to get students the help they need. Problems are often not apparent until they come to a head, so finding appropriate help early on may be difficult or impossible to do. Therefore, teachers need to be prepared for a student who suddenly becomes violent and dangerous.

When an individual is in crisis, what should you do? First, for your own safety, do not violate his or her space. When people are emotionally distraught, frequently they do not think clearly and are not themselves. You cannot rely on their past behavior as a guide to what they might do. Many teachers make the mistake of trusting students because they have never experienced the erratic nature of violent behavior. Unfortunately, under extreme pressure, people do not act in character. You cannot assume that a student in crisis won't hurt you.

Because you cannot rely on your past experience with a student, you will need to rely on other cues to tell you whether a student is about to become dangerous to themselves or others. Nonverbal cues may signal that something is wrong and an attack is coming. Be aware of (a) resistive tension—when you touch a student, he or her tenses up, (b) feigning ignorance—students conspicuously ignore you when you give them a command, (c) a sudden cessation of motion, (d) clenching hands into fists or clenching their jaw, (e) stance—students may shift their shoulders as if ready to punch someone, (f) staring—students may stare as if lining up a target or stare through someone as if ready to run through the person to reach a distant goal.

4.15, p. 189

If you think you are facing a crisis, chances are you are! Listen to that tickling feeling in your stomach and take the necessary precautions. First, secure your own safety because the entire class depends on it. If you are not safe, you cannot use your expertise and composure to defuse the situation. Once you are safe, attend to the safety of the other students in the classroom, including the student(s) about to blow and begin to stabilize the situation. Keep the situation as contained as possible. It might be helpful to understand the student before you try to deal with him or her. An individual in a crisis situation usually reacts emotionally to things, experiencing a roller coaster of emotions, and is unable to process information or think about even the near future. Therefore, if you try to reason with an individual by threatening him or her with future consequences for his or her behavior, you will often be unsuccessful.

Begin by reviewing the crisis situation from the student's point of view. In most cases the individual is having an intense emotional reaction to something that has probably been bothering him or her for a long time and recently has been set off again. The student is unable to get any perspective on the problem and knows no other way to deal with it. In many cases anger is aimed at an authority figure, and the student feels outnumbered and alone. The student probably is suffering from an adrenalin dump, causing him or her to feel a surge of energy from their anger and a need to act. It is common for students in this state to embarrass themselves because they are not thinking clearly and may try to gain control by testing alternative behaviors. Unfortunately, they are probably also experiencing tunnel vision and audio exclusion, so listening to reason is more difficult than normal for them.

4.16, p. 190

With all this going on, you can see that the problem is serious. You must focus on getting the student back on track. When dealing with individuals in crisis situations, remember some tips to help you break through to them. If you have already given them instructions that they have so far not followed, repeat the instructions slowly and calmly. (Always try to remember that because their concentration is not up to par, they are not able to process information well, so information is not getting through to them.) You need to break through their wall of emotional turmoil, so be patient and try to get them to focus on what you are saying so that they can process it. (Continue to speak slowly, carefully, and directly to them. Look them in the eye and model what you want them to do—which is slow down, calm down, and cue into you.) You are their emotional lifeline. If you keep the conversation off emotions and help them slow down their heartbeat, they may be able to follow your calm lead.

For example, Mrs. Preston was working with a high school history class when Tyler walked into her room swearing about another teacher who had kicked him out of class. He was pacing and punched the file cabinet, perhaps breaking some bones in his hand. Mrs. Preston said to Tyler, "Let's go out into the hall." Tyler remained in the classroom pacing and swearing. Mrs. Preston repeated herself, "OK Tyler, you are upset. Let's go out into the hall." When he looked at her as if he was contemplating her request or at least questioning what to do, she said, "Come on. Let's see what I can do to help."

Tyler slowly turned and preceded her out of the room. She closed the classroom door. (This gave Tyler less of an audience and the history class had the protection of a door between the students and Tyler.) She then very calmly said to Tyler, "I know history class has been frustrating for you, but I am so pleased with your progress in my class. You did an excellent job on your paper on the Civil War veteran's feelings when he returned to his home in Virginia. Let's walk down to see the guidance counselor and we will find out what options we have. You have done some excellent work for me, so I know what you are capable of. Did you go to the dance last weekend?" By getting Tyler out of the classroom, empathizing with him, remaining calm, and switching the subject, Mrs. Preston was able to get Tyler to the guidance counselor for help. The problem situation was diffused.

Luckily you have two weapons (perhaps this is a bad choice of words) at your disposal: time and distance. Your first weapon is time. If an out-of-control individual hasn't done anything violent in 1 to 3 minutes, chances are good he or she won't. Your second weapon is distance. The farther away you can keep the violent student from yourself and your other students, the more time you have to react and flee if necessary.

Your next actions can work toward resolving the problem and returning the situation to normal as soon as possible. During your actions, be personable. Don't corner the individual or add to his or her stress in any way. You want to calm the person down so that the adrenalin level in their body decreases. You should think about your presence and how you display yourself. Don't cower in front of the individual, but don't appear so authoritative that you set off the individual. At this point you are acting as a mentor—a counselor who will help the person think through his or her options. Individuals in this predicament need calm and caring reassurance that neither are they at the end of the rope nor are things out of control. Don't let them give up hope of a positive resolution. Show them a way out of the predicament, and help them see the positive.

When working with potentially violent students, put your hands in a presentation stance, meaning folded in front of you at your hips perhaps. Give them space and time to think things through and calm themselves. The appropriate use of space is very important when dealing with angry individuals, especially when violence might be an issue. Remember, acquaintance space is 4 to 12 feet; confidential/conversational space is 1 to 4 feet; and intimate touching space is 1½ feet or less. You want to give an angry or upset student a minimum of 4 or more feet of acquaintance space distance. This helps alleviate the threat of violence, and it gives you more time to react and get away if a student lunges at you. (You want to be more than an arm's length away.)

Other strategies may also protect you from physical harm. For example, a well-placed piece of furniture between you and the angry student may make the difference. A desk may be strategically placed between both of you. Best of all would be to position yourself behind your desk because it is probably too heavy for the student to push or throw at you. Try to stand to the front and side of the student. If another adult is in the room, have him or her stand to the back and side of the student. Prepare your students to go and get help in the event that you are unable to alert anyone of your predicament. Your goal is to throw off the student's intention to strike. You may call the student on his or her behavior to show that you are aware of what is being planned and that you are ready. You may say something like, "Now you do not want to hit me—that would be foolish." Remember to pull out your list of things to do in a crisis.

So far we have discussed measures to calm down an angry individual who is not completely out of control. But what can you do if the student does not calm down or if an angry, out-of-control individual is nearby? At this point, the safety of your classroom depends on your quick thinking, so you need a plan in advance to guide you. If the individual is not in the classroom or if you can remove him or her from the room, you should immediately barricade the door to keep out the individual. The heaviest, moveable object in the room is your first choice, if it is close enough to the door to block it quickly. Have students help you move the object in front of the door and then stand away from the doorway.

If a truly dangerous individual is in the classroom, the first thing to do is to get everyone down on the floor. This is the safest place to be because on the floor you are less conspicuous and threatening, so less of a target and less likely to get hurt from flying objects. If you cannot get the violent individual to leave, find areas in the room that you can control. This may mean keeping students at the back of the room if the person is at the front by the door. If the person is farther into the room, try to get him or her away from the door so you can usher the class out of the room. If anyone can get out, assign two students the task of getting help to you in the event that you are left in the room.

By having a preset plan and preparing students to know what to do in an emergency, the chances of having a positive outcome are highly increased. A run-through of what to do in an emergency can be very helpful. If students know you have a plan for their safety, they will be able to follow your instructions more quickly and confidently. A preset plan is the best insurance you can have for avoiding violence in your classroom. For more information about protecting your school or classroom from violence, contact information is provided:

National Alliance for Safe Schools
P.O. Box 290
Slanesville, WV 25445
(888) 510-6500

HELPING CHILDREN DEAL WITH SEPARATION AND LOSS

Dealing with loss is very difficult, especially for children, who are often unable to understand the reasons for the loss. Children may experience separation from important people in their lives through death, illness, divorce, military duty, or even a prison sentence. Whatever the reason for separation or loss, children must go through the grieving process, just as adults do, and this interferes with their ability to concentrate in school, enjoy normal activities, and fulfill routine requirements. When working with a child in the classroom who is undergoing the difficult process of grieving, a teacher can be an invaluable source of support. However, many teachers feel ill prepared for the challenge.

To help any individual who is dealing with a loss, it is most important to be open with the individual and encourage him or her to talk about the person when and if he or she is ready. Showing students you are available to talk to them about their loved one and able to handle talking about loss is the first crucial step. Many people are so uncomfortable with loss that they do not want to discuss it. This makes the grieving process especially difficult for children to handle. Often, the significant adults in the child's life are grieving through the loss as well. They may be trying so desperately to be strong and in control of their own grieving that the child is left to cope on his or her own, frequently with an unhealthy model of repression.

A teacher may be one of the few people in the child's life who knows the child well enough to see his or her pain and who is removed enough from the loss to be able to help the child cope. Teachers need not wait for a parent or guardian, or even for the child, to ask for help. The first step in helping a child may simply be asking the child what he or she is experiencing or how he or she is coping with the loss. Often, the individual who is gone is a taboo subject not only in the home but also in society. This leaves the child with no one to share his or her thoughts and feelings.

Even though speaking about the person the student has lost is an important part of the grieving or coping process, some children may find talking about this person difficult. It may help children to bring to school pictures of the individual so they can tell you about this person and the feelings they have for him or her. Children may need to have some form of physical contact while talking about their loss, or they may need to be physically doing something while they talk to help them express themselves. The photos may also help the child feel that they have something concrete to secure the memory of the individual, which can be a significant source of relief for the child, even if the individual does not return.

Some children feel the need to keep a journal to share with the person they are separated from or unable to contact. To preserve their memories, they can write in the journal as if they were talking to the person, or as if it were just an account of things they enjoyed doing together. One of the great fears children have who are separated from someone they love is that either they will forget the individual or the individuals will forget them, or both. Therefore, memory preservation is especially comforting. It may also be helpful for the child to build some form of memory box. This box could contain items of special significance to both of them, such as pictures, stories, audiotapes, videotapes, or letters about things they enjoyed doing together. If the individual is going away, such as for military duty or because of divorce, the child can make a memory box to give to the individual to remind him or her of the many things they shared together. This box can match one kept by the child, symbolically creating a link between the two.

With the help of a caring teacher, a child can learn to cope with this extremely difficult process, which, unfortunately, is a part of life. The lessons learned about coping and grieving can be of value to children throughout their lives and will never be forgotten.

CHAPTER

Analyzing Behavior in the Classroom

5

The educated differ from the uneducated as much as the living from the dead.

—Aristotle

- When to Use Behavior Therapy Techniques
- Positive Reinforcement
- Negative Reinforcement
- Token Economies

- Contingency Contracts
- Corrective Techniques to Stop Negative Behavior
- Time-Out Strategies

Dear Mrs. Loichinger,

I want to thank you because you are the best teacher I ever had. I really liked our science class. The best thing we did was play kickball each Friday. Thanks so much for all the times you helped me with my homework.

Love,

Patrick

WHEN TO USE BEHAVIOR THERAPY TECHNIQUES

The idea of analyzing students' classroom behavior to effect changes may be considered controversial. Students are not puppets or animals to be controlled or trained to behave in certain ways just to please us. Obviously such manipulation would be cruel and unethical. However, in the past 10–20 years it has become more common for students who detest school who fill classrooms only because they are forced to attend school. Schools can also be forced to keep students. At present students with very difficult behaviors can be found in any teacher's classroom, and educators need tools to help teach out-of-control students to control themselves. Otherwise, these students' opportunities to participate and succeed in society will be limited, and the concentration that other students need to facilitate learning will increasingly be disrupted. Teachers must face this reality and strive to fully integrate these students into classrooms with their peers.

It would be wonderful to have students find our classrooms so inviting and stimulating that they would be happy to learn and grow with us. Unfortunately, some students have had so many bad experiences in their life that they may not yet be capable of adopting this disposition. Many of us learned at a very young age about consequences: when we did certain things, bad things happened. So we learned not to do those certain things again. Often, the basic motivation for how we behave initially comes from an external source—something outside ourselves. Slowly we learn personal control for our behavior, often by internalizing the initial external source of motivation. We begin to make choices, some of which may defer immediate gratification for future gain. Some children may never have learned the self-control to do this. The lesson is a hard one and may demand an external source of motivation.

Teachers may be able to provide that motivation by teaching children about making choices, one valuable way to help them gain self-control. Life is full of choices for all of us, and we must often choose the lesser of two evils. Teachers can make the difference between a child making a good choice or a bad choice. If children are not socialized at home or in school, they will probably be socialized through the court system. These children have every right to an education and deserve all the help they can get to become self-actualized. Management techniques have been developed solely for such children who need a great deal of assistance to take part in our educational system. These techniques are offered as interventions to help these children learn to make choices that will improve the quality of their life. However, the techniques should not in any way abdicate our responsibility to make classrooms interesting places where students have opportunities to investigate and learn according to their own interests and talents.

POSITIVE REINFORCEMENT

Do you ever ask yourself why your students behave as they do? According to Mr. Winslow, a seventh-grade science teacher, Shawna always plays the class clown, disrupting the class; Maria rarely opens her mouth in class; and Linwood tries to be his best on everything he does, no matter how hard it is for him. Mr. Winslow reports that he cannot understand why these students misbehave. If we have some understanding of what motivates an individual's behavior, we stand a chance of helping them change their behavior to serve their needs more effectively. Positive reinforcement probably affects behavior more than anything else. As classroom teachers we are in the position of setting up an environment that reinforces our students' positive behaviors to increase the frequency of them occurring in the future. We want to increase appropriate behavior and decrease inappropriate (nonfunctional) behavior in our classrooms. We must be aware of the power of reinforcement. A behavior that is positively reinforced occurs more often in the future, as long as the reinforcer still seems to be available, because the reinforcement, or our positive response, strengthens the probability that the behavior will be repeated. When Amanda works really hard on her science project, her work is praised, she's given a high grade, and her parents receive a letter about the nice job she did. As long as the praise, good grade, and letter home are positive things to her, she is more likely to work hard on her next science project as well.

We can judge whether our attempt at reinforcement is effective only by the outcome of our student's response. If the positive reinforcement is working, the probability of the student's response should increase; in other words, the response will be more likely to happen again. Also, the probability of the student repeating the positive behavior must increase because of the reinforcement only, and not for some other reason. So if a teacher says very good after the student performs a new behavior well, these words become positive reinforcers only if they cause the favorable behavior to be performed more often.

Positive reinforcement is an easy concept to understand. What is difficult to understand is the student's point of view. If you ask most teachers about their own academic success, you will find that most of them were successful in school and in most cases probably enjoyed school. If a student had the unhappy experience of finding school to be difficult, they would probably not continue in school to become an educator. The majority of teachers today probably had at least one parent at home supporting and encouraging their academic achievements.

Children and adolescents today have more distractions, social diversity, and entertainments than in the past. Unfortunately, today's students expect and demand more from school than traditional schooling can provide. The challenge to meet these demands and expectations can be a good thing because teachers want to give students more information and better, more useful skills to survive in the complicated world in which they live. We also have to prepare them for a world that is less factory oriented and more service oriented, more likely to value communication and group interaction skills, and more interested in rewarding creativity than ever before.

Thus, a teacher's job is probably harder than it was when most of us were growing up. If we do not give students the time, curriculum, and attention they need, they are sure to let us know, often by being difficult. Our job is to set up a program that teaches them the skills they need and engages them in material that is at the appropriate level and pace, with enough support to maximize their involvement and growth.

The Do's of Positive Reinforcement

When using reinforcement you must use it mindfully. Reinforcement is a powerful tool. If you do not think carefully before you begin about the complications and ramifications of the changes you are trying to establish in behavior, you might heighten the individual's difficulty. Take your time deciding whether you want the student's behavior modified for your sake or for the sake of the student. Use reinforcement only if you need to correct problematic behavior that is highly disruptive to the student. If this is the case, look for a way to reinforce appropriate behavior until the student learns to reinforce it him- or herself. Once the behavior becomes intrinsically motivated, versus extrinsically motivated, the student will be able to behave without needing to get something from you or to please you.

If you need to use a program of reinforcement, you must first decide what you will use to reinforce the student. Involving the student from the beginning is the best way to use a reinforcement system. Doing so helps the student learn how to reinforce him- or herself. In fact, you should switch the student to a system of self-reinforcement as soon as he or she is ready.

Once a system is set up and a reinforcer is chosen, work with the students to update the reinforcer as often as necessary. Changing reinforcers often reduces the likelihood students get tired of the reinforcer and quit working. New behaviors should be reinforced constantly until they are so well learned that they become habitual. After students learn new behaviors, up the ante for receiving reinforcement. Teachers should slowly demand more and more learning from the students each time they teach and reinforce new behaviors.

The Don'ts of Positive Reinforcement

Do *not* continue tangible reinforcers indefinitely. Students should be weaned from primary reinforcers, such as food and objects, and move on to secondary reinforcers such as praise and high fives. Eventually they should be weaned from your extrinsic reinforcements altogether. Remember the end goal: you want students to learn to reinforce themselves. As soon as students can do so, you should withdraw the program so they do not come to depend on your reinforcers and on pleasing you to value themselves.

Avoid reinforcing children to produce perfect work only, especially if they are perfectionists. Teach them to enjoy the process, not just a perfect product. They may already have enough people in their lives telling them they must be perfect if they want to be praised. Children do things they like because they are meaningful to them and not because they must please someone else.

Advantages and Disadvantages of Positive Reinforcement

Positive reinforcement is versatile and can be used in many ways. Many kinds of positive reinforcers are easy to acquire, dole out, and keep on hand. Examples of these reinforcers include tokens, such as points or chips, and verbal praise. Tangible reinforcers include food and drinks, favored activities, and privileges. Positive reinforcement is also a behavior modification method that children can be taught to use themselves, for example, when they want to change a very ingrained habit.

Using positive reinforcement has its disadvantages as well. Students can become dependent on the positive reinforcement they receive from adults and go to extreme lengths to get it. Unfortunately, they may cease to have any desire to do anything at all if they feel they will not be rewarded.

Using positive reinforcement to manipulate the environment has another disadvantage. Because both appropriate and inappropriate behavior can be positively reinforced, you could inadvertently reinforce behavior you would rather eliminate. Therefore, teachers need to take care to reinforce the desired behaviors, not only in individual students but also in the classroom as a whole. In some cases, even though a teacher may have control over what he or she intends to reinforce, the teacher may find it difficult, if not impossible, to control all the other variables in the classroom environment, including the rest of the class.

Examples of Positive Reinforcement

Remember Shawna, who always plays the class clown, disrupting Mr. Winslow's science class? Several observations revealed that the class is rather slow paced, and Shawna is highly reinforced by her classmates to liven up the class. The more attention she receives for her jokes and antics, the more she is reinforced and motivated to think up even more interesting diversions.

Mr. Winslow also reports that even though he tries to reinforce Maria's participating in class, by praising her in front of the class when she answers him, she rarely raises her hand or opens her mouth. However, she often stays after school to talk to him about the experiments they did in class. He cannot understand why his reinforcement does not work with her. Do you think Mr. Winslow's praise in front of the class is reinforcing? (Remember, only reinforcement causes the desired behavior to increase.) Does Mr. Winslow's praise satisfy the condition of increasing Maria's behavior? We can assume that Mr. Winslow's praise does not increase this behavior.

Mr. Winslow's student Linwood gives every project all he has, no matter how hard it is for him. Because he has some learning problems, his work quality is not as high as the average student in his classes, but his grades are high and he seems to be every teacher's favorite. Can you imagine what keeps him working so hard?

Every time Andrew sits down to read, his teacher gives him a token for extra time to play ball in the gym. Lately Andrew has not been reading as frequently. Is Andrew being positively reinforced for reading in class? What accounts for his change in reading behavior?

Erica giggles during science class. Her teacher puts her in the time-out area in the back of the room whenever this happens; however, she continues to giggle in science class. Is positive reinforcement taking place? How can you tell?

NEGATIVE REINFORCEMENT

If you ask your students whether they would like to be negatively reinforced most of them would probably decline because most people think negative reinforcement is punishment. But as a type of *reinforcement* it is actually the opposite. Most of us appreciate negative reinforcement as much as positive reinforcement. For example, if the air conditioning in your classroom broke on a very hot day, you would be negatively reinforced to get the janitor to fix it. Negative reinforcement reinforces behavior (getting the janitor) that eliminates something negative (the uncomfortable heat) thereby reinstating the comfortable (positive) environment (the air conditioning). If you told your class that they could skip the exam you planned on the presidents of the United States if they did a nice job on their individual reports of one president of their choice, you would be negatively reinforcing them to produce good reports.

Negative reinforcement is an easy way to reinforce students in the classroom. We all use it, often not fully realizing the power of what we are doing. Once we understand the process of negative reinforcement, we can use its power more consciously and effectively. Negative reinforcement can be defined as motivating a behavior that reduces or eliminates something negative and increases the likelihood of the behavior occurring again under similar conditions. We use the term *negative* not to signify anything bad, but rather to indicate that the reinforcement motivates behavior that *removes* something negative, in contrast to positive reinforcement, which motivates behavior that *produces* something positive.

Consider another example. You get a $50 parking ticket because you parked in a no-parking zone when you took a sick child to the doctor. You are unhappy about the ticket and decide to go to court. In court you explain to the judge that you had an emergency. The judge reduces your ticket to $25. He has negatively reinforced you to go to court. The next time you get a parking ticket you probably will again go to court to see whether you can get the fine reduced. So if someone asks you whether you would like to be negatively reinforced, say yes!

The Do's of Negative Reinforcement

Always use negative reinforcement in a positive way. It is a wonderful tool for motivating behaviors that reduce or eliminate unwanted effects or conditions that impair students' ability to learn, thus helping students learn. It is especially effective when paired with positive reinforcement. Together, the combination of these two behavior modification techniques increases the power of each.

The Don'ts of Negative Reinforcement

Do not bring negative things into your classroom only to remove them for reinforcement. One teacher developed a very complicated and punishing demerit system for her class. The students lived in constant dread of making mistakes on their work or in their behavior. In concert with her demerit system, she used positive reinforcement by having students earn away their demerits. This procedure for handling students' behavior made the classroom a dismal place to be, and soon she found her classes very poorly attended. Try not to use negative reinforcement too often because it is counterproductive. Your students might begin to associate you and your classroom with bad things happening or try to avoid you to rid themselves of the negative association.

Advantages and Disadvantages of Negative Reinforcement

The advantage of negative reinforcement is that it can be used to increase the probability of a behavior that is meant to get rid of something negative. The disadvantage is that it is based on something negative occurring, which must then be removed or reduced.

Examples of Negative Reinforcement

Josh forgot his track shoes for physical education one day. The teacher told him he must leave class and go to study hall for the entire period. Josh forgot his shoes the rest of the semester. Is negative reinforcement occurring? What is reinforcing Josh's behavior? (Hint: What is Josh's attitude toward physical education?)

When Caroline, a first-grader, is in reading group, she always pokes other children. This particularly upsets her teacher, Mr. Mealy, because Caroline is a poor reader and needs to follow along even more than the other students in the class. When Caroline is called on to read, she doesn't know where to read, so Mr. Mealy skips her turn and calls on someone else. If positive reinforcement were occurring, which behavior(s) would you expect to increase in the future? (Mr. Mealy thinks he is punishing Caroline by skipping her turn. Is he?) What might Mr. Mealy do instead to be more effective?

TOKEN ECONOMIES

Token economies reinforce acceptable behavior with items students exchange for something they find desirable, such as privileges, activities, events, or material objects. Teachers like to use token reinforcement systems because primary reinforcers can be difficult to keep on hand and have available each time a teacher wants to reinforce a child's behavior or academic performance. By having a "back-up" reinforcement system, in this case a token economy, teachers are free to continue whatever they are doing without having to stop continually to locate and use a specific reinforcer for each individual student. Such a system also allows students more control in deciding what they desire to work toward. Because tokens can later be exchanged for something the student wants, teachers are released from the chore of constantly reassessing what a particular student might want at a particular moment.

The Do's of Token Economies

Always have a fair and consistent method of giving tokens along with an adequate supply of tokens, and items or privileges for which they can be exchanged. You can help your system run smoothly by developing a manageable way for students to store their tokens that is safe and nonintrusive. Teachers need to set aside specific times for students to exchange tokens for rewards. Otherwise, students will continually disrupt class to cash in their tokens immediately every time they have earned enough for a desired reinforcer. To avoid disorder, set up a store, treasure chest, or exchange box in which the reinforcers are kept for which students can exchange their tokens.

The Don'ts of Token Economies

Teachers soon discover that everyday objects such as marbles or paper clips can easily be counterfeited. Therefore, it is not advisable to use objects that your students can obtain on their own. Teachers report that some tokens are so valuable to a particular student that he or she may like the token better than the rewards to be exchanged for the token. In this case the individual may not enjoy exchanging their tokens for the reward, rendering the token system ineffective. Also ineffective is permitting students to stockpile too many tokens. If students are allowed to gather so large an amount of tokens that they need no longer work or behave, their incentive to do so will subside.

Advantages and Disadvantages of Token Economies

The advantages of token economies are many. They are particularly effective tools for modifying behavior because they are highly motivating. They can create a fun atmosphere in a classroom. They teach students about working toward rewards that are not immediate. Finally, token economies are especially appealing to students who are unmotivated or disruptive. Teachers often find that setting up a token reward system makes their classroom a better place to teach.

Disadvantages may also accompany token economies. Students may be encouraged to work only for tokens or rewards, and not for the fun of learning. This consequence may increase the difficulty of the already difficult talk of discontinuing the token economy when you feel it is time to try to maintain the behavior you were reinforcing without this reward system. Therefore, if you choose to use a token reward system in your class, don't forget to withdraw the system slowly as soon as students seem ready to work or behave without the extra reinforcement.

CONTINGENCY CONTRACTS

A contingency contract is a written agreement between two or more parties establishing student performance, teacher and/or parent performance, and reinforcing consequences. When developing a contract, each task and corresponding reward for each party is specifically described. A well-written contract should have something for everyone.

The Do's of Contingency Contracts

Each part of a contract must be well thought out. The teacher or contract author should first indicate the target achievement in detail. Everyone should be clear about whether and when the student's and teacher's targets have been successfully achieved. Second, ensure that the timing of rewards, also a very important part of a contract, is appropriate and acceptable to all concerned. To be most effective, the reward should come as

5.7, p. 199

5.8, p. 200

5.9, p. 201

5.10, p. 202

soon as possible after the task/or behavior has been accomplished. Third, decide in advance on a date for review and renegotiation of the contract. Include these details in the written contract. Finally check and double-check that each party feels that the contract is fair and clear. Always provide each participant with a copy of the contract, and keep a copy in the student's file. All parties mentioned in the contract, including, parents or guardians, the principal, all teachers involved, and the student, must sign the contract to activate it. This contract will best succeed as a powerful tool when it has the endorsement of all concerned. When it does succeed, award your student a certificate to honor his or her success.

The Don'ts of Contingency Contracts

Although a good contract is a powerful tool, it will not succeed if misused or used inappropriately. Never allow the contracting procedure to become a power struggle. Never initiate a contract when one person is being pushed or forced to comply. This will result in grief, and resentment, and failure. Never begin a contract by giving large rewards; otherwise, there is little incentive to work harder. If it is obvious that the student will fail, end the contract and try something else. (Perhaps even draw up a new contract.)

Consider an example of a successful contract. Justin is a junior in high school with attention deficit disorders. He had a very poor start in his English literature class. He had always had difficulty taking notes and taking tests, and his grade in the class depended on these skills. He was also too embarrassed to answer questions in class. His teacher could have sent home a first semester Poor Progress Report and let him fail. However, she expected more from her students than sitting through her class without participating fully.

Justin's teacher invited Justin to stay after school and discuss with her the problems he was having. Together they came up with some solutions in the form of modifications of his course requirements. They developed and drew up a contract that spelled out exactly what each party needed to do. Justin was able to do the work, earn a B in the class, and learn something along the way. All parties were much happier with this solution than they would have been with the failure Justin was sure to experience if neither the requirements nor the student's behavior had been modified.

Advantages and Disadvantages of Contingency Contracts

The advantage of using a contingency contract is that it is a positive, reward-based system of managing behavior. Contracts can be very useful because they help form partnerships between the student, teachers, and parents. The specificity of contract agreements hold parents, teachers, and students accountable for their part of the contract. Therefore, consistency is increased and ambiguity is further decreased in a contract. All parties have the choice of fulfilling their part of the bargain or forfeiting their gain.

The disadvantage of contracting with a student is the amount of time it takes on the part of all individuals to develop the contract. A contract must be very well planned, well written, and precise, or it will not be effective. Another unintended, disadvantage of a contract is that unfortunately it focuses attention on the student who is misbehaving in some manner.

CORRECTIVE TECHNIQUES TO STOP NEGATIVE BEHAVIOR

5.11, p. 203

Many people think they are using corrective techniques—or punishment—to stop inappropriate behavior even though they are not. Punishment can be defined as presenting something negative or aversive. For example, when Gwen says "Hi" to Jonathan, he responds by poking her in the stomach. If the poke is painful and Gwen does not like it, she will probably experience his action as a punishment and stop speaking to him. But if Gwen is a sixth-grader who likes Jonathan and he pokes her as a friendly sixth-grade response, she might continue to talk to him and be reinforced by his attention.

A corrective technique is meant to punish misbehavior to eliminate it. Using corrective techniques is very difficult in a school setting because the punishment must be accomplished within the legal constraints of the law. Therefore, teachers must exercise extreme caution when they use such techniques. Furthermore, it is very difficult to find consequences that are truly punishing and that will eliminate misbehavior. The only way to know if an action is serving as a punishment is to study the subsequent behavior of the individual was being "punished."

Punishment is only effective if it occurs immediately. For example, if Sasha is trying to take a toy from a peer, she should be punished before she gets the toy. Once she gets it and plays with it, her behavior of taking the toy is reinforced. Stopping her from doing this again will be much more difficult because you will have to overcome this reinforcement.

The effectiveness of punishment in decreasing unwanted behavior depends on the intensity and frequency of the punishment. Is it severe enough to cause someone to stop doing the unwanted behavior? Also important is the timing of the punishment. Being sent to the back of the room would be much more punishing for Sunita during a game than during spelling class, which she dislikes.

Another deciding factor in the effectiveness of punishment is whether the person has the opportunity to choose alternative responses. You may need to teach alternative behaviors to your students *before* you try to eliminate the misbehavior in question. If you take away a behavior without giving the student a replacement activity, you risk getting worse behavior in its place.

The effectiveness of using punishment to change behaviors also depends on the strength of the behavior being punished. (By *strong* we mean that the student has been doing the behavior for a long time, probably because it has been especially effective for them.) Some behaviors are much stronger than others because they have been extremely rewarding to a student. If this is the case, a great deal of reinforcement must be added to the punishment to have any success in changing the behavior.

Consider an example of just such a case. Piper loves to sing. Whenever she is happy, sad, excited, or bored, she breaks out into song. (Usually one she has made up.) Her parents always thought this was cute and never stopped her. Consequently, she does it whenever she wants, including at restaurants, the movies, while shopping, while eating, or during naptime. Mr. Holmes, her first-grade teacher, is very frustrated because Piper sings through announcements, teacher presentations, reading groups, silent work time, and tests. He and the students in his class find it very disruptive.

Punishing consequences may either occur naturally or be devised by a person. Naturally occurring consequences include getting a stomachache after eating too much candy and falling and breaking an arm after disobeying the teacher and climbing to the top of the playground equipment on a wet day. These punishing consequences usually need no intervention from adults. The unpleasant consequences of behaviors such as these are likely to prevent the inappropriate behavior from being repeated. Most students easily give up behaviors that have painful natural results.

However, sometimes no unpleasant natural consequences follow misbehavior, so a person, such as a parent, teacher, or guidance counselor may need to arrange punishing consequences. These consequences may consist of social living rules; if you hit a peer, you will be sent to the office to see the principal; if you forget to return the ball to the closet after recess, you will not be permitted to take it out for the rest of the week. Social living rules should not be arbitrary nor extremely punitive. Instead, they should be logical and easily understandable. The student should feel that he or she has a clear choice. By following the rules, good things happen and bad things are avoided.

Unfortunately, the presentation of aversive consequences may or may not result in relatively permanent behavior modification. Sometimes the behavior is only temporarily suppressed and comes back later on in a stronger form. This is especially true when the misbehavior is very exciting or pleasant. Before using any form of punishment, the teacher should first consider whether the child needs to learn a new behavior to replace the old one or needs to be more effectively reinforced for using the alternative behavior.

Remember, whenever you are trying to eliminate misbehavior, first teach the appropriate behavior and have the student practice it. Then reinforce the new behavior whenever you see it occurring. Ensure that you are using the best possible reinforcer by choosing one you know the student will enjoy. Once the misbehavior seems to be inhibited, continue to reinforce alternative behaviors on an intermittent schedule. You no longer need to reinforce the good behavior every time. You may reward the student for the good behavior any time, but the student should not know for which occurrence of the behavior.

Sometimes, after being punished, misbehavior stops for a period of time only to reappear a short time later, as soon as the specific conditions are removed or changed. The misbehavior was probably habitual, and most behaviors change slowly, just as they develop. This can be very frustrating for a teacher, or parent but don't give up. Just follow the procedure already outlined.

Unfortunately punishment has many negative side effects. Students may begin to avoid or fear the person who punishes them. Students may avoid places where they have been punished. They may become aggressive and learn to use punishment on others to get their way. Any of these reactions can interfere with students' progress in school and their ability to get along with others in the school building.

Sometimes, when punishment isn't administered each time the misbehavior occurs, the misbehavior is reinforced. The student realizes that he or she can get away with the misbehavior sometimes, and it becomes a challenge to test the punisher and see how often the misbehavior can go unpunished. It becomes an exciting gamble for the student to see whether he or she will win. In these circumstances the individual might continue the misbehavior despite the threat of punishment.

For some children the only time they get attention is when they are being punished for misbehavior. This is a serious problem with using punishment. If the teacher is paying attention to a student only when he or she is punishing the student, the misbehavior is likely to increase instead of decrease. If so, the teacher is not really punishing but reinforcing the behavior.

One way to punish students without giving them something negative is to remove positive consequences. When Sunita is taken away from her friends to sit by herself at the back of the classroom, she may feel punished. Again, this can only happen if Sunita views being with her friends in the class as a positive thing. Another student might not feel this way at all. Being sent to the back of the class might be viewed as a positive thing for a student who doesn't want to be involved with the academic material and who enjoys being alone to do as he or she wishes. Again, remember that the only way to know whether an action is punishing is to study the subsequent behavior of the individual who was "punished."

For example, in the beginning of the year, Rebecca began to get out of her seat 2 or 3 times a day. Each time Mrs. Donapple saw her out of her seat, she would verbally reprimand Rebecca. By January, Rebecca was spending a large amount of her time out of her seat. Mrs. Donapple decided to increase her efforts to get Rebecca to remain in her seat. First, Mrs. Donapple counted the average number of times Rebecca was out of her seat. It appeared to be 6 or 7 times a day. Second, Mrs. Donapple decided that each time she found Rebecca out of her seat, she would guide her back to her seat and verbally reprimand her. Since Mrs. Donapple began guiding Rebecca to her seat and reprimanding her for being out of her seat, Rebecca has been getting out of her seat 12 or 13 times a day. Is Rebecca's out-of-seat behavior being punished?

TIME-OUT STRATEGIES

Time-out is a strategy whereby a child is removed from a reinforcing environment and placed in a nonreinforcing environment. Teachers can use time-out as a consequence for a student's misbehavior. Teachers can also use time-out to remove students from an environment in which they cannot behave appropriately. Such a time-out area can be useful for a child who is upset and needs quiet space in which to calm down. Time-out may be used in the home, school, or any other environment, such as day-care centers and after-school activities in which children are being cared for by adults. This procedure is useful because it is not as negative as punishing procedures used in the past, yet can effectively help change student misbehavior without being extremely harsh or negative. Time-out strategies can be divided into many different types. The main types are nonexclusionary, observation, exclusionary, and seclusionary.

Nonexclusionary Time-Out.   The first level of time-out is removing materials being inappropriately used by a student. The child's chair can be pulled away from a group in which he or she was not behaving well. A child may be required to put down his or her head for a designated period of time. Teachers often use this procedure for mild misbehaviors, such as talking out and distracting other learners.

Observation Time-Out.   In observation time-out a student is excluded from group involvement. He or she may, however, still see and hear the activity. This is especially positive because it allows the student access to the information that the other students are receiving so the student can avoid falling behind.

Exclusionary Time-Out.   In exclusionary time-out the student is denied access to reinforcement. To use this procedure in a classroom setting, most teachers screen off a corner of the classroom. (Some teachers use a study carrel.) There the offending child can neither see nor be seen by the rest of the class. Furthermore, students being punished with exclusionary time-out are not allowed to be a part of the activity for a designated period of time. Students who are excluded often gain an additional incentive to practice self-control because they are not allowed to participate in the classroom until they do.

Seclusionary Time-Out.   In seclusionary time-out a misbehaving student is moved completely out of the area where the other students are. Students are removed to a time-out area. This space must be supervised by a staff member. It is used for serious, out-of-control misbehaviors, such as physical harm to self or others, trashing the room, and so forth.

If you move a child into a seclusionary time-out area, it is important to maintain the safety of all concerned. It is recommended that teachers follow certain guidelines in respect to the location and attributes of the time-out area. For example, the room should have appropriate lighting, temperature, and ventilation, and it is highly recommended that the room not be locked. The room should be at least 6 × 6 feet in size, to provide comfortable access by the student and staff. Remember, students should not be left unmonitored and should always be safe. If the student is likely to be highly aggressive or physically threatening to self and/or others, the floor, door, and walls should be padded or carpeted. Check the entrance to the room to ensure that it can be easily entered and accessed when necessary. The room must be within view of the teacher or teaching support staff.

To use a seclusionary time-out area correctly, a time-out log or record should be developed. The log should include when the child went to time-out, when the time-out ended, the behavior that preceded time-out, and the behavior during time-out. Analyzing this ongoing record can provide clues as to why time-out is or is not effective for

5.12, p. 204

5.13, p. 205

5.14, p. 206

5.15, p. 207

any particular student. It is also helpful in documenting the student's behavior and alerting parents to the type and occurrence of problems their child has. Using time-out correctly is a very effective tool for changing behavior.

The Do's of the Time-Out Procedure

Begin using time-out by selecting one specific misbehavior and explain to the student the behavior you would like to see instead. Then gather information on how often and under what circumstances this misbehavior is occurring. As you do this, you must choose the type of time-out that works best for the offending student. Learn all you can about this student so you can make informed judgments. Time-out procedures should be well defined to the child and the parents before it can be implemented. Whenever you use a time-out room, you must obtain informed consent from the student's parents. Explain to students what your expectations are and post them for readers, in the time-out areas. Hold "practice" sessions on how to get to and behave in time-out. Do this when the child is not in crisis.

Reinforce positive behaviors that occur after a time-out. Remember to be consistent so that the student always knows when and why they are being timed-out. If you find that time-out is effective, use it throughout the child's school day to increase its effectiveness. The student should be told only once to go to time-out. If the student does not comply, the teacher should unemotionally place the student in time-out, if this can be easily done. However, it would be unwise to gather a group of other teachers to help you force the student into time-out unless the student is being dangerous to him- or herself and others. (Some teachers choose to call the police or school security when students are being extremely destructive and refuse to be timed-out. If this happens parent or guardians must be notified.)

The Don'ts of the Time-Out Procedure

Never use time-out sporadically or without first thinking it out carefully. Never leave a student in time-out without carefully monitoring him or her. Do not permit the student to talk or interact with others during time-out because this interferes with the magnitude of the punishment. Commenting on or discussing the offender's inappropriate behavior upon returning from completing a period of time-out is also negative. This would be doubling the punishment. It is more effective to let the punishment stand alone. Some teachers slowly increase the amount of time the student must serve in time-out, mistakenly thinking that they need to make the punishment stiffer to make it work. However, by slowly increasing the amount of time, the student becomes acclimated to the time-out, and it loses its punishing power. Never leave any student in a time-out room for more than 15 minutes. (For some students 5 minutes is too long, so teachers must know their students well and accordingly adjust the punishment to fit the needs of the child.) Periods of time-out should be brief. A very rough guideline used by some teachers is 1 minute for every year of a student's age.

It is also inappropriate to use time-out with a student if it appears to be ineffective for them. Some children are not able to accept the conditioning. Also, do not overuse time-out. Any procedure used too often loses its effectiveness. Even for students who seem to learn from the time-out procedure, there is a limit to how often it will work effectively. Discontinue altogether the use of time-out procedures if they seem to cause fear in a student. Educators are not in the business of terrorizing children.

Advantages and Disadvantages of the Time-Out Procedure

Most important to the successful use of time-out is the teacher's ability to ascertain whether the environment the student is leaving is reinforcing and the time-out environment is not. This is easier said than done. Unfortunately, some children find the classroom an uncomfortable or difficult place to be, especially when they have problems with academic achievement or sitting still. (Often these are the very same students that teachers need to discipline.) So before using time-out with any student, the teacher must evaluate the impact of the environment the student is leaving. If the classroom or activity is rewarding to the student and the time-out area is not, then using the time-out procedure with that student can be a very effective means for reducing a target behavior.

Another advantage of using time-out is that it requires record keeping. Careful record keeping documents when and why a student is failing in a classroom situation and when and why a student must be removed or secluded from the class. These records help the staff carefully examine what the student finds positive or negative in the environment. This understanding can enable us to better design our classrooms for learning and better design an environment free of as many distractions as possible.

One disadvantage of the time-out procedure is that teachers are not always able to seclude a child. Some children are very resistant to being timed out. If this is the case, the teacher should have back-up consequences ready. Furthermore, if a student resists or refuses to go to time-out and the teacher or staff member continues to try to place him or her in seclusion, an upsetting and distracting commotion can ensue. This commotion may be reinforcing for the student, which is exactly what you do not want.

Time-out loses its effectiveness when the period of time is either too long or too brief. Teachers may find it difficult to remember that the duration should be short and consistent. Some teachers find that they want to leave the behaviorally disruptive student in seclusion for long periods of time. It may seem pleasant to have misbehaving students removed from the classroom and from the other students in the classroom. However, don't tempt yourself. Get yourself a timer and limit the time-out with the help of a bell or ringer that sounds when the designated amount of time is finished.

Time-out is often misused as a form of school suspension with teenagers. School suspension is usually ineffective because students come in contact with outside reinforcers. Does it not seem strange that we often like to punish students who do not come to school by not allowing them to come to school? Similarly, outside reinforcers also play a counterproductive role in some time-out situations in which students are placed in an area where other children walk by and talk with the timed-out student. Or, they may be placed in an area such as the school office, which can be more interesting to some children than their original classroom because a great deal of drama transpires in the school office.

Unfortunately the effectiveness of time-out as an intervention is contingent upon the characteristics of the student. Time-out can be very effective with an acting-out, aggressive, group-oriented child who wants to be with the group and attended to by the teacher. However, time-out is probably less effective with a quiet or withdrawn student who enjoys the quiet of being left alone to daydream.

For a time-out procedure to have full effect, the student should always be held responsible for class work that was interrupted by the time-out; otherwise the child may learn that time-outs can be used as a means of avoiding difficult or undesirable assignments.

CHAPTER

6

Techniques for Handling Students with Distinct Abilities and Challenging Needs

People seldom see the halting and painful steps by which the most insignificant success is achieved.

—Anne Sullivan

- Children and Adolescents with Learning Disabilities
- Students with Attention Deficit Hyperactivity Disorder
- Children and Adolescents with Emotional or Behavioral Problems
- Students Who Are Frequently Truant or School Phobic
- Students Who Are Gifted and Talented
- Students with Cognitive Disabilities
- Children Who Are at Risk in Our Schools
- Useful Resources

To the greatest teacher ever—

You have taught me so much in the time I have known you. Not only did you constantly help and support me with school, but you also taught me about life and what it means to be a good person. You have inspired me to do my best and be my best. Much of what I learned from you I learned from the example you set and the way you live your life. Grace under fire, patience, kindness, giving, not giving up, how to work hard but always have time for the important things, how to be a good person, that loving others is the most important thing in life, that knowledge is the key to your future, and most of all that no matter what happens you would always be there for me. Who I am today is shaped by what you taught me, and if I grow up to be even a fraction of the person you are, I will be happy.

Thank you,

A. A.

CHILDREN AND ADOLESCENTS WITH LEARNING DISABILITIES

Definition of Learning Disabilities

The term *learning disability* was first coined by Kirk in 1963 as a compromise term for kids with learning problems. Other terms used at the time to define these children were *minimally brain damaged, slow learner, dyslexic*—(which means inability to read), and *perceptually disabled.*

Students with specific learning disabilities show a significant difference between their academic achievement and their overall intelligence. They often have severe difficulties learning in one or more of these areas: oral expression, listening comprehension, written expression, basic reading skill, reading comprehension, mathematical calculation, and mathematical reasoning. They may be successful in some school subjects yet have extreme difficulty with certain skills, such as decoding words, calculating math facts, or getting their thoughts into writing. Teachers usually recognize them as being significantly behind their peers in these skills. Specific learning disabilities are believed to be caused by problems with the brain's ability to process information. Most processing problems continue throughout a person's lifetime. However, over time most individuals will successfully adapt to their differences with coping skills that help them lead normal lives.

Causes of Learning Disabilities

A central nervous system dysfunction has always been presumed to be the cause of learning disabilities. According to recent research, processing disorders cause difficulty in the ability of different regions of the brain to interact. In particular, genetic links, problems during pregnancy or delivery, toxins in the environment, alcohol or other drug abuse, and stress in the child's life can all adversely affect neurons and brain cell growth.

Approaches to Teaching Students with Learning Disabilities

Many teaching approaches seem to help students succeed academically and socially. In today's world, technology can help students perform tasks they find difficult. For example, students with learning disabilities often find that writing is made more manageable with computers loaded with a word-processing program featuring spell checkers. Other students use palm pilots with timers to help them remember what they need to do and when they need to do it.

Many individuals are helped when teachers use multisensory teaching approaches whereby multiple senses are involved in the presentation and manipulation of information. When teaching the class to work a problem in math, the teacher can talk about the procedure, give a physical demonstration of why the procedure works, work the procedure on the overhead projector, list the steps in doing the procedure on the board, and have the class take places at the board to work problems themselves.

Providing a high degree of structure in the classroom helps students with learning disabilities learn a routine, for example, where they need to be, when they need to be there, and how they need to act once they are there. A teacher who is highly organized can help a student become organized. Check the organization of students' materials periodically to help them stay on track. Eliminating distracting stimuli can have a very positive effect. A teacher who reduces the quantity of stimuli in the classroom helps students with learning disabilities concentrate. Similarly, telling the class specifically when a message is important helps students with learning disabilities know when to attend and what to attend to.

A teacher's willingness to be flexible can also be a great asset to students with learning disabilities. If the classroom teacher is flexible enough to allow students to learn in whatever way they can, the end will justify whatever means are necessary. Some students may need video or audio recordings of lectures to review at a later time when they are less distracted. Others may benefit from an outline of the lecture that they can review before it starts. This way, they have extra time to review and retain information.

Cognitive training is another method of helping students with learning disabilities. Students may profit from instruction in learning how to learn and in what is involved in being a good student. Study skills, such as how to take notes, tricks for memorizing facts, how to underline and then outline a chapter, studying for tests, getting organized in life, and how to keep assignments straight, can all provide excellent support. By showing students how to develop information webs, learn mnemonic devices, correct and revise their work, and break up difficult tasks into smaller parts, teachers often see great improvement in students' achievement and understanding of material.

Much can be done to help students with learning disabilities succeed academically even though researchers still have a lot more to learn about their abilities and disabilities. You can find more information on this subject in the last section of this chapter, Useful Resources. In this section lists of suggested readings and organizations are provided for further research (see pages 66–67).

6.1, p. 209

6.2, p. 211

STUDENTS WITH ATTENTION DEFICIT HYPERACTIVITY DISORDER

Definition of Attention Deficit Hyperactivity Disorder

Students with attention deficit hyperactivity disorder (ADHD) often have trouble focusing and attending to relevant, important information. They also have a difficult time inhibiting their behavior. Because of this, they tend to blurt out things that get them in trouble and dive into things without a plan. They may seem to be in constant physical motion, focusing their attention only briefly on one thing after another. More boys than girls seem to be affected by this condition. But no matter what the gender of the student, having ADHD makes achieving and learning in school very difficult for students and their teachers.

Causes of Attention Deficit Hyperactivity Disorder

The most probable cause of attention deficit hyperactivity disorders is neurological. ADHD is most likely caused by an imbalance in neurotransmitters. Because neurotransmitters are important in regulating and focusing behavior, high or low levels of neurotransmitting chemicals may affect a student's ability to regulate themselves. Perhaps the chemical dopamine, which helps the brain focus, is less effective or deficient in children with ADHD. Scientists suspect that this disorder is inherited genetically.

Approaches to Teaching Students with ADHD

Before any student walks through the classroom door, his or her teacher should look at the student's medical records to see what needs he or she may have. Teachers need to be informed about allergies, vision or hearing problems, immunization records, and any medication being taken by their students. If any of your students need medication it would be very helpful for you to know their medication schedule. You can be a much more effective instructor with this information.

To help students with ADHD, and possibly others, provide students with a clear structure and routine schedule, posting rules, schedules, and assignments in the same place each day. Use a routine attention-getter before beginning a lesson, and invite students with ADHD to attend if they are not already doing so. Have routines for students to enter the room, to leave the room, and turn in assignments. This will make it easier (and therefore more likely) for a student with ADHD to keep up with the other students and to be in the right place at the right time.

How you handle distractions and lesson time also makes a difference. Try to limit distractions such as fans or machinery both in the classroom as well as directly outside your door. However, students should be given optimal sensory stimulation. Use lots of visual aids and give the class a variety of multisensory, kinesthetic, and hands-on activities whenever possible. Also remember that students should have 20 minutes maximum of sitting time. If you must go longer than this, have students stand up and stretch at their seats. Mix up sitting time and active time, allowing for frequent breaks. Mix high-interest and low-interest activities as well as easy and difficult tasks. Finally, break down tasks into small segments and help students know which task must be done in which order. With all these approaches, always monitor behavior and give appropriate feedback.

Students with attention deficit disorders often profit from social skills training. In particular, they may need to be taught how to work in groups. Using cooperative learning groups can be especially useful in classroom settings. Teach all students the specific roles they are to play in the group.

A comprehensive behavior management program should be developed for use at home and at school. Parents of students with ADHD might find that management techniques used in the classroom are helpful at home as well. For example, when a parent request a child with attention deficit disorder to perform a chore, the parent will find it just as useful to break down the steps of the chore as a teacher finds doing so with large classroom assignments. Because of the high level of physical movement associated with ADHD, providing a physical outlet for the individual, especially one that is noncompetitive, is also helpful. Although medical intervention, such as drug therapy, can be helpful, it needs to be closely monitored by the doctor, the student, the parents, and the classroom teacher.

Students with ADHD benefit from individual counseling to learn coping techniques, problem-solving strategies, and how to deal with stress and self-esteem. Students with ADHD need coping strategies to regulate personal behavior as well as "stop-and-think" techniques. The pressures caused by ADHD affect not only the child, but the family as well. Therefore, it is often helpful to involve the family in counseling as well. A greater understanding of the disorder can improve the entire family's ability to cope with the child in a positive and supportive manner. More information on the material in this section is provided at the end of this chapter. Lists of suggested readings and organizations can be found in Useful Resources, on page 67.

CHILDREN AND ADOLESCENTS WITH EMOTIONAL OR BEHAVIORAL PROBLEMS

Definition of Emotional or Behavioral Problems

Students with emotional or behavioral problems have significant difficulties in one or more of the areas of emotional, behavioral, or social functioning. These difficulties interfere with their ability to learn. They may have difficulty making or keeping friends, showing or perceiving emotions, and controlling anger or fear. This emotional disability is evident in multiple environments, including school, home, and community. Students with problems in these areas generally show signs of difficulty over a long period of time, often beginning at school entrance, if not before. Students with emotional disturbance have problems that are so severe in strength and severity that they stand out from their peers.

Causes of Emotional or Behavioral Problems

Causes of behavioral and emotional disabilities may be biological, environmental, or a combination of both, which is often the case. Biological causes include genetics, damage to the brain or central nervous system, and chemical imbalances. Environmental causes include, but are not limited to, extreme poverty, stress, violence, and significant personal loss.

Approaches to Teaching Students with Emotional or Behavioral Problems

6.4, p. 213

6.5, p. 214

When it is known or suspected that a student in your class has a behavioral or emotional problem, the first thing you need to do is define the problem as it relates to your classroom. Watch carefully and begin to isolate the problem behaviors that need to be addressed. Before you begin to address the behaviors, you need to observe and document when and how they occur. For this reason, it is recommended that teachers use an ABC (antecedent-behavior-consequence) Observation Form.

Keep copies of the ABC form on a clipboard on your desk so that you can readily access it and carefully describe the situation in which the child's problem occurred. List the problem behavior on the form under Behavior of Interest (see Teacher Resource 6.5). In the second column, Behavior, list and describe in detail the behavior of concern. In the first column, Antecedent, fill in the circumstances that preceded the behavior. Again, use as much detail as possible because it may take you more than a few observations to discover what is triggering the behavior. In the last column, Consequences, list in detail what happened after the behavior occurred. Continue to document at least four or five occurrences of the behavior. The more information you have, the better able you will be to unlock the mystery of why the student does what he or she does.

Next, look at all the entries in the antecedent column. These entries need to be compared to see what they may have in common. Sometimes it is very easy to discern.

For example, whenever the teacher tells her class it is time to correct their homework, Manuel somehow bothers his neighbors, poking, hitting, and teasing them. This suggests that Manuel is trying to avoid homework correction.

If you are unable to find any patterns that make sense to you in the antecedent column, check the consequence column. Usually, when a behavior persists over time, it is rewarding the student with exactly what he or she wants. If it were not rewarding, that behavior would eventually disappear. Often "punishments" are the reason students continue to misbehave. (Remember our discussion of punishment in Chapter 5?) Although you may think that the consequences a student pays for misbehaving are punishing, the student may not experience those consequences quite that way.

For example, Tamara's teacher always sent her to a time-out area in the back of the room when she was found swearing. She continued to swear and seemed always to lose her temper and swear during intense academic activities. Her teacher noticed this but assumed it was due to academic frustration. Although this was probably partially true, Tamara learned, more importantly, that by causing a scene and disrupting class, she would be left alone and probably get out of doing the academic activity altogether. Students tell us more about what they want and need than we might realize, but we must crack the code they use when speaking to us.

Once you discover what is causing the behavior, you are well on your way to finding solutions to the problem. Sometimes solutions involve rearranging the reinforcers in your classroom; sometimes the problem goes deeper and solutions require outside intervention. Whatever the problem is, it must be addressed and a good place to start usually is getting good information or evidence of the problem. You may want to videotape the class to evaluate what is going wrong and to capture the evidence on tape. After watching the tape, you may get a better idea of what is happening.

After honing in on the problem and gathering further information about it, you are ready to find a technique to modify the behavior. (See Chapter 5 for more information on modifying behavior.) Were you able to identify what precluded the behavior? Is there any way to head off the problem before it starts? For example, if you suspect that Manuel misbehaves when it is time to correct homework because he is trying to avoid turning in or correcting his homework, you can require him to turn in homework assignments as soon as he enters the classroom—before class starts. In this way, you will discover right away whether he did the assignment. At this time he can be rewarded if he turns in his homework; otherwise, he can be sent somewhere to complete it if it is not done, thereby missing a favorite activity, for example, the morning quiz show, as a consequence.

Once you distinguish the misbehavior from the situation in which it normally occurs, you can positively reward or punish the behavior to help the student make better choices in the future. If Manuel learns that he will be rewarded if he does his homework and that he will lose something he desires if he doesn't do his homework, he will probably learn to make the correct choice in the future. Setting clear and fair consequences for behavior helps children learn to behave in ways that lead to success in your classroom and presumably throughout their lives. Never leave a student's success to chance. Doing all you can to help a student succeed does both of you a favor.

When problems are so serious that a child seems to have no control over his or her behavior, even when the behavior does not elicit the desired results, it is time to call in reinforcements. Talk to past teachers. One or more of them might have found ways to work with the child in the past. Arrange to meet with parents to see what they do at home that might work for you. You may want to contact school psychologists or social workers. If necessary, enlist the aid of the principal to discover other school district resources. Or, investigate whether community support services are available that you or the school cannot provide. Try not to let problem behavior disrupt you, the student, or the rest of the class. For further information about these problems, see the list of suggested readings and organizations in Useful Resources at the end of this chapter (pages 67–68).

STUDENTS WHO ARE FREQUENTLY TRUANT OR SCHOOL PHOBIC

Definition of Truancy and School Phobic

Students who are school phobic and students who are truant both often miss school without good reason. Because they miss so much classroom information, they rarely do well in school or learn what they need to learn to succeed in life. Accordingly, these absences are of great concern to teachers and their schools. However, whatever other similarities these two groups of students share, their absentee behavior has one important difference: the two groups miss school for completely different reasons. Therefore, we now examine by comparison the causes of absenteeism that distinguish these two groups of students.

Causes of Truancy and School Phobia

Students who are school phobic miss school because they are either afraid of school or afraid to leave home whereas truant children are usually happy to leave home (pretending to go to school) and go off with their friends to do something they find more exciting. To ascertain which type of student you are dealing with, you must find out what the individual is doing when he or she is not in school. If the individual is to be found mostly at home, chances are that the factor determining his or her behavior is fear, not disinterest.

Not only does the location of the absent student signify his or her reason for missing school, but the particular school years during which the student is most often absent may also signify the reason. Therefore, you must examine a student's school attendance records. Identify the years when a student was absent the most. Do you see any patterns? If you discover that a student missed the greatest number of school days in kindergarten and first grade, at the beginning of middle school, and again at the beginning of high school, you have evidence that this students has phobia stemming from a fear of school. If absences don't seem to follow this or any other pattern, but are more or less constant, you probably have a case whose school phobia stems from a fear of leaving the home.

They might be afraid of leaving home for many reasons. School phobic children might stay home from school because they are afraid to leave their parents alone at home. They might fear their parents will fall ill and need them. They might fear their parents will be lonely without them. They might fear their parents will be angry or hurt if they leave them. Some children are overly attached to their parents. They might feel insecure and frightened without them. They might fear their parents will go away while they are at school. In most cases these fears are probably unreasonable. However, the first step to overcome these fears is to ascertain whether they have any basis in reality.

Consider Vicky, a 17-year-old high school student who was constantly missing school. Often her mother wrote her notes so that she would be excused for her absences. Soon the school required a doctor's confirmation of her illnesses, which never was obtained. Other times her mother would drive her to school in the morning and then pick her up at lunch, presumably because her daughter felt ill.

Vicky's teacher knew that if Vicky did not come to school more often, she would never graduate. (After 2 years in driver's education courses, she had not been able to attend enough classes to pass the course and so was not permitted to drive.) The teacher tried to make school more accommodating, putting Vicky in special classes—even in classes with constant individual help. Nothing seemed to help.

On one of the few days when Vicky attended school, she received a phone call from her father. He had been out of town on a business trip and her mother had gotten so upset that she attempted suicide. The reason Vicky stayed home became clear. It was not because Vicky had any problem at school; it was because her mother was making her feel guilty for leaving her at home alone. Without knowing the reason for constant absences, it is very difficult to find a cure.

Students who are truant from school usually do so to be off with their friends, and not out of any fear. These individuals can often be found at local hangouts or at places where students are known to gather to drink or do drugs. If you or the police cannot find them there, they can be identified by where they are not: they are not at school and they are not at home. Children who are constantly truant often have conduct disorders. They may be involved with a gang of friends with whom they are off doing things. They are often the children who are out late at night and return home only to sleep, if they return home at all.

Approaches to Teaching Students Who Are School Phobic

A child with school phobia often displays school refusal behaviors. Such children may refuse to go to school. They may leave home for school but soon return home. They may say nothing but have certain physical complaints, such as headaches, stomachaches, or racing hearts. The behavior they exhibit in front of their parents may come in the form of tantrums, physical resistance, pleading or tears. The treatment for this condition must be progressive.

Approaches to Teaching Students Who Are Frequently Truant

When students are absent because of truancy, you can help them comply with school attendance rules in two main ways. First, help students enjoy being in school by increasing academic success and positive reinforcement. Second, do not allow students to gain positive reinforcement from skipping out of school. You increase the student's positive rewards in school by meeting often with the student to discuss his or her progress and to ensure success. Always try to get the student's parents involved in the child's academic progress, and notify them regularly of their child's successes.

To decrease satisfaction that the child obtains from being absent from school, school officials need to do all they can to ensure the student arrives at school. This may entail picking up students at their door and escorting them to school, or having parents, siblings, or relatives drive the student to school. If for some reason it is impossible to get the child to school, send home the student's work and insist upon its completion. It is always best to involve the student's parents or guardians in as many ways as possible. This is especially necessary because you need to work closely with them to eliminate reinforcements for not coming to school. For example, parents may agree not to allow their child to watch television, play video games, or receive an allowance if the child does not go to school. For more information on this subject, see Useful Resources at the end of this chapter (pages 68–69).

STUDENTS WHO ARE GIFTED AND TALENTED

Definition of Gifted and Talented

Individuals who are gifted and talented demonstrate superior ability in one or more of the following areas: intellectual, visual or performing arts, creativity, or leadership. These individuals use higher-level thinking skills than those typical for their age. They are able to manipulate information in new and unique ways to solve complicated problems beyond the understanding of their peers. They also often show a remarkable determination to complete tasks.

Causes of Being Gifted and Talented

An important factor in giftedness seems to be genetics. However, social factors also are important in the development and use of high intellectual capacity. Parental support seems to be especially influential in developing high potential.

Approaches to Teaching Students Who Are Gifted and Talented

Students who are gifted progress best when taught with strategies consistent with their individual learning rates. Therefore, it is suggested that teachers pretest learners who are gifted to avoid reteaching already learned skills. When students are given unknown material to learn, it is usually most beneficial to deliver the material in a self-paced mastery instructional format. This way skills can be absorbed at an individualized, probably increased, rate. For example, when a new concept is being learned, these students may not need to practice it as frequently or extensively as more typical learners. Nor may they need as many illustrations or examples to understand it. The idea of placing a child who is gifted ahead 1 year is not well founded and doing so is often not successful. Students 1 year older do not necessarily learn at a faster rate than do the students in the preceding grade, especially if those younger students are gifted. Such an idea also neglects to take into account the social, emotional, and behavioral maturity of the student who is gifted. Superior intellectual or creative ability in no way guarantees advanced maturity.

Most helpful when working with a child who is gifted in a typical grade-level classroom is developing an independent curriculum and a learning contract. With a learning contract a student can be assigned certain portions of the curriculum for mastery, given a timeline to master them, and allowed an objective way to demonstrate mastery. Such a contract also gives the student the opportunity to study in greater depth once mastery is met. This in-depth study may involve bringing in parents, mentors, and/or community experts to assist the student who is gifted in pursuing further information in fields that interest the child. A learning contract helps the child delve more deeply into topics than other students do, preventing the child from being bored with a typical pace. For further information about these students, see the lists of suggested readings and organizations in Useful Resources at the end of this chapter (page 69).

STUDENTS WITH COGNITIVE DISABILITIES

Definition of Cognitive Disabilities

Students with cognitive disabilities are usually evaluated by a psychologist using an instrument called an IQ test. The IQ score, or intelligence quotient, obtained from the test is currently considered a useful evaluative predictor of school performance. Children whose test score indicates cognitive disabilities have been found to be significantly delayed from their same-age peers. However, the IQ measure alone is not enough to constitute a determination of cognitive disability. Students must also be delayed in adaptive behavior. Therefore, individuals with confirmed cognitive disabilities must also have been identified as having a disability to function in society. Such individuals are evaluated using an adaptive behavior test. Individuals with cognitive disabilities are therefore also deemed to be significantly delayed in two or more of the following areas: communication, social skills, self-care, home living, community use, functional academics, self-direction, health and safety, leisure, and work. Adaptive disability should be evident before the age of 18.

Causes of Cognitive Disabilities

The cause of mild cognitive disabilities in most students is unknown. However, most of these individuals have these factors in common: at least one parent and one sibling also have mild cognitive disabilities, and brain damage is usually not evident. Despite the lack of evidence of brain damage, whether environment or heredity is the cause of mild cognitive disabilities is still hotly debated. Environmental causes would include environmental deprivation, diet and toxins in the environment. If the cause of a mild disability is heredity, it may be useful to study organic phenomena such as genetics, infections, and drugs. Perhaps for many children, the cause is a combination of lacking of appropriate stimulation in the environment and lacking the genetic ability to gain, interpret, or regain information and skills as quickly as the average individual in society. Whatever the cause, it is interesting to note that most individuals who are considered to have mild cognitive disabilities were not so considered before they started school.

Approaches to Working with Students with Cognitive Disabilities

In general, students with mild cognitive disabilities can learn much of what other students learn in a typical classroom at the elementary school level. However, they may need more review and multiple examples to arrive at the same place. In addition, some of these children may have the information-processing deficits characteristic of individuals with learning disabilities. If a child does have difficulty processing information, the tasks that cause them difficulty in school should be familiar to everyone working with the child.

Deficits in processing information may affect one or more areas of the child's capabilities. Problem areas include: short attention span, distractibility, impaired abstract thinking, and poor short-term or long-term memory. However, something else may be causing the child's particular problem. For example, the child may be experiencing difficulty in school because of a mismatch in his or her curriculum. If so, rethinking the curriculum materials and your teaching methods might result in a better fit for the child and a reduction in school difficulties.

If teachers could give their students PET scans, they could see whether an area of the brain lit up when a child performed a task. Unfortunately, this technology is not available to students on a routine basis. PET scans are rare, most likely a factor of the high cost of the expensive machinery and of employing a neurologist. They usually are administered only in cases of serious trauma to the head and/or some other medical exigency or emergency. At this time, teachers' most valuable tool is careful observation. They need to watch students' behavior during academic tasks and look for clues to possible processing and other problems.

Whether teachers are able to gather enough information about a student's academic problems is not, however, the total answer. Teachers need to discover which techniques pique a student's interest and enable the student to flourish in the school setting. Perhaps the student needs more hands-on learning and is best able to grasp concepts when given ample time to manipulate objects and ideas with concrete, multisensory instruction. For many students, it is helpful to break down tasks, including directions, into steps that are explained one at a time. As with all students, always try to connect what the student is currently learning to the real world and to what the student already learned in the past. Doing so makes new skills and information easier to learn as well as more meaningful.

When teaching older students with cognitive disabilities, the curriculum may need to be broadened even further into the community. By the time students reach high school, it may be wise to decide whether the school curriculum is appropriate or whether a more functional curriculum would be advantageous. This question needs to be decided by the student, his or her parents, and the teachers who know the child well. It is very important to help the child imagine his or her possibilities for the future. Then, help them see how they can realize those possibilities. See the lists of suggested readings and organizations in Useful Resources for more information about the material in this section (pages 69–70).

AT-RISK CHILDREN IN OUR SCHOOLS

Definition of Being at Risk

The term *at risk* is applied to students when they are at risk for school failure. These students constitute a very large group of learners, and, depending on the point of view of the individuals using the term, children who are involved in special education may be included in the definition. In general, this term refers to children whose life experiences and/or conditions interfere with their ability to succeed in school.

Causes of Being at Risk

The reasons for being placed in the at-risk category vary widely from one child to another. However, in general children are at risk for school failure because some condition(s) and/or experience(s) in their life or in utero makes academic success very difficult for them to achieve. The causes for this situation are numerous, and a child may suffer not only from a single cause, but from any combination and number of these causes. For example, a child may live in substandard housing or be homeless; a child may have been neglected or physically or sexually abused; a child may have parents who are drug users or alcohol dependent; a child may have been born with very low birth weight; and/or a child may have been exposed to toxins in utero.

Procedures and Interventions for Students Who Are at Risk

6.10, p. 219

6.11, p. 220

6.12, p. 221

Research suggests that one of the best ways to help students at risk for school failure is to intervene with additional supports early in life. Teachers must watch the behavior of students in their class very carefully to identify these students. Students who are at risk often have few friends, are excessively quiet, frequently miss school, and have poor academic success. Placement in programs such as Headstart and/or early intervention programs is a good way to give students opportunities to succeed in school. Early success for these children is an excellent predictor of positive outcomes all throughout life.

When working with students who are at risk, try to be patient and flexible. Creating a classroom where students are interested and free to learn at their own pace greatly increases both the possibility and likelihood of success. Have students work collaboratively with other students. However, these students need not be grouped with children who have learning or cognitive disabilities and be given easier assignments. Instead, teachers should set high yet realistic expectations and develop tasks to pique the student's interest and to motivate the student's natural curiosity. Give these students more control over what they learn and how they learn it. Accordingly, establish peers as teaching partners so students can teach and learn from each other's experiences.

If problems in the child's home or social situation seem to be ongoing, seek collaboration with other helping professionals while working closely with parents or other caregivers. If a problem of neglect or abuse in the child's home comes to your attention, call the appropriate authorities. In most states, teachers are required, by law, to report suspected abuse to child protective services. Signs of possible physical neglect such as malnourishment or undernourishment include: slow growth rate, constant hunger, and begging or stealing food. Signs of neglecting health needs include poor personal hygiene, frequent or constant uncleanliness, frequent or constant fatigue (perhaps indicating poor or no supervision of children who may be out late each evening after curfew or all night long), and unattended medical needs. Other signs indicate a neglect of social responsibilities such as parents whose children have poor school attendance or who are abusing drugs and/or alcohol.

Even more serious than neglect is abuse. Possible indicators of physical abuse include, but are not limited to, unexplained bruises or welts, burns, fractures, cuts or scrapes, stomach injuries, visual or hearing defects, human bite marks. Some behavioral manifestations of physical abuse are fear of adults, fear of going home, fear of parents, or excessive aggression or withdrawn behavior. Possible indicators of sexual abuse include difficulty in walking or sitting, pain or itching around genitals, stomachaches, bed-wetting, sleep problems, depression or withdrawn behavior, poor peer relationships, sudden onset of behavior problems, or unusual knowledge of or interest in sex.

Students whose parents have drug or alcohol problems are much more likely to develop problems with substance abuse themselves. Teachers are in a unique position to observe students in the school community with little or no personal bias. Therefore, their observations about changes in student behavior can be essential in helping students overcome debilitating problems of chemical misuse and abuse. Teachers should report any observations that arouse their suspicions.

Changes in school attendance, schoolwork, falling grades, and increased disciplinary problems are common signs of alcohol or drug use and abuse. Physical signs of drug or alcohol abuse and misuse include poor grooming; red and/or wet eyes; sleepiness or overactivity; dilation or contraction of pupils; and detachment, disinterest, and disorientation. Behaviors to look for in students heavily involved in drugs or alcohol include change of friends, increased paranoia, secreting of possessions, and ambiguous information about activities and whereabouts of new friends, especially those who are known drug or alcohol users. Symptoms such as stealing, theft, borrowing money constantly, or possession or obsession with drug paraphernalia are also signs of problems with chemical abuse. If alcohol or other drug abuse seems to be a problem, refer the student to an alcohol and other drug abuse (AODA) wellness program. For more information about students who are at risk, lists of suggested readings and organizations are provided in Useful Resources (page 70).

USEFUL RESOURCES

Suggested Readings: Students Who Have Learning Disabilities

Bos, C. S., & Vaughn, S. (2002). *Strategies for teaching students with learning and behavior problems.* Boston: Allyn & Bacon.

Carnine, O., Silbert, J., & Kameenui, E. J. (1990). *Direct instruction reading.* Columbus, OH: Merrill/Macmillan.

Cavey, D. W. (2000). *Dysgraphia: Why Johnny can't write.* Austin, TX: Pro-Ed.

Diamond, M., & Hopson, J. (1998). *Magic trees of the mind: How to nurture your child's intelligence, creativity, and healthy emotions from birth through adolescence.* New York: Dutton.

Dixon, B., & Engelmann, S. (1979). *Corrective spelling through morographs.* Chicago: Science Research Associates.

ERIC Clearinghouse on Disabilities and Gifted Education. (1996, spring). Beginning reading and phonological awareness for students with learning disabilities. *Teaching Exceptional Children, 28*(3), 78–79.

Fowler, C. L., & Davis, M. (1985). The storyframe approach: A tool for improving reading comprehension. *Teaching Exceptional Children, 17,* 296–298.

Frost, J. A., & Emery, M. J. (1995, August). Academic interventions for children with dyslexia who have phonological core deficits (*ERIC Digest* E539). Reston, VA: ERIC Clearinghouse on Disabilities and Gifted Education. (ERIC Document Reproduction Service No. ED 385 095).

Goswami, U., & Bryant, P. (1990). *Phonological skills and learning to read.* Mahwah, NJ: Lawrence Erlbaum.

Griffith, P. L., & Olson, M. W. (1992). Phonemic awareness helps beginning readers break the code. *Reading Teacher, 45*(7), 516–523.

Hallahan, D. P., & Kauffman, J. M. (2000). *Exceptional learners.* Boston: Allyn & Bacon.

Levine, M. (1993). *All kinds of minds.* Cambridge, MA: Educators.

Lieberman, A. (1998). *Active learning.* New York: The Brain Shop; Longmont, CO: Sopris West.

Lovitt, T. C. (1995). *Tactics for teaching.* Englewood Cliffs, NJ: Prentice Hall.

Maheady, L., Harper, G. F., & Sacca, M. K. (1988). Peer-mediated instruction: A promising approach to meeting the diverse needs of LD adolescents. *Learning Disability Quarterly, 11,* 108–113.

McBride-Chang, C. (1995). What is phonological awareness? *Journal of Educational Psychology, 87*(2), 179–192.

McCarney, S. B., & Bauer, A. M. (1995). *The learning disability intervention manual.* Columbia, MO: Hawthorne.

Nadeau, K. (1998). *Help4ADD@high school.* New York: Advantage Press.

O'Connor, R., Jenkins, J., Slocum, K., & Leicester, N. (1993). Teaching phonemic manipulation skills to children with learning handicaps: Rhyming, blending, and segmenting. *Exceptional Children, 59,* 532–546.

Oldrieve, R. N. (1997, March/April). Success with reading and spelling: Students internalize words through structured lessons. *Teaching Exceptional Children, 29*(4), 57–64.

Quill, K. (1995). *Teaching children with autism: Strategies to enhance communication and socialization.* Albany, NY: Delmar.

Richards, R. G. (1998). *The writing dilemma: Understanding dysgraphia.* Riverside, CA: RET Center Press.

Rief, S. F. (1998). *The ADD/ADHD checklist: An easy reference for parents and teachers.* New York: Prentice Hall.

Silver, L. (1998). *The misunderstood child: Understanding and coping with your child's learning disabilities* (3rd ed.). New York: Time Books.

Sousa, D. A. (2001). *How the special needs brain learns* (2nd ed.). Thousand Oaks, CA: Corwin Press.

Swanson, H. L. (1999). *Interventions for students with learning disabilities: A meta-analysis of treatment outcomes.* New York: The Guilford Press.

Winebrenner, S. (1996). *Teaching kids with learning difficulties in the regular classroom.* Minneapolis, MN: Free Spirit.

Organizations: Students Who Have Learning Disabilities

Council for Exceptional Children
1920 Reston Drive
Reston, VA 20191-1589
www.cec.sped.org

Council for Learning Disabilities
Division of Learning Disabilities International
P.O. Box 40303
Overland Park, KS 66204
www.cldinternational.org

International Dyslexia Association
Chester Building, Suite 382
Baltimore, MD 21286
(800)222-3123
www.interdys.org

Learning Disabilities Association of America
4156 Liberty Road
Pittsburgh, PA 15234
www.Idanatl.org

Learning Disabilities Research and Practice
Lawrence Erlbaum Associates Inc.
10 Industrial Avenue
Mahwah, NJ 07430
(210)236-9500

National Center for Learning Disabilities
381 Park Avenue
New York, NY 10016
(888)575-7373
www.ncld.org

Suggested Readings: Students Who Have ADHD

Dowdy, C. A., Patton, J. R., Smith, T. E. C., & Polloway, F. (1997). *Attention-deficit hyperactivity disorder in the classroom: A practical guide for teachers.* Austin, TX: Pro-Ed.

Fowler, M. (1992). *CH.A.D.D. educators manual: Attention deficit disorders.* Plantation, FL: Children and Adults with Attention Deficit Disorders.

Fowler, M. (1999). *Maybe you know my kid: A parent's guide to identifying, understanding, and helping your child with ADHD* (3rd ed.). New York: Birch Lane Press.

Gordon, S. B., & Asher, M. J. (1994). *Meeting the ADD challenge: A practical guide for teachers.* Champaign, IL: Research Press.

Greene, R. W. (1995). Students with ADHD in school classrooms: Teacher factors related to compatibility, assessment and intervention. *School Psychology Review, 24,* 81–93.

Nadeau, K. (1998). *Help4ADD@high school.* New York: Advantage Press.

Reeve, R. E. (1990). ADHD: Facts and fallacies. *Intervention in School and Clinic, 26,* 70–76.

Rief, S. (1993). *How to reach and teach ADD-ADHD children.* West Nyack, NY: Center for Applied Research in Education.

Rief, S. (1998). *The ADD-ADHD checklist: An easy reference for parents and teachers.* New York: Prentice Hall.

Ross-Flanagan, N. (1995, June 14). Learning to live—and succeed—with attention deficit disorder. *Saint Paul Pioneer Press,* p. EB.

Zeigler Dendy, C. A. (1995). Teenagers with ADD: A parents' guide. Bethesda, MD: Woodbine House.

Organizations: Students Who Have ADHD

Attention Deficit Disorders Association (ADDA)
P.O. Box 972
Mentor, OH 44061
1(800)487-2282

The Attention Deficit Resource Center
1344 Johnson Ferry Road, Suite 14
Marietta, GA 30068

Children and Adults with Attention Deficit Disorders
   (CH.A.D.D.)
499 Northwest 70th Avenue, Suite 109

Plantation, FL 33317
1(800)233-4050
(Local chapters exist around the country.)

National Attention Deficit Disorder Association
P.O. Box 1303
Northbrook, IL 60065-1303
www.add.org

Suggested Readings: Students Who Have Emotional or Behavioral Problems

Alberta, P. A., & Troutman, A. C. (1999). *Applied behavior analysis.* Upper Saddle River, NJ: Prentice Hall.

Airasian, P. W. (2001). *Classroom assessment concepts and applications.* Boston: McGraw-Hill.

Algozzine, B., & Kay, P. (2002). *Preventing problem behaviors.* Thousand Oaks, CA: Corwin Press.

Bodine, R., Crawford, D., & Schrumpf, F. (1994). *Creating the peaceable school: A comprehensive program for teaching conflict resolution.* Champaign, IL: Research Press.

Bos, C. S., & Vaughn, S. (2002). *Strategies for teaching students with learning and behavior problems.* Boston: Allyn & Bacon.

Charles, C. M. (1996). *Building classroom discipline.* White Plains, NY: Longman.

Coleman, M. C., & Webber, J. (2002). *Emotional and behavioral disorders: Theory and practice.* Boston: Allyn & Bacon.

Doyle, T. (1991). *Why is everybody always picking on me? A guide to handling bullies.* Middlebury, VT: Atrium Society Publications.

Garrity, C., Jens, K., Porter, W, Sager, N., & Short-Cammilli, C. (1994). *Bully-proofing your school: A comprehensive approach for elementary schools.* Longmont, CO: Sopris West.

Goldstein, A., & Conoley, J. C. (1997). *School violence intervention: A practical handbook.* New York: The Guilford Press.

Grandin, T. (1996). *Thinking in pictures: And other reports from my life with autism.* New York: Vintage Books.

Grapes, B. J. (2000). *School violence.* San Diego, CA: Greenhaven Press.

Hallahan, D. P., & Kauffman, J. M. (2000). *Exceptional learners.* Boston: Allyn & Bacon.

Harrington, K. (2000). *For parents and professionals: Autism in adolescents and adults.* East Moline, IL: Lingui Systems.

Jenson, W. R., Sloane, H. N., & Young, K. R. (1988). *Applied behavior analysis in education: A structured teaching approach.* Englewood Cliffs, NJ: Prentice Hall.

Kids of survival: Real-life lessons in resilience. (1998). *Reaching Today's Youth: The Community Circle of Caring Journal, 2*(3).

Long, N. J., & Morse, W. C. (1996). *Conflict in the classroom.* Austin, TX: Pro-Ed.

Molnar, A., & Lindquist, B. (1989). *Changing problem behavior in schools.* San Francisco: Jossey-Bass.

National School Safety Center. (1989). *Set straight on bullies.* Westlake Village, CA: Author.

Quill, K. (1995). *Teaching children with autism: Strategies to enhance communication and socialization.* Albany, NY: Delmar.

Repp, A. C., & Horner, R. H. (1999). *Functional analysis of problem behavior,* Belmont, CA: Wadsworth.

Rhodes, W. C. (1967). The disturbing child: A problem of ecological management, *Exceptional Children, 33,* 449–455.

Rhodes, W. C. (1970). A community participation analysis of emotional disturbance. *Exceptional Children, 36,* 309–314.

Richards, G. (1997). *The source for autism.* East Moline, IL: Lingui Systems.

Rutherford, R., Nelson, C. M., & Wolford, B. (1986). Special education programming in juvenile corrections. *Remedial and Special Education, 7,* 27–33.

Shore, K. (1998). *Special kids' problem solver.* Paramus, NJ: Prentice Hall.

Szasz, T. (1966). *The myth of mental illness.* New York: Hoeber-Harber.

Walker, H. (1999). The present unwrapped: Change and challenge in the field of behavioral disorders, *Behavioral Disorders, 24*(4), 293–304.

Wicks-Nelson, R., & Israel, A. C. (2000). *Behavior disorders of childhood.* Upper Saddle River, NJ: Prentice Hall.

Wunderlich, K. C. (1988). *The teacher's guide to behavioral interventions: Intervention strategies for behavior problems in the educational environment.* Columbia, MO: Hawthorne Educational Services.

Organizations: Students Who Have Emotional or Behavioral Problems

Asperger Syndrome Coalition of the United States
P.O. Box 49267
Jacksonville Beach, FL 32240
www.asperger.org

Center for Effective Collaboration and Practice
www.airdc.org/cecp/cecp.html

Cognitive Therapeutics Catalog
(800)444-9482

Illinois Emotional/Behavioral Disabilities Network
www.ebdnetworkil.org

National Mental Health Information
(800)772-1213

National Alliance for the Mentally Ill
(800)950-NAMI

National Institute of Mental Health
6001 Executive Boulevard, Room 8184, MSC 9663
Bethesda, MD 20892-9663
(310)443-4513
www.nimh.nih.gov

National Technical Assistance Center for Children's Mental Health
Georgetown University Child Development Center
deacon@gunet.georgetown.edu

Research and Training Center on Family Support and Children's Mental Health
Portland State University
www.rtc.pdx.edu

SOS Self-Help Programs
Parents Press
(800)567-1582

Suggested Readings: Students Who Are Truant or School Phobic

Coleman, M. C., & Webber, J. (2002). *Emotional and behavioral disorders: Theory and practice* (pp. 189–192, 243–244). Boston: Allyn and Bacon.

Hartman, D. (1987). *Motivating the unmotivated: A practical guide for parents and teachers to help teenagers through the tough years.* Lakeland, FL: Valley.

King, N. J., Ollendick, T. H., & Tonge, B. J. (1995). *School refusal: Assessment and treatment.* Boston: Allyn & Bacon.

Kremer, B., & Farnum, M. (1985). Dropouts, absentee and Illinois education policy. *Illinois Association for Counseling and Development Quarterly 97,* 19–26.

Mandel, H. P., & Marcus, S. L. (1996). *Could do better: Why children underachieve and what to do about it.* New York: John Wiley & Sons.

Nowicki, S., & Duke, M. P. (1992). *Helping the child who doesn't fit in.* Atlanta, GA: Peachtree.

Raffini, J. P. (1994). *Winners without losers: Structures and strategies for increasing student motivation to learn.* Boston: Allyn & Bacon.

Rutherford, R., Nelson, C. M., & Wolford, B. (1986). Special education programming in juvenile corrections. *Remedial and Special Education, 7,* 27–33.

Suggested Readings: Students Who Are Gifted and Talented

Clark, B. (1992). *Growing up gifted; Developing the potential of children at home and school* (4th ed.). New York: Merrill/Macmillan.

Cox, J., & Daniel, N. (1985). *Educating able learners.* Austin, TX: University of Texas Press.

Daniel, N., & Cox, J. (1988). *Flexible pacing for able learners.* Reston, VA: Council for Exceptional Children.

Davis, G. A., & Rimm, S. B. (1998). *Education of the gifted and talented* (4th ed.). Boston: Allyn & Bacon.

Halsted, J. W. (1994). *Some of my best friends are books: Guiding gifted readers.* Scottsdale, AZ: Gifted Psychology Press.

Macker, C. J., & Nielson, A. B. (1995). *Teaching models in education of the gifted* (2nd ed.). Austin, TX: Pro-Ed.

Schmitz, C. C., and Galbraith, J. (1985). *Managing the social and emotional needs of the gifted: A teacher's survival guide.* Minneapolis, MN: Free Spirit.

Treffinger, D. (1986). *Blending gifted education with the total school program.* East Aurora, NY: D.O.K.

Winebrenner, S. (1992). *Teaching gifted kids in the regular classroom.* Minneapolis, MN: Free Spirit.

Organizations: Students Who Are Gifted and Talented

The American Association for Gifted Children
Duke University
1121 W. Main Street, Suite 100
Durham, NC 27701
1(919)683-1400

Association for Gifted
The Council for Exceptional Children
1920 Association Drive
Reston, VA 22091
(703)620-3660

Association for Gifted and Talented Students
P.O. Box 16037
Louisiana State University
Baton Rouge, LA 70893
(800)626-8811
(504)388-2469

National Association for Gifted Children
1155 Fifteenth Street, N.W., #1002
Washington, D.C. 20005
(202)785-4268

National Research Center on the Gifted and Talented
University of Connecticut
362 Fairfield Road
Storrs, CT 06269-2007
(860)486-4676

Wisconsin Center for Academically Talented Youth
2909 Landmark Place
Madison, WI 53713
(608)271-1617

Suggested Readings: Students Who Have Cognitive Disabilities

Bender, M., & Valletutti, P. C. (1990). *Teaching functional academics.* Austin, TX: Pro-Ed

Cunningham, C. (1996). *Understanding Down syndrome: An introduction for parents.* Cambridge, MA: Brookline Books.

Gable, R. A., & Warren, S. F. (Eds.). (1993). *Strategies for teaching students with mild to severe mental retardation.* Baltimore: Paul H. Brookes.

Hallahan, D. P., & Kauffman, J. M. (2000). *Exceptional learners.* Boston: Allyn & Bacon.

Lovitt, T. C. (1995). *Tactics for teaching.* Englewood Cliffs, NJ: Prentice Hall.

Matson, J. L. (Ed.). (1990). *Handbook of behavior modification with the mentally retarded* (2nd ed.). New York: Plenum.

McBride-Chang, C. (1995). What is phonological awareness? *Journal of Educational Psychology, 87*(2), 179–192.

McCormick, L., Loeb, D. F., & Schiefelbusch, R. L. (1997). *Supporting children with communication difficulties in inclusive settings.* Boston: Allyn & Bacon.

McDonnell, J., Wilcox, B., & Hardman, M. L. (1991). *Secondary programs for students with developmental disabilities.* Boston: Allyn & Bacon.

Oelwein, P. (1995). *Teaching reading to children with Down syndrome: A guide for parents and teachers.* Rockville, MD: Woodbine House.

Robinson, G. A., & Polloway, E. A. (Eds.). (1987). *Best practices in mental disabilities* (Vol. 1). Des Moines, IA: Iowa State Department of Education, Bureau of Special Education.

Schloss, P. J., & Sedlak, R. A. (1982). Behavioral features of the mentally retarded adolescent: Implications for mainstreamed educators. *Psychology in the Schools, 19,* 98–105.

Schultz, J. B., Carpenter, C. D., & Turnbull, A. C. (1991). *Main-streaming exceptional students: A guide for classroom teachers* (3rd ed.). Boston: Allyn & Bacon.

Shalom, D. B. (1984). *Special kids make special friends.* Bellmore, NY: Association for Children with Down Syndrome. (This book is intended to teach young children about Down syndrome, and can be obtained by calling 1(516)221-4700.)

Smith, R. (Ed.). (1993). *Children with mental retardation: A parents' guide.* Bethesda, MD: Woodbine House.

Sousa, D. A. (2001). *How the special needs brain learns* (2nd ed.). Thousand Oaks, CA: Corwin Press.

Stone, P. (1988). *Blueprint for developing conversational competence.* Washington, DC: Alexander Graham Bell.

Trainer, M. (1991). *Differences in common: Straight talk on mental retardation, Down syndrome, and life.* Rockville, MD: Woodbine House.

Organizations: Students Who Have Disabilities

American Association on Mental Retardation
444 North Capitol Street, N.W., Suite 846
Washington, DC 20001
(800)424-3688

The Arc
500 East Border Street, Suite 300
Arlington, TX 76010
(800)433-5255
Fax (817)277-3491

The Association for Persons with Severe Disabilities
29 Susquehanna Avenue, Suite 210
Baltimore, MD 21204
(410)828-8274

Mental Retardation Division Council for Exceptional Children
1920 Association Drive
Reston, VA 22091
(703)620-3660
www.cec.sped.org

Mental Retardation Association of America
211 E. 300 Street, Suite 212
Salt Lake, UT 84111
(801)328-1575

National Association for Down Syndrome
P.O. Box 4542
Oak Brook, IL 60522
(708)325-9112

Suggested Readings: Students Who Are at Risk

Brophy, J. F. (1997). *Motivating students to learn.* New York: McGraw-Hill.

Hartman, D. (1987). *Motivating the unmotivated: A practical guide for parents and teachers to help them help teenagers through the tough years.* Lakeland, FL: Valley Hill.

Kremer, B., & Farnum, M. (1985). Dropouts, absentee and Illinois education policy, *Illinois Association for Counseling and Development Quarterly, 97,* 19–26.

Mandel, H. P., & Marcus, S. L. (1996). *Could do better: Why children underachieve and what to do about it.* New York: John Wiley & Sons.

Nowicki, S., & Duke, M. P. (1992). *Helping the child who doesn't fit in.* Atlanta, GA: Peachtree.

Raffini, J. P. (1994). *Winners without losers: Structures and strategies for increasing student motivation to learn.* Boston: Allyn & Bacon.

Sanders, M. G. (2000). *Schooling students placed at risk.* Mahwah, NJ: Lawrence Erlbaum.

Wlodkowski, R. J., & Jaynes, J. H. (1990). *Eager to learn: Helping children become motivated and love learning.* San Francisco: Jossey-Bass.

Organizations: Students Who Are at Risk

Alcohol and Other Drug Abuse Prevention and
    Referral Information
(800)729-6686

Alcohol Treatment Referrals
(800)662-HELP or (800)662-4357

Runaway National Switchboard
(800)621-4000

CHAPTER 7

Grading and Measurement Techniques for Teacher Effectiveness

When children sound silly, you will always find that it is in imitation of their elders.

—*Ernest Dimnet*

- Grading and Assessment
- Curriculum-Based Assessment
- Curriculum-Based Assessment of Reading
- Curriculum-Based Assessment of Writing
- Curriculum-Based Assessment of Math
- Instructional Assessment
- Performance Assessment
- Portfolios
- Using Contracts for Grading
- Self-Assessment

Dear Mr. Sheets,

I don't think I ever thanked you for being such an effective teacher. You were strict but caring, demanding but fair, and concerned yet not intrusive. When you saw me trying to conform to fit in with the crowd, you encouraged me to be different so that I could be better. And when I had difficult challenges in my life, you were the one who helped me find ways to cope.

I am so lucky that you were my teacher. As a teacher myself, I look back on your classes as a model of good instruction. I remember so clearly how you realized the importance of individualization and let us choose what we would do to show you we understood the material. You let each one of us be graded in our areas of strength. I really loved the classes you taught and I also became a teacher because of the effect your compassionate teaching had on me.

Thanks so much,

Courtney

GRADING AND ASSESSMENT

Unfortunately for most of us, grades are an integral part of our current educational system. However, this may not always need to be so. Perhaps some day grades will be a thing of the past and students will be enthusiastically involved in learning in their classrooms without fear of being harshly judged by teachers, parents, administrators, and higher educational institutions. Research tells us that overemphasizing performance achievement is dangerous because it causes students to focus on how well they are doing as gauged by adults, and not on what they are learning for their lives.

If you have spent any time lately in a classroom at any level, you have probably seen the obsessive emphasis placed on grades. Students from grade school through graduate school have become so hung up on what they need to do to get an A or a perfect score that the idea of learning for the pleasure has almost disappeared. Grades are now interfering with learning for pleasure and learning to know instead of motivating learning, as they were probably originally intended. Students now no longer ask, "What would I like to learn more about?," but rather ask "What do I need to do to get an A?" The student who attends class only to compete with the rest of the class is not open to new ideas, cooperative learning, or lifetime learning. Instead, this student is crippled by needing to know what is on the test and how he or she will be judged. One suggestion for turning around this dangerous mind-set is to allow and encourage the student to set up and evaluate the fruits of his or her learning. If a student's learning belonged to the student and was not something imposed on him or her, perhaps our classrooms would be more joyful places for all of us to grow.

Perhaps you currently work in a system where grades are required. If so, you must decide what grades will stand for and how they will be used in your classroom. Whatever your decisions, these questions can be highly debated by teachers at all grade levels and in all topic areas. One need only look at the plethora of grading systems used across your state, in your town, and even within your school to see that grading styles and grading systems are as diverse as educators themselves. Therefore, the grade a student receives is not necessarily an objective or accurate portrayal of that student's achievement, effort, or standing in relation to his or her peers. It is difficult to see the value of a system that is so irregular. Whatever an A means to you, it may not mean at all to the teacher across the hall. This is true at all levels: elementary school, middle school, high school, technical school, college, graduate school, workshops, and seminars.

Before even considering a grading scale, teachers must decide what they want the grade to mean or stand for. Do you want to show how a student scores on standardized tests of achievement in comparison to others in the student's classroom? Or do you want to show the student's progress from the first month of class, assigning grades that reflect where they stand on attaining the skills?

Consider Mr. Noble. He has developed a skill level for the social studies chapter "Living in Communities" that he expects all students taking that chapter test to achieve. If students pass the chapter test with at least 80% correct, they can proceed to do the more in-depth exercise for the chapter "Living off the Land" for which they choose a county they would like to visit and report on the productivity of the land.

Or perhaps you will prefer Mrs. DeLong's teaching methods. Her students are working in cooperative groups to find a fair way to distribute resources in an imaginary town where they must feed everyone all year long. After the students develop their plans, they will self-evaluate their contributions to the group and the finished project. The choices you make in consideration of the end product will considerably change how you evaluate your units.

If you are like many teachers, you dread grading students because your idea of fair and useful grading may not fit the typical grading format of a typical U.S. school. If this is the case for you, or if you have not yet decided how you will set up your grading system, perhaps you need more information. If you must use a standardized system in your school, you should familiarize yourself with it immediately. Perhaps the principal or an experienced teacher can show you the ropes. You also would do well to check the district's curriculum guides for their goals and objectives for your particular topics or grade. This might be an excellent place to start when deciding what you will expect of your students.

Many educators are moving to competency-based assessment. Teachers in many different subjects are not happy having some students get good grades and learn the material and having others get poor grades, learn very little, and move on. If something is worth the time and effort to teach, it ought to be worth continuing to teach until it is learned. Teachers are increasingly expected to be accountable for their students' achievement, and students are now more than ever being asked to prove what they have learned. A good way to do this might be pairing curriculum-based testing with competency-based grading.

CURRICULUM-BASED ASSESSMENT

Curriculum-based assessment is a system of repeatedly testing the skills students have been learning from the curriculum in which they are taught. In good teaching, teachers use this form of assessment to decide where to start teaching, what exactly to teach, and when they can move on to teach something else. Curriculum-based assessment is the best way to measure students' progress because it corresponds with the teachers' preferred learning outcomes of his or her instruction. Unfortunately, norm-referenced testing, the form of testing recently favored by districts, uses standardized tests, which are estimated to assess information in the curriculum only 10%–20% of the time. Therefore, although standardized tests do not provide an overall picture of what students have been learning in a classroom, they have their place because they help us compare students in one locale to students across the country.

Many teachers prefer to use curriculum-based assessment on a routine basis because the advantages of using these measures are many. The greatest advantage to the classroom teacher is that it can be used as a guide in determining what to teach. For example, instead of teaching the entire Dolch word list, the teacher can first test the student and then teach only those words the student does not know. Moreover, studies report that in a typical school day only 15%–20% of the time is spent on academic learning. With so little time spent on academics, efficiency is especially important to teachers. Testing students before teaching, and then teaching only what students need to know saves teachers valuable time. This is a plus for students too because in many classrooms too much of the students' time is wasted on going over material they have already mastered.

Curriculum-based assessment is both valid and reliable. It is valid because it tests from the curriculum, and reliable because you do it again and again. It helps teachers improve their teaching because it gives teachers precise information on what the students have learned so that teachers can judge their effectiveness and adapt their teaching style to what works best for the students. This form of assessment increases student achievement and motivation as well: when students see their progress and become our partners in the learning process, they are inspired.

To implement a curriculum-based assessment, you first need to look over your curriculum carefully. What do you want students to learn? Once you decide, establish a beginning point in the assessment process. One likely beginning is the material with which you intend to begin teaching. (Having a textbook with pretests makes this task easier.) Next, administer the assessment and analyze your students' responses. In your analysis of student responses, move from general to specific and analyze all errors and successes. Depending on what each student's response shows, select appropriate instructional strategies in accordance with each student's preferred learning style. Often this means using multisensory teaching.

7.1, p. 223

When you want to use multisensory teaching, take any curriculum you have and give it the SHOT test. This means evaluate whether it uses the Seeing or visual modality, the Hearing or auditory modality, or the Touching or manipulative modality. For example, Mr. Moyer is teaching basic subtraction facts. He designs a lesson that involves both whole-class and individual instruction methods to teach the fact $7 - 5 = 2$. He writes the fact in large letters on the board as well as on a sheet of paper at each student's table. Next he says the equation $7 - 2 = 5$ and has the whole class repeat it after him. Last he has each student manipulate crayons. Each student takes seven crayons from their coloring box and puts the box away. The remaining crayons are lined up on the table in front of them. He has each student take the red and green crayons out of the line-up and count how many are left. This lesson uses all three modalities and is likely to help most children better remember the math fact because each modality complements, supports, and reinforces the learning taking place in the other modalities.

Schedule intense, short, instructional sessions and use the Good Teaching Checklist in Teacher Resource 2.7 to ensure effective teaching. Each student must be taught until his or her understanding is firm. To confirm a student's knowledge, the student has to be tested until a result of 100% correct is achieved. Only information that is important enough to be taught well is worth teaching at all. Assess the teaching process throughout the school year by scheduling frequent curriculum assessments. Each student's instructional needs must be monitored on an ongoing basis. Plot each student's learning on individual graphs for each subject so both you and the students can see the course of the students' progress toward mastering the skills that they need.

7.2, p. 224

CURRICULUM-BASED ASSESSMENT OF READING

Reading can be assessed in many ways. You can assess any number and combination of reading skills, including decoding skills, sight vocabulary, phonetic analysis, structural analysis, and/or ability to derive word meaning. Many teachers begin with an informal reading inventory. You can easily prepare material for informal reading inventories using your own classroom curriculum. Choose material that is from one of your own classroom textbooks such as a history or social studies text. (The material should be a little difficult so you can evaluate the student's word attack techniques.)

7.3, p. 225

7.4, p. 226

To begin the inventory, mark a passage of 100 words and have the student read the passage aloud to you. While the student is reading, mark his or her mistakes using a code such as the one in Teacher Resource 7.3 or one of your own choosing. (If you have difficulty marking while the student is reading, tape record the student's reading; later play it back more slowly and mark the passage as you listen.) When the student finishes reading, have him or her answer comprehension questions about the passage. Record the student's answers. You might evaluate the student's comprehension ability by asking the student to explain the title of the story or to cite examples of cause and effect.

As you assess the student, compare his or her reading skills to the current curriculum requirements. Evaluate whether the student's decoding skills are adequate for the demands of the curriculum. Are the student's comprehension skills adequate? Next, describe the strengths and weaknesses of the student's decoding skills. Finally, describe the student's strengths and weaknesses in comprehension.

CURRICULUM-BASED ASSESSMENT OF WRITING

Written expression is a visual representation of thoughts, feelings, and ideas using symbols to communicate. It is a highly useful form of communication. One study found that most employers ranked "the ability to write accurate messages" as the number 1 skill required for their employees. Throughout their lives individuals need to express themselves effectively in writing. The need for written communication skills is growing as a result of increased reliance on computers.

7.5, p. 227

To assess the written expression of your students, a graph of skills is commonly evaluated and then benchmarks are set to which each writer's level of ability is compared. Once again, you need to choose the level and skills you consider most important. For example, you might want to evaluate organization of writing by looking at paragraph structure and sequencing of events. Or you might focus on ideas and content, creativity of expression and along with vocabulary, handwriting, spelling, or any combination of these skills. Each area you assess needs to be compared to a current curriculum standard to determine the student's overall success. Once the student meets the required standard, he or she can then move on to explore a higher-level writing curriculum. You might be very surprised to find how talented your students are.

CURRICULUM-BASED ASSESSMENT OF MATH

The most elementary components of the school mathematics curriculum are computation and problem solving. Computation is the result of manipulating numbers according to given rules to produce predictable outcomes. A single computation results in one correct outcome (answer). Computations consist of three components: readiness skills, readiness facts, and whole number computations. Readiness skills include comprehension of numbers, use of number lines, and skip counting. Students often move directly to memorization of tables and never learn about or understand these skills, which are the basics of our base 10 number system. Readiness facts are the specific computations of numbers found in the tables and must be memorized to be immediately and accurately recalled during computations. These facts require knowledge of the operations addition, subtraction, multiplication, and division. Whole-number computations are simply tools for solving problems. What is most important about this skill is the student's ability to use readiness facts to find answers to mathematical questions. Basic problem solving entails applying readiness facts and computational skills in a logical order to find solutions.

Problem solving involves five important steps. First, the student must read and understand the problem to ascertain find what is being sought. Second, the student must select the correct operation to develop an action strategy for solving the problem. Third, the student must organize the facts correctly by arranging them according to the information given in the problem. Fourth, the student must compute the answer by selecting and applying the correct computational operation. Last, the student's answer must be evaluated for correctness and reasonableness.

Teachers must carefully evaluate error patterns to ascertain whether their students are learning the required skill incorrectly, or not at all. Student mistakes must be evaluated to determine the source of the problem, whether stemming from a fact-related skill or strategy, or something else, before they can be retaught correctly. These errors are clustered into groups for ease of teaching and understanding. The clustered errors help teachers see the patterns students use to solve problems and help teachers formulate ideas about what went wrong and where the student needs the most reteaching. For example, a teacher might cluster math mistakes into six groups based on the similarities of these mistakes. The teacher could then develop six lessons—one lesson to cover each cluster of mistakes—instead of trying to address each particular mistake individually.

7.6, p. 229

7.7, p. 230

INSTRUCTIONAL ASSESSMENT

Instructional assessment is testing the individual students' understanding of what is being taught while it is being taught to help teachers become better facilitators of future learning. This does not mean that, as students are working away on projects or discussing ways to find more information about a topic of interest, the teacher stops everything and gives them a written quiz or exam. What it does mean is that teachers constantly evaluate the understanding and learning that is taking place while it is taking place.

For many teachers this is probably not easy to do because teachers can get so involved in the material they present to their class that they can forget to take into consideration where the students are at. Whenever a teacher is teaching, it is necessary for him or her to gauge where each child is to see whether the information or concept is connecting or getting through to each individual student. If a teacher can correctly discern the students' understanding of the material, he or she can begin to guide or adjust the task, project, or procedure appropriately to fit the needs of the students.

The greatest value of instructional assessment is that it enables the teacher to revise the instrument of learning while it is in progress. After beginning a project, a teacher, along with the class, may decide to step back and review prerequisite skills, to find more examples, or perhaps to change to a different project altogether. Making changes is often difficult, and teachers may find it painful to give up their plans and to try something different. But teaching is a form of communicating ideas; if the teacher is not communicating, teaching is not occurring.

PERFORMANCE ASSESSMENT

Instructional assessment is an excellent tool for evaluating the efficacy of instruction during instruction, but it is also necessary to evaluate students' ability to apply what has been taught. Teachers may do so using a procedure called performance assessment. In performance assessment the evaluator sets up a situation that simulates as closely as possible a real-life situation in the community. For example, if you were teaching your students how to make change but could not take them all to the local hamburger joint, you could set up a simulated store in your classroom and have students practice making change as they wait on each other at the counter. In performance assessment you evaluate a student actually performing a task versus giving them a pencil-and-paper test or asking them to describe how they would perform a task.

PORTFOLIOS

A portfolio is a collection of student work that highlights a student's growth over time. The student's work can be kept in a notebook, folder, file, or anything else that can contain the original pieces of work. Portfolios come in many different shapes and sizes. They can consist of journals, self-reflections, homework, essays, tests, artwork, course disks, audiotapes, videotapes, CDs, and group work. When evaluating a student's portfolio one can look at the student's progress over any period of time to determine how he or she personally improved. Furthermore, the progress can be measured in comparison to peers in the same class or grade.

The portfolio also is an excellent progress record to share with parents and other interested parties. It can be the focal point of a parent–teacher conference (i.e., Portfolio Conference), or it can be used for a student's show-and-tell time, either with their peers or with parents. Having children show others what they have done helps them engage more fully in the process of evaluation. In addition, students can use the portfolio to set goals and reflect on their own work. When doing a self-reflection of their work, students can be assigned to think about how they will practice responsibility and goal setting. This task is especially useful in helping students feel ownership of their work. They can use the skills they learned while compiling the portfolio to solve problems that arise as they learn.

When putting together a portfolio, students can be involved in selecting their own work. Every week they can add their best work of the week to their portfolio. (Work not selected can be sent home.) Student selection and evaluation of the materials in the portfolio are very important. They give the student control over his or her own progress evaluation. It also gives teachers another way to connect a child's progress to the classroom. If you use a portfolio approach, be sure you regularly collect work and evaluate it in a timely fashion. The younger children are, the more often you need to collect their work and have them reflect on it. The portfolio becomes a useful document that helps the student and the teacher be better able to gauge what the student needs to learn in the future.

A good way to help students evaluate their work is to teach them about rubrics and criteria. Rubrics are templates of standards against which evaluators compare performance. Together, the class as a whole may develop their own group-evaluation rubrics, or different rubrics may be developed for each child. In higher grades, students can be evaluated using a three-pronged evaluation: peer evaluation, self-evaluation, and teacher evaluation. You might think that students are not able to rate themselves and their peers accurately. However, students rarely overrate themselves. They are fair and in fact sometimes are harder on themselves than their teacher is.

USING CONTRACTS FOR GRADING

Once you have selected the skills you want your students to learn, assessed their present skill level, and decided how to begin instruction, you are almost ready to begin teaching. However, one more thing is needed: how will you motivate the students in your classroom to learn? Some students will find the curriculum very exciting and are already motivated. Unfortunately, other students are not as motivated or interested as you would like. As discussed in Chapter 5, establishing a contract is a good technique for inspiring individuals to fulfill their commitments and to achieve their goals. The grading contract is like any other contract except that the end result is a grade toward which the student works. As with any contract, the reward is in the hands of the contractors; therefore, the student and the teacher become partners in the grading process. The student chooses his or her grade, and the student and the teacher come to an agreement about what the student needs to do to earn that particular grade. Sharing the responsibility for earning the grade helps the student become part-owner of that grade. In this way, contracting makes grading easier and fairer by taking the guesswork out of grading and eliminating the fear of grades that many students have.

One of the most interesting things I have come across was a modest study of students who were admitted to college conditionally. When their first semester was half over and the students were asked how they were doing, most reported that they were doing just fine. Unfortunately, the opposite was true. Most of them were failing most of their subjects and had no idea that their grades were so low. If such a lack of knowledge and awareness can occur among college students, imagine how a primary or secondary school student who is at-risk for school failure might have no idea what it takes to succeed in school.

In grade contracting the teacher and student discuss what needs to be achieved for the student to earn a particular grade—before the grading period begins. The contract is signed by teacher and student both. It is also often signed by parents as well. The key to successful grade contracting is ensuring that everyone knows what is expected of each party involved. Having parents involved gives the teacher another partner in the education of the student. Very often, parents can be quite effective partners because they can initiate strategies at home, such as awarding the student certain privileges for adequate completion of academic tasks, to motivate the student to honor the grading contract.

Suppose you have certain skills that two students in your class must obtain. One student masters these skills immediately and the other takes two months to achieve the same level of proficiency. Do you grade students by how fast they learn or by the skills they have mastered at the end of the grading period, no matter the speed? Why?

SELF-ASSESSMENT

We begin at the beginning, deciding first what we want our students ultimately to be and do. Then we think about students becoming lifelong learners—individuals who study and learn for their own satisfaction, not just to get a grade. What can teachers do to facilitate this? Perhaps we need to teach students how to teach themselves. When I want to improve myself, I set a goal, set a time limit, and then aim for it, evaluating myself as I go. It might be useful to teach students this process.

For example, remember Mrs. DeLong, who had her students working in cooperative groups to find a fair way to distribute resources in an imaginary town? She had her students choose what they wanted to do, set a time for the project, and evaluate themselves on their contributions to the group and the finished project. Her students probably learned more about lifetime learning than they did about distributing resources fairly. By evaluating their own progress students can learn to develop their own standards and personal assessment tools. Ultimately, the individual who is self-evaluating and self-motivating will always be needed in this world.

8

Political Awareness for the Successful Professional Educator

The whole art of politics consists in directing rationally the irrationalities of men.

—Reinhold Niebuhr

- The Educational Structure at the Federal Level
- The Educational Structure at the State level
- Local School Boards
- The Superintendent of Schools
- The Local School Principal
- Education Department Heads and Administrators
- Politics in the School
- Teachers' Roles and Relationships Outside the Classroom
- Teachers' Unions

Dear Mr. LaPointe,

I want to thank you for everything you taught me. I really loved your class—it was more fun than any other class I have had. It is nice to know that learning can be fun! The "Kandy Kane" mock trail was really a great way to learn about the American justice system. I still remember it today. I just wish more of my teachers were like you. I hope you know how much all the students loved you! You are a really great teacher.

Thank you—

Ashley

It is imperative to recognize and understand that politics permeates all levels of the educational structure. Those who learn this early in their careers are much more successful in using the system to their advantage. Many of us are not interested in politics; we try to ignore it because we believe the system is corrupt and should be avoided at all costs. Unfortunately, if we buy into this way of thinking we put ourselves at a great disadvantage in any career path we choose. This chapter is designed to give an overview of the political structures at various levels of the educational system, how teachers fit into these structures, and how they affect teachers in the everyday world of education.

THE EDUCATIONAL STRUCTURE AT THE FEDERAL LEVEL

The Secretary of Education is a cabinet position in the executive branch of the government appointed by the president and approved by Congress. The Secretary is responsible for educational policy, for research on all levels of education, for budgeting that includes gifts and grants, and in recent years for broad testing programs to raise academic competency at all grade levels. It should be noted that in the last three presidential elections both political parties placed education as one of the top priorities in their party platform. This has resulted in increased federal oversight together with enhanced federal funding. It naturally follows that each state is forced to compete more vigorously for its share of the federal dollar. Lobbying for federal dollars has created an industry all its own. The writing of federal grants and programs has created thousands of administrative positions at the state and local level.

Politics in education at the federal level can be illustrated by the following example. According to Andrew Rotherham, who directed Educational Policy at the Progressive Policy Institute, the National Education Association (NEA), a union of teachers across the country, approved at its annual convention in Los Angeles a resolution effectively supporting parents who boycott standardized tests. The NEA directed its lobbyists to work against mandatory testing provisions before Congress (*Wall Street Journal*, July 2001).

THE EDUCATIONAL STRUCTURE AT THE STATE LEVEL

Most states have a department of public instruction (DPI), which is staffed by the superintendent of public instruction, an elected official who reports to the governor. The department oversees and administers educational policy, teacher certification, and educational standards through testing, together with developing the governor's educational budget. In recent years these departments have been instrumental in passing state laws that put caps on budgets for local school districts. Politically, caps were instituted to control school board spending and, in turn, hold down property taxes, which are used largely to fund education at the local levels.

Politics at the state level can be illustrated with two examples. One example involves the recent election of a superintendent of public instruction in a Midwestern state. The winner, a well-liked teacher and public school administrator, picked up all but one of the state's counties to gain a 4-year term. The winner's campaign was helped along with the financial support of the state's largest teachers' union, along with this union's support at the ballot box.

The second example involves a medium-sized Midwestern capital city that hired a new superintendent a few years ago. The new superintendent's primary objective was to rebuild relationships between the very strong and politically active teachers' union and the school system. The president of the local teachers' union came from an extensive background in industrial unionism. He was adroit in using the media to enhance the union's position, while putting the school administration on the defensive. The new superintendent decided to "take on the Union" and used the media to create a war between the two factions.

The union retaliated by stalling contract negotiations, by using sickouts and 1- and 2-day work stoppages, and by attacking the superintendent's power base and personal credibility with a negative media blitz. After 3 to 4 years of conflict, her school board support gradually eroded and she was forced to resign. A new superintendent was hired to be a peacemaker. After 1 year he succeeded in rebuilding relations between the school system union and the teachers and the teachers' union. He renegotiated a new contract and restored peace and tranquility to the beleaguered parties. This school system learned a lesson about power: it is not a good idea to try to ignore the power and strength of politics in the school system.

LOCAL SCHOOL BOARDS

Most local school and district boards are elected by popular vote. In many communities these elections are hotly contested. Even though most elections are nonpartisan, the process is not kept free of politics. These boards make local educational policy, control finances, and hire and fire superintendents, one of their biggest responsibilities and possibly one of their most difficult and contentious tasks. In addition, decisions on building schools, athletic facilities, and educational recreational facilities are all part of their responsibilities. It goes without saying that many educational issues become politicized along racial, ethnic, and religious lines. In our litigious society, legal issues frequently come to the forefront and consume prodigious amounts of board hours. In some districts getting qualified board candidates to run for office is a difficult undertaking. Many board members use this experience and public visibility to move on to other political positions and eventually a political career.

THE SUPERINTENDENT OF SCHOOLS

The position of the superintendent of schools is generally considered to be the chief operating executive of the local school district. Superintendents are hired under contract and report to the school board. Their responsibilities include staffing the administration, hiring and evaluating principals, preparing budgets for the board, handling finances, negotiating contracts with teachers' unions, providing custodial and maintenance personnel, and safeguarding physical resources for the school district. Maintaining high standards of quality education is paramount in the job description.

Community and union relations are a high priority on most superintendents' agendas, along with carrying out policies and maintaining close relationships with the school board. Positive media relationships are a must in this sensitive position. It takes a very special executive personality to manage a successful school district in today's world. In large cities this position has heavy turnover. Many contracts have buyout clauses, and the burnout rate is high. Successful superintendents generally move on to larger school districts with more attractive compensation packages. The keys to this job are twofold: getting and keeping the school board's political support and maintaining a positive and productive relationship with the unions.

THE LOCAL SCHOOL PRINCIPAL

Whether you are a new teacher beginning to work with a seasoned principal or an experienced teacher beginning to work with a new principal, it is essential to know the management style of the school principal. Is this person a hands-on administrator, or a delegator who isn't concerned with everyday details and workings of the school? Along with maintaining the high educational standard of the school, foremost in this position is selecting, training and managing, and retaining qualified and professional teachers.

EDUCATION DEPARTMENT HEADS AND ADMINISTRATORS

As a teacher in a large school you will probably be closest to your department head. Grade schools may have team leaders for each grade level. Middle and high schools may have subject chairmen. These individuals are the most likely candidates for your mentor, if you would like one. If they do not agree to mentor you, they may assign someone else in the area to do it for them. Mentoring new faculty is becoming increasingly popular, and many states are beginning to require that teachers have mentors to help them along as they begin teaching.

If you have such a mentor, this individual can help you learn about your school. You need to know what is the exact school routine, and what are your responsibilities beyond teaching. You need to find out who will be doing your yearly evaluations and what standards they will be using to judge you. Also you need to find out who holds power in the school and who makes which decisions. Often, the individual you think is making decisions is not the one who is really making them. Certain individuals can be very influential in the school decision-making process. Find out who these people are as soon as possible. Your knowledge of how things work will make you more effective in the classroom.

POLITICS IN THE SCHOOL

It is always interesting to look at the political structure of a school. Somehow certain teachers seem to know how to make the political structure of their school work for them whereas others find themselves on the outside looking in. If you want to help the children in your classroom get the best possible services, you must pay attention to your school politics.

It is important that from the very beginning of your post, before you may even have formed any opinions about how things should be, you are seen as a positive person who will help the school improve. Never appear to be a negative person who

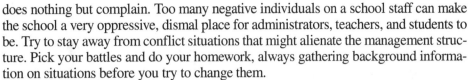

does nothing but complain. Too many negative individuals on a school staff can make the school a very oppressive, dismal place for administrators, teachers, and students to be. Try to stay away from conflict situations that might alienate the management structure. Pick your battles and do your homework, always gathering background information on situations before you try to change them.

If you have disagreements with school or school district policies or practices, find out how other schools operate and offer helpful alternative solutions. Criticizing without offering possible solutions can be counterproductive, making a bad situation worse. The art of politics is based on compromise and understanding of all factors involved. Keep your eyes and ears open and try to find someone who can mentor you in the classroom and introduce you to the power structure of the school. Knowledge is power, and such information can make you a more effective teacher (as noted in Chapter 1). Teachers who understand how to get things done have a much better chance of being satisfied and successful in their school.

One of the first lessons you need to learn is whom to go to to get things done. The teachers who know whom to seek for help will get more support than those who do not. You can get a good idea of who can help you do what by watching those teachers who seem to get what they want. With whom do these teachers spend a lot of time? Where do they go when they need something? Hang around them for a while and you might learn something. This may seem rather crass, but it is an effective way to learn the ropes. Remember, part of your job is getting the materials and services your students need. Try not to let embarrassment or pride interfere with helping your students get what they need.

Once you know which people can best help you, how do you approach them? Do they mind discussing school during lunch or would they rather talk in private after school? Knowing whom to ask, when to ask, and where to ask are important hurdles in your search for help. If you can't get over these hurdles, you are likely to get nothing. If you can, you have a much better chance of getting what you need, knowing when you might get it, or at the very least learning why you couldn't get it.

TEACHERS' ROLES AND RELATIONSHIPS OUTSIDE THE CLASSROOM

Maria seemed always to get the best students assigned to her class. Students with behavior problems seemed always to end up in everyone else's class. She seemed never to get recess duty in the cold of winter. In fact, her turns for recess and bus duty seemed never to come up. After watching her, it began to become clear to the newest teacher in the building, Danielle, that Maria was different from the other teachers. For example, Maria always wore beautiful suits to school even though she was a first-grade teacher. Most of the teachers in the early grades wore clothes in which they could easily move around. In fact, the rest of the teachers wore clothes in which they could sit on the floor with their students. Maria also wore nylons and heels every day. She seemed to see herself differently than the other teachers saw themselves.

Maria took her job very seriously. She often was busy after school giving in-service training of some kind to other teachers. She was known to be associated with the local college. Interestingly, on closer inspection, the college had her come in as a guest speaker once every few years or so. But she carefully let everyone know that she taught at the college. She also decorated the teachers' lounge weekly, remembered and celebrated teachers' birthdays, and handled all the social activities (such as the school Christmas party). It slowly dawned on Danielle that Maria took care of many things that made the principal's job easier. Because of all she was doing, and perhaps because of the superior way she dressed and acted, the principal listened to her advice and sought her assistance.

Danielle soon realized that even though she did not particularly like Maria, she did not want her as an enemy. She could see why the principal would appreciate her help. Clearly, if Danielle complained to the principal that she had recess duty once a week, as did all the other first- and second-grade teachers (except Maria), it would not get her very far. In fact she would need to be careful about stepping on toes, especially if they were the toes encased in Maria's heels. Many schools have teachers like Maria who seem to have power beyond their job descriptions. Watch for these teachers or you may alienate the wrong person and have a very unhappy year. As with people in any other occupation, teachers who take on extra responsibilities and perform tasks and services without being asked usually are rewarded in one way or another.

New teachers (and veterans) can also learn about their fellow teachers at faculty meetings. Most principals call together all their teachers for meetings at least once a month. Teacher meetings are an easy and efficient way to impart information, clear up confusions, and discuss issues and problems among all teachers. Teacher meetings are a good time for new teachers to learn about the rest of the faculty and for faculty to get to know them. Although usually they are not a favored activity among teachers, they are necessary and much can be learned if you are alert.

Scott was in his first year as a math teacher at Langdon High School. He knew the other math teachers because he had met with them on several occasions. He was also acquainted with some of the science teachers, and the special education teachers had already come to him concerning the students in their program that he had in his classes. However, most of the teachers at the first few faculty meetings were basically strangers to him. A few certainly stuck out though. A very large older man complained about everything, and a young English teacher seemed to have a question about everything. Many of the other teachers did not seem to have much to say.

After speaking to his mentor and watching the action for a few weeks, he came to realize that the teachers' meetings did not show the whole story. Often, the people who spoke up continually complained about the same things over and over again. Their favorite complaints targeted the awful students. Other teachers took up valuable time concerning the rest of the faculty with their specific problems. Neither the large man nor the English teacher, he found out, had any clout. No one cared to listen to these kinds of comments. Most of the teachers wished they would just be quiet because they all had so much work to be done to prepare for the first weeks of school.

What Scott did begin to notice was who sat with whom and who stayed after the meeting to discuss problems in small groups or individually with the principal. As it turned out this principal preferred not to deal with problems that lacked ready solutions during faculty meetings. (He did not like to be blindsided.) He was much more amenable to small-group discussions in which key teachers offered up and discussed the merits of different courses of actions. If Scott had not watched carefully and discussed the faculty meetings with his mentor, he might have come away from them thinking that all the teachers felt the students were awful and that none of them had answers to even the most basic questions. He began to realize that the meetings after the faculty meeting were indeed interesting and worth attending, so he began to stick around, slowly voicing his opinion as he learned the ropes.

TEACHERS' UNIONS

The two major teachers' unions in the United States are the American Federation of Teachers (AFT) and the National Education Association (NEA). Both unions were formed to support educators at all levels of education, from preschool to graduate school. Many school districts belong to one union or the other, and teachers can choose to belong or not. When a school district is a member of a union, teachers in that district often have membership dues withdrawn from their paychecks monthly, whether or not they are members. They pay these dues because they reap the benefits of contract negotiations. As a "fair share" dues payer (nonmember), however, they don't have a say in contract priorities and don't get representation if and when it's needed. These organizations offer professional development opportunities, support for school staff, contract bargaining, political and financial assistance for lobbying state and local legislators, and numerous other benefits for their members, such as insurance and vacation/travel discounts.

The American Federation of Teachers was founded in 1916 and has approximately 1 million members. The mission statement follows:

> is to improve the lives of our members and their families, to give voice to their legitimate professional, economic and social aspirations, to strengthen the institutions in which we work, to improve the quality of the services we provide, to bring together all members to assist and support one another, and to promote democracy, human rights and freedom in our union, in our nation and throughout the world. (*Futures II,* July 5, 2000)

The AFT reports a union philosophy with a commitment to higher pay, better benefits, and educational reform.

The National Education Association was founded in 1857 and reports more than 2.6 million members. To become a member of the NEA you must work for a public school district or be involved in a student NEA organization if you are training to be a teacher. The NEA offers scholarships and teacher training opportunities as well as job search assistance. They currently stand in opposition to privatizing public education. The NEA Code of Ethics of the Education Profession can be viewed at the NEA web site. For more information about the NEA and AFT unions, please visit the web sites. Other contact information is provided here:

The National Education Association
1201 16th Street, N.W.
Washington, D.C. 20036
(202)833-4000
(Toll free) (800)637-4636
www.nea.org/

American Federation of Teachers
AFL-CIO
555 New Jersey Avenue, N.W.
Washington, D.C. 20001
(202)879-4400
www.aft.org

CHAPTER

9

Materials for Use in the Classroom

We think of schools as places where youth learns, but our schools also need to learn.

—Lyndon B. Johnson

- Reading Materials
- Writing Materials
- Mathematics Materials
- Social Skills Materials

- Science Materials
- Social Studies Materials
- Other Materials

The materials teachers use in their classroom have a great deal to do with their personalities and the skills and interests of their students. It is therefore difficult for one person to judge which materials are "good" materials and which ones are not. It is probably best to offer suggestions for interesting textbooks, curriculums, and software that teachers and their students have found useful and enjoyed working with together. This chapter does just that. It includes materials that many teachers recommend as very student friendly and useful for specific needs in the classroom.

The materials are grouped by subject into six categories: reading, writing, mathematics, social skills, science, and social studies. Descriptions are provided by teachers in the field and organized in the following categories: title and publisher, estimated cost, a brief description of the material, appropriate age level and readability, durability, student adaptability, teacher versus student directed, and a brief critique of how they can be best used. Hopefully everyone can find materials of interest to them that will be useful in their classroom.

READING MATERIALS

ACCELERATED READER (AR)

Renaissance Learning Incorporated
P.O. Box 8036
Wisconsin Rapids, WI 54495
(800)338-4204
Or (866)846-0760 Department #5766

Description.   Accelerated Reader is a well-developed reading management software program designed to help teachers track their students' reading and improve students' reading skills. The program can be used at all grade levels and is designed to give realiable, objective information on each student's reading skills and ability. The program helps teachers manage students' reading by supplying over 50,000 computer-based quizzes and assessments. This series of quizzes is based on population and classic children's literature. Accelerated Reader includes fiction and nonfiction books. If teachers find a book that does not have its own assessment, they can create their own. Students begin by reading a book. After the quiz has been taken, both teacher and student get information about the student's level of understanding of the book, and average reading level. The program assesses 24 literacy skills.

Age and Readability.   This program is geared for all students in first through twelfth grade. The readability of the questions coincides with the reading level of the book being tested.

Durability.   As a computer program, Accelerated Reader is very durable. Because the material is computer based, however, it is vulnerable to problems. Good software instruction for teachers and students alike is imperative, and regular support for the computers is also necessary.

Adaptability.   This program is available in Mac or Windows format. One benefit of this program is that it allows each student to work at his or her own level. The computer then gives the student immediate individualized information about his or her progress.

Teacher / Student Directed.   Because of its nature, this program is very student directed. However, teachers need to help students choose books, set their own personal goals, and monitor their test taking.

Critique.   Accelerated Reader is an exciting aid to teachers working with students at any age or grade level. It requires computer support but is easy to use and is a great help to teachers and students wanting immediate feedback on their progress. The record-keeping aspect of this material is also very helpful.

HORIZONS: READING TO LEARN

Science Research Associates
McGraw-Hill, Open Court Division
(888)772-4543
www.sra4kids.com

Description.   This direct instruction reading series is intended for students who are experiencing difficulties in learning how to read. The program starts at approximately a third-grade reading level and works to develop vocabulary, reading fluency, and comprehension. The series consists of a textbook, a workbook, and a teacher's manual to guide the student through the learning process. The lessons in the textbook begin with vocabulary lists and then move into a segment that discusses facts that appear in the reading section. The reading sections begin with short passages in beginning levels and gradually become longer and more detailed. After the reading passages, the students are led through skills exercises in the textbook and the workbook that relate to the facts of the story and to other details concerning objects or places mentioned within the story. The lessons build on each other and facts about previous stories are referenced throughout the 100 lessons in each textbook.

Age and Readability.   This series is intended for a late-elementary/middle school population. If used beyond the middle school years, the series may not be as effective because the stories are geared toward a younger population.

Durability and Usability.   This series appears to be well made and should hold up well over the course of time. The textbooks are hardbound, and the teacher's manual is a large spiral-bound book with a hard cover. The series should last longer than typical textbooks because the students have no reason to carry the books back and forth to school in a backpack. The series is very easy for the teacher and student to use together. The teacher's manual has step-by-step instructions that delineate how the lessons should proceed, even including when to take breaks and to inject comprehension questions. The only drawback to this program is that students need a teacher to administer the lesson, so students have no opportunity to read on their own when using this program.

Adaptability.   Unfortunately it would be difficult to adapt this series to readers who are below a third-grade reading level. It would probably be more appropriate to use different material for those students. For students who at a third-grade level and higher, the teacher can adjust the starting point in the series as necessary for the student.

Teacher / Student Directed.   The teacher does need to be present to lead the student during the entire lesson. The student is highly involved through the format of oral questions, written comprehension questions, and reading aloud.

Critique.   This material would be most useful for students who are having difficulty learning to read and comprehend. The stories build on each other and refer back to each other, prompting the student to think about and remember details in reading. The vocabulary sections in the beginning of each lesson are instrumental in expanding the decoding skills of each student. The students must know the vocabulary words, both definition and pronunciation, before they can move onto facts concerning the theme of the story and on to the story itself. For students who are struggling with reading, this series provides modest successes that the student can build on to increase confidence and reading enjoyment.

The format of the textbook is well done. The print is large enough for students to read the text easily. The sections are short enough for students to finish a section without becoming frustrated. In addition, the skill areas are varied enough that students have opportunities to speak, read, and write words to build their vocabulary. Another positive feature of this series is timing. Lessons take approximately 45 minutes to administer, so students can work at a pace of one lesson per reading period and really feel like they are making rapid progress through the material. [Critiqued by Peter Thompson]

MACMILLAN CONNECTIONS READING PROGRAM

McGraw-Hill
(800)442-9685
Science Research Associates
McGraw-Hill, Open Court Division
(888)772-4543
www.sra4kids.com

Description. This material contains workbooks, skill practice exercises, teaching charts, test masters, placement tests, reteaching masters, vocabulary strategies, challenge masters, and parent–child activities. The workbooks and guides work together to build on what is being taught and learned.

Age and Readability. The age level is first grade. The material is appropriate for this age group, because it uses large easy-to-read print and has helpful pictures for students to learn. The material is user friendly.

Durability and Useability. The material is safely contained in a three-ring binder. The material is easy to use in the binder, or the workbooks can be taken out of the binder and used individually.

Adaptability. No adaptation is needed for the material.

Teacher/Student Directed. Macmillan Connections is both teacher and student directed.

Critique. This book contains many practical activities that reinforce reading. The worksheets are user friendly. They have cute pictures to help students learn. The workbooks also teach the student writing skills. The book provides other ideas on how to use direct instruction. For example, you are directed to cut out different shapes in three different colors to teach the students shapes and colors using direct instruction. [Critiqued by Terri Lattimer]

MAKING WORDS

Good Apple Publishing

Description. Making Words is a manipulative, developmental, multilevel activity that teachers and children both can enjoy. More importantly, children explore words and discover patterns, increase word knowledge, and become better readers and writers.

Teachers can choose lessons having words that can be integrated with their curriculum or that teach the letter–sound patterns that they want the students to focus on. Lessons are arranged alphabetically by the big word that ends each lesson, but they can be arranged in any order. Teachers may teach several lessons in a row that concentrate on particular patterns students may need to practice.

Each Making Words lesson is multilevel in two ways. The children begin by making very simple, short words and then make more complex, long words. The sorting is also multilevel in that children sort for consonants, blends, and diagraphs, as well as phonograms, suffixes, compound words, and homophones. Because most primary classrooms contain children at all different stages of spelling/decoding ability, provisions for making easier and more difficult words and for sorting easier and more difficult patterns allow all children to increase their word knowledge. Asking children to spell two or three words based on the sorted patterns increases the possibility that children will transfer their knowledge to real reading and writing.

Age and Readability.   Making Words is intended for children in grades 1–3. Readability is appropriate for this age group. Words are provided that can be used at each of their grade levels.

Durability and Useability.   Making Words is very durable and easily used. It can be integrated into a variety of lesson plans and doesn't have a strict order that needs to be followed.

Adaptability.   Making Words fits easily into many different lesson plans. Nothing needs to be changed in either the curriculum already in place or with the Making Words lesson for the teacher to integrate the two.

Teacher/Student Directed.   The teacher must be present to facilitate the lesson; most students cannot do these lessons on their own. Each lesson requires the constant participation of both the students and the teacher. It is highly interactive.

Critique.   This activity was used in conjunction with a Project Read lesson and the children involved seemed very enthusiastic. Students were able to use tactile, visual, and auditory learning. The students were constantly busy doing something and so were able to pay attention and stay on task throughout the lesson. Especially impressive about this material is the continual interaction between the teacher and students. It involves everyone working together. Moreover, this material makes use of every student's own way of learning by making use of different teaching styles, making it possible for all children to learn. The activity, with its varied levels of words and use of different teaching styles, seems to be well designed to facilitate every student's success. [Critiqued by Rachael Schroeder]

PROJECT ACHIEVEMENT: READING

George D. Spache and Evelyn B. Spache
Scholastic, Inc., 1987
Budget Text: (800)642-2665

Description.   The Project Achievement: Reading series is a direct-instruction independent learning program designed for students experiencing difficulties or having deficiencies in reading at grade level. The program begins with short stories and questions dealing with reading comprehension, emphasizing the need to pay attention to details to obtain information while reading. The second unit of study examines vocabulary. This includes looking at context clues, word parts, words with the same meaning, and words with opposite meanings. Again, short stories and multiple-choice questions are used. Another unit focuses on study skills with visual materials, such as maps and tables, and reference skills. The reference skills cover alphabetizing, using a table of contents, choosing a reference, using an encyclopedia, etc.

Age and Readability.   The Project Achievement: Reading series would be appropriate for late-elementary/early–middle school ages. The text is simple and easy to follow. The stories are interesting. The lessons are quick and to the point. Photographs and illustrations further enhance the text and maintain the students' interest.

Durability.   Although not a hardbound series, the cover is sturdy and the size of the book makes it less cumbersome and easier to transport. Because each lesson is only two to four pages long, stress from holding the book open should be minimized, and the book should withstand a fair amount of use. (The low price makes replacement costs a bit less frightening as well.)

Adaptability.   This book, which is already simplified, could be broken down even further to facilitate students with special needs. It is presently being used in a middle school at-risk program. This book complements multiage and multiability-levels settings.

Teacher/Student Directed.   The program presents flexible possibilities for presentation. It can be used both with complete direct instruction—the teacher leading all aspects of the lesson—and as a supplementary independent study unit. The lessons are self-explanatory, and group participation is not required.

Critique.   This program has been successfully used in the at-desk setting. For students who tend to need "quick" learning, it hits the mark. Students are drawn into the interesting and varied stories, and the questions at the end of the story are easy to follow. Photographs add a little spark to get curiosity juices flowing. Many of the articles offer insight into history, which prompts some thoughtful discussion beyond the reading lesson itself. Also, because the book is smaller in size and weight, it seems less threatening. This program works well with populations with special needs; however, it can easily be an added bonus in a regular education setting. [Critiqued by Jennifer Solomon]

PROJECT READ

Mary Lee Enfield and Victoria Greene
LanguageCircle Enterprises
P.O. Box 20631
Bloomington, MN 55420
(800)450-0343
FAX: (651)406-8788
www.projectread.com

Description.   Project Read is described as an early intervention program designed to help students learn to read, particularly those with reading problems or learning disabilities. The program is divided into three parts: decoding, reading, and comprehension. They encompass systematic learning, direct instruction, and multisensory strategies.

Workbooks are available to use with this program. The program has many creative, and multisensory ways of teaching phonics, using kinesthetic techniques such as "air writing," "felt writing," and "sand writing" to help children grasp the look and feel of letters. After students study and comprehend the sound and look of letters, they begin to learn to blend letters. Letters are "pounded out" letter by letter and sound by sound to teach this skill. Next, children are taught to blend together these letters into whole, complete words. The program can rapidly increase the reading ability of children who were previously unsuccessful at breaking the reading code.

Mary Enfield, Ph.D., and Victoria Greene, who also do trainings on how to use the materials effectively, originated this material. Enfield is an educational psychologist at the University of St. Thomas in St. Paul, Minnesota. Her coauthor, Victoria Green, has been an ED/LE teacher for many years in Minnesota. The cost of the materials is minimal, and many of the materials can be teacher made to cut down the expense for the school or district. The most important part of the material is the manual, which describes the procedures in detail. A set of stories is also important to have.

Teachers can provide the letters of the alphabet, which can be self-made, the box of sand, and the felt for writing letters.

Age and Readability.   The grade level of this program is first through sixth. The material is very appropriate for this age group if it is used as suggested. The vocabulary, story plots, and teaching methods are intended for elementary schoolchildren.

Durability and Useability.   Project Read has a fairly durable set of materials. Some parts, however, may need to be replaced regularly. For example, the sand can be messy and at times can be lost when tipped and spilled. The letters may also need replacing because they can be easily torn. However, the manual should last for many, many years.

Adaptability.   This program would need to be adapted for use with an older child. The material may still be useful but would need to be presented in a more age-appropriate manner for most middle school and probably all high school students.

Teacher/Student Directed.   This program is very teacher directed but has a lot of student involvement. However, the material is so teacher directed that it could be difficult to use with students who are absent a lot; it would be hard for the child to catch up without individual help.

Critique.   Project Read is a great program for children who are having difficulty learning to read. It does, however, take a lot of teacher time and energy and is easiest and most effective when used with a small group of children. [Critiqued by Melissa Viola]

WRITING MATERIALS

EXPRESSIVE WRITING

Science Research Associates
McGraw-Hill, Open Court Division
(888)772-4543
www.sra4kids.com

Description.   Developed by Sigfried Englemann and Jerome Silbert at Science Research Associates, Expressive Writing is a scripted material written in direct instruction format. The material was designed to take students through each step of the writing experience and ensure success using direct instructions and repetition. This book contains student workbooks teaching sentence-writing mechanics, paragraph writing, proofreading, reporting with and without inference, past and present tense forms, and the parts of the sentence.

Age and Readability.   This material is designed to be used with students from fourth through eighth grade. Each lesson has a picture to help students understand the content and tell the story. Expressive Writing 1 is designed to be used with students in third through fourth grade as well as students who are delayed in writing skills. This program can be followed with Expressive Writing 2, which is designed for students with higher skills and abilities.

Durability and Useability.   The teacher material is durable and developed to save and reuse, whereas the student workbooks are consumable with perforated pages and meant for one time usage. This makes the teacher's and the child's work easier.

Adaptability.   This program works best when the entire lesson can be used. As a result it might not be as useful for teachers who have only 15-minute reading periods. Because it is a scripted text, the material is easy for a teacher to use without complicated preplanning—once the material becomes familiar. The material includes suggestions for correcting students' errors. It can be used with regular education students and students with special needs.

Teacher/Student Directed.   To successfully use this program, the teacher needs to use the entire lesson. The direct instruction material is highly scripted and interactive. The material is to be used with a combination of teacher-directed lessons and students working on their own to produce the writing. It may not be a good choice for teachers who are not available to teach students directly.

Critique.   This material is a worthwhile investment for teachers who have students with expressive writing difficulties. The program is structured in a clear and precise manner and does not leave unanswered questions for the teacher to worry about. It is an excellent aid for covering the many important aspects of expressive writing. It is very useful for students who have failed to learn the basics of writing in the past. [Critiqued by David A. Puls]

SPELLING MASTERY

Science Research Associates
Macmillan/McGraw-Hill
220 Easy Danieldale Road
DeSoto, TX 75115-2490
(888)SRA-4543

Description.   This direct instruction spelling series is a six-level (A–F) basal spelling series designed to achieve student mastery. The Spelling Mastery series blends together three approaches: phonemic, morphemic, and whole word. These three approaches are put together according to the students' skill development. The phonemic approach is used to help beginning spellers generalize the spelling of regular phonemic patterns. The morphemic approach is used to help more advanced spellers learn multisyllabic words. Finally, the whole-word approach is used at all levels to teach common words that cannot be taught with the other strategies.

Spelling Mastery consists of procedural details such as signals, group and individual responses, scripts, pacing, and corrections. This spelling series helps students transfer the spelling skills they learn to writing skills for other academic work. The teacher uses a scripted format while the students pace along in their workbook. The students work on skills such as reading target words, spelling target words while looking at them, spelling target words without looking at them, and writing target words. These skills are completed under the direction of the teacher instead of all independent work. After every five lessons a list of words studied is presented to be used as a resource for a spelling test. Spelling Mastery guides the teacher with scope and sequence, as well as objectives, and can be used when the teacher wants to enhance a particular skill.

The series consists of a teacher's manual and a student workbook. Each lesson takes about 15–20 minutes (depending on the level of ability the teacher is currently working with). Each level should be taught daily for consistency and mastery of spelling skills.

Age and Readability.   This series can be used in general education, in special education, and with those students who are nonnative English speakers. Teachers may use the series for first-year up to sixth-year students. However, depending on students' ability level, older students can use the program as well. Students' ability level determines which spelling level to place them in. Spelling Mastery can be used with the entire class or with a small group of students. If students are low performers, a smaller group is more beneficial for the students' learning.

Readability is on a per-level basis and appropriate for the age level you decide to use it for. Because the teacher performs most of the modeling, students follow the teacher's directions. The work done in the workbook is based on what students already know from past learning or from learning it as they go.

Durability and Useability.   The teacher's manual is bound together and will hold up for a while, but in time the pages may begin to tear from the binding and fall out. The students' workbooks are durable and hold up well. Pages can be pulled out if students wish to take them home. The students' spelling workbook does stay at school so there is no reason for it to get worn out or torn up being carried in a backpack.

Spelling Mastery is a very user-friendly program. The program is all scripted so the teacher knows what to say to the students and what the students are supposed to do in their workbook. The teacher's manual has step-by-step instructions about how to test students, how to correct wrong answers, how to use the scripted format, how to place students in a spelling group, what words to use for a spelling test, how to transfer spelling skills to writing, and much more. One drawback is that because the program is teacher directed, students are only able to do the spelling lesson when the teacher is present.

Adaptability.   At times procedural details need to be adapted, such as signals, pacing, and different wording. The program can be easily adapted for students and their ability level. If too many spelling words are included for the spelling group, the teacher can omit words or add words appropriate for the specific lesson. If the lesson seems too long, the teacher can omit parts that are repetitious. At times separate lessons—one in which students perform one skill on the board and another in which they perform the skill orally—can be combined into one, or one of them may be omitted. This series is flexible to adapt to the type of learners teachers have in their class.

Teacher/Student Directed.   The teacher must be present for the entire lesson. The lesson consists of a scripted format that the teacher follows when teaching the students. Students must follow the teacher's presentation of the format to know what to do. The teacher directs students when to perform certain skills, such as oral work or book work. Many of the skills students learn are first modeled by the teacher and then performed independently by the student. The lessons consist of more than one rule, pattern, or new skill being taught. The student is highly involved in the lesson with direction from the teacher.

A student's absence can create a problem for the teacher and the student. The student will fall behind in spelling when absent because the other students will have learned a new skill or moved on while the absent student will have missed a whole lesson. The teacher's goal should be to help the student catch up on some of the missed work. The teacher should focus on new rules that were introduced and a quick review of old material. The teacher may direct the student to perform the independent portions of the work only, looking at the word list, or arranging for a tutor. This will help the absent student learn and understand any missed material without falling behind.

Critique.   I have used and am still using Spelling Mastery and really like the program. It combines into different lessons three approaches to spelling that commonly cause difficulties for students. I like how the format of the lesson is set up; everything is scripted for the teacher and teachers know ahead of time what the lessons contain, so if they want to modify the lesson, they can plan for it. I think this program is especially useful when working with students at lower spelling levels. It allows the teacher to model skills first, then have children practice spelling on their own. Having students repeat back to me enables me to see where they are having success and where their area of difficulty is. From this feedback I can modify certain areas of the lesson. I think the repetition is great because it allows time for information to be stored in a student's long-term memory.

I really like the program's versatility—allowing students to perform oral work and then perform written work in their workbook. At the end of some lessons, independent work is provided for the student as well. This allows me to see how well my students work on their own and whether they are mastering the skills. In addition, the lessons really teach students skills, rules, and word patterns on which they have been working for the week or even in the past. I like the way the program provides words for the teacher to use as a reference for spelling tests. In other spelling programs, words are tested and never seen again. In this program, words are tested but reappear later in other lessons, encouraging greater mastery. The program provides opportunities for group responses and individual turns as well.

I believe the teacher's manual has a wonderful set-up as well. It really goes through step by step what the teacher has to do, how to present the script, how to correct students' work effectively, what objectives the students will meet, and how to place students correctly in a group. I will keep using Spelling Mastery with all my students because of the success they have achieved. [Critiqued by Tara Niesen]

MATHEMATICS MATERIALS

BASIC MATHEMATICS, 2nd Ed.

Globe Fearon
Upper Saddle River, NJ
www.globefearon.com

Description.   These basic mathematics materials are designed "to develop math skills to succeed as well as survive" (*Basic Mathematics,* p. 1). Their goal is to help students reason, think, and make good judgments. We are reminded that calculators are machines that can only do what they are told. Students completing this curriculum will master a solid background in lifelong decision making in any area.

Age and Readability.   *Basic Mathematics* and resource worksheets are used successfully in high school. However, they are appropriate for middle school–aged students as well. The readability level is grade 3.5. This combination of book and resource binder is written in an easy-to-follow format. A simple color scheme of black and blue is less distracting than other commonly used materials. Vocabulary is boxed and located in the same place on the page each time it appears. The format is clear and concise, enhancing concepts.

In these materials the teachers will find basic math concepts; whole numbers, addition, multiplication, fractions, decimals, percentages, graphing, probability, measurement, metric system, polygons, circles, equations. Each section also has a short segment titled Mathematics in Your Life and may cover anything from saving money to life insurance to recipes, and figuring your salary or home repairs. The relevance cannot be overstated as teachers often hear students' lament, "Why do we need to learn this?"

Durability and Useability.   This text is a sturdy hardcover text; handy worksheets make this a great choice for the student in need of a basic course. The binder also contains a student assessment record, unit-by-unit class chart, and, lastly, a reproducible certificate of achievement. All these features make learning and teaching a coordinated effort.

Adaptability. *Basic Mathematics* could well fit into the curriculum of the student with special needs and may benefit the student who needs to review certain chapters or the student who did not previously master vital math concepts. This text can be used for a quick review, work on specific topics, or completion of whole coursework.

Teacher/Student Directed. The teacher may need to be present to teach or tutor the student. Also, the student may proceed as directed in the course of schoolwork. Teachers may correct work or students may be directed to correct incorrect problems. This is a typical book/worksheet arrangement of outstanding quality.

Critique. This book has proven to be an excellent resource. I have found it especially helpful with students who do not understand the concepts behind mathematics. As stated earlier, often students yearn for knowledge that is applicable to life, not just to school.

As mentioned earlier, the text is clear and not overburdened with bright photos, many colors, or types of print, which are often confusing to learners. It stands as a text for the serious student. The worksheets have variety and combine work problems (critical thinking) crossword puzzles, vocabulary, and comprehension. Students will appreciate the variety as well as the teacher presenting complete coverage of concepts.

Mathematics is a subject whereby concepts build on each other. Coursework must be mastered before the student may proceed to other material. The student completing this coursework is ready to undertake further study. This material may be below the needs of many high school students, but for the students mentioned it can provide the necessary background into the world of mathematics. I recommend both the hardcover book and the classroom resource binder for *Basic Mathematics*. [Critiqued by Brenda Carlson-Hahn]

MATH WARM-UPS FOR JR. HIGH (7–9): SHORT EXERCISES FOR REVIEW AND EXPLORATION

Scott McFadden, 1983
Dale Seymour Publications
P.O. 10888
Palo Alto, CA 94303

Description. *Math Warm-Ups* can be used as a workbook or as a set of black-line masters for junior high through high school math students. Seventy warm-ups each consist of five problems with a bonus problem. The main topics contained in the warm-ups include whole numbers, fractions, decimals, money, percents, measurement, and geometry.

Age and Readability. Although the materials are listed for use with junior high students, I have found them particularly effective with high school students in our extended algebra courses, which often contain many students with learning disabilities and emotional disturbances. These warm-ups provide special education students with the important practice they need to be able to integrate complex math topics. It also readily highlights for students that proficiency in math is often based more on practice than on the ease of initial learning. For some students it provides a daily predictable transition from other academic subjects to the language and activities of math. Students report that they enjoy starting the lesson with review materials.

Durability. The edition that we use was published in 1983 and is still very useful. Unlike other academic areas, the language of math remains consistent and the majority of problems are not word problems.

Adaptability. The material is adaptable to many different populations. One adjustment we make for the high school level is to remove the clipart or pictures that are included with many of the worksheets. These pictures might be perceived as somewhat childish by high school students and may distract from their comfort level when doing the math problems. The Extended Algebra class teacher has used the warm-ups for more than 4 years with few adaptations. The material as written is very readable for students with reading difficulties. Extended Algebra is a regular education class that is offered for 2 hours every day. Students receive two math credits for successful completion. As standards and benchmarks raise the expectation of algebra competency for all students, it is important for students who have previously been less successful in math (sometimes due to the written language component, sometimes due to behavior or other concerns) to experience success through use of well-written materials and classes structured to meet their needs.

Teacher/Student Directed.   The materials are designed to be completed individually at the beginning of math class, to provide practice with recurring topics, and to "warm up" the students for the upcoming lesson. The warm-ups take only about 10 minutes and allow students to focus on math topics.

Critique.   We have students complete the worksheets independently at the beginning of class, and later participate in group correction to explain concepts and mistakes. The worksheets can also be used as a teacher-directed activity. One of the side benefits of this strategy, however, is the quiet and focus achieved at the beginning of class with this independent work. I highly recommend these materials and am currently investigating parallel materials for another math course to incorporate some of the positive features I have described here. [Critiqued by Maribeth Malnor]

MIDDLE GRADES MATHEMATICS: AN INTERACTIVE APPROACH

Prentice Hall, 1995
(800)848-9500

Description.   *Middle Grade Mathematics* was developed for middle grade students and is a student-centered program. The program uses real-life situations to help students experience math by incorporating active learning and problem solving. The goal is to build a partnership with family and community that increases the student's math ability through experience.

Contents consist of classroom resources, teacher's communication kit (Spanish and English), tools for smarter studying, overhead transparencies, Spanish resources, and a teacher's answer book. Eleven chapters develop specific math skills, including "Algebraic Equations and Inequalities," "Probabilities," and "Rational Numbers."

Durability and Useability.   Each lesson is organized with the following sections: What's Ahead, Teacher Materials, Student Materials, Introduction/Interaction, Facilitate, Follow Up, Assignment Options, and Self-Evaluation. This math series helps students master math using several methods: introduction, instruction, discussion, worksheet, and alternative activities (at school, at home, and/or in the community). *Middle Grades Mathematics* should be teacher directed, but lessons are easily readable and understandable if the student needs to work independently. Prior to each chapter, letters are sent home to parents that encourage parental involvement to enhance students' mastery of the skills being learned.

Adaptability.   Adaptations include Spanish supplements for teachers and alternative lessons. Also, the Tools for Studying section encourages students to explore their learning style and to become active participants.

Teacher/Student Directed.   At the beginning of each lesson teachers should introduce the new material and give examples; otherwise, students have one ready example to refer to and to learn by on their worksheet. To master the new material the students complete a worksheet and choose from alternative assignments that can be completed in school, at home, or in the community.

Critique. *Middle Grades Mathematics* looks more like a supplement or an overview than a teaching tool. This series has a lot of good ideas, and although the lessons are very well organized, they are somewhat brief. Program strengths include a well-organized text, encouragement of learning styles, and tools for learning. Not only are students active participants, but they can apply these skills to their other environments, use alternative activities, and record their progress on an assessment sheet. The main weakness is that only the teacher's materials are provided in Spanish, not the students' worksheets. Another weakness is that each lesson worksheet provides only one example and most of the questions have a word problem orientation versus practicing equation skills. Unfortunately, not enough equations are provided for students to solve to master the new knowledge and/or skills at all levels. In general, this book provides many wonderful ideas and tools to make learning math more fun. [Critiqued by Mary Neuman]

MATH IN ACTION

Jim Overholt
Center for Applied Research in Education
Professional Publishing
West Nyack, NY 10994

Description. *Math Wise* is a student-based hands-on math program that is adaptable to the programming needs that a district, school, and individual classroom might have. The material can be used with students in all grades and levels. It has a problem-solving component including real-life situations to solve, as well as a cooperative learning component.

Teacher/Student Directed. Many parts of this program can be used with either teacher leading, in cooperative groups, or with students working alone for further enrichment.

Age and Readability. The material reaches students' needs in multiple areas and at multiple ages. Each activity level is delineated by skill and level in the front of the book.

Durability. Math Wise is a teacher's book in paperback form and bound in a spiral for easy use.

Adaptability. It is very adaptable to a wide range of teaching styles. Each activity ends with a list of extension activities to be used for enrichment.

Critique. I like this book because it is practical, easy to use, and adaptable. It is teacher friendly and excellent for classrooms with multiage or multiskilled students. The hands-on/manipulative activities are especially good for young students or students with special needs. [Critiqued by Missy Hilliard]

SOCIAL SKILLS MATERIALS

READY-TO-USE SELF-ESTEEM ACTIVITES FOR YOUNG CHILDREN

Jean R. Feldman, Ph.D., 1997
The Center for Applied Research in Education
West Nyack, NY 10994

Description. Self-esteem is essential for a child's success in life. Children with high self-esteem are leaders, team players, and the type of people other children want to be around. Children with low self-esteem are more likely to abuse drugs or alcohol, join gangs, or do poorly in school. Teachers play an important role in raising a child's self-esteem. This book demonstrates many different activities to help in this process. It consists of different areas for developing positive self-esteem.

1. Activities such as art projects, stories, and songs to help children appreciate themselves and find their strengths
2. Developing social skills and helping kids have fun with friends
3. Recognizing feelings and showing them in appropriate ways
4. Seeing similarities and differences in everyone and appreciating them for who they are
5. Instruction on wellness, including health, safety, and fitness, to help students learn how to look out for themselves and deal with changes
6. A parent section with activities for parents and students to do at home to improve a child's self-esteem

Age and Readability. The activities in this book are most appropriate for younger children, probably through third or fourth grade. However, some activities can be adapted for older elementary-aged children or older students with lower skills. Students are not required to do any reading with this book, but younger kids may need some teacher assistance to complete some of the worksheets. The activities vary from needing lengthy preparation to little preparation.

Durability. This manual is set up to be very user friendly for the teacher. The activities are outlined very simply with objectives, materials needed, directions, and variations/tips. These activities can be implemented into a variety of subject matters, and most are intended to be applicable to the student's life.

Adaptability. Many of the projects can fit into different lesson plans and subject areas. The easiest way to adapt the activities for younger children or children with lower abilities is to pair or group the students so they can work together, which many of the plans suggest as a variation. As mentioned earlier, some activities can be adapted for older children. These projects also enlist many different learning styles using reading, art, music, experiences, and stories to help students understand the concepts.

Teacher/Student Directed. The *Ready-to-Use Self-Esteem Activities for Young Children* curriculum needs a teacher to present the activities. Some lessons can be done in large groups, some in small groups or pairs, and others independently. Many of the activities are interactive, creative, and short, so they keep students' attention. Also provided are activities for parents/caregivers to implement at home to help reinforce the lesson.

Critique. Many of these activities should be very useful for increasing students' self-esteem. It is important to have students reflect independently as well as work with teachers and other students. This book gives students a good balance of both types of activities. I especially like the activities that teach students to develop friendships and to take care of themselves in today's world. Because these activities can be used in many subject areas, they can help many different students. [Critiqued by Jennifer McCann]

SKILL STREAMING THE ELEMENTARY SCHOOL CHILD: A GUIDE FOR TEACHING PROSOCIAL SKILLS

Ellen McGinnis, Arnold P. Goldstein, Robert P. Sprafkin, and N. Jane Gershaw
Research Press
P.O. Box 9177
Champaign, IL 61826
(800)519-2707
www.researchpress.com

Description.   This paperback book is intended as a resource book or guide for teachers working with elementary students. It has good ideas about how to assess students' skills and then work with students on social skill concepts that are not yet attained. It gives many examples of how to teach the skills in social groups.

Age and Readability.   This material is intended for teachers working with children in first through sixth grade. This book is designed to assist teachers in teaching and evaluating the social skill needs of their students. It should be especially useful for working with elementary-age students with or without physical disabilities who continually deal with everyday events in an immature manner, with aggression, or with withdrawal. This program is also appropriate for students who show these behaviors less frequently because these behaviors still affect their personal happiness and relationships with others.

Durability.   As a teachers' resource material this book is fairly durable. However, it is a paperback. No handouts or students' useable parts are supplied.

Adaptability.   If a teacher wanted to use this material with high school students, some of the items could easily be adapted. A book called *Skill Streaming the Adolescent* (by Arnold P. Goldstein) would probably be more effective in most cases.

Teacher/Student Directed.   This material is a resource for teachers to use as a springboard for their class. It is not written for students to read.

Critique.   This book, especially in conjunction with the book for adolescents, can be the basis of a highly effective social skills program throughout a school district. It has nice assessment materials that can be easily used to pre- and posttest skills, pinpointing skill strength and weaknesses for students' social skills training programs. The ideas given to help teachers teach the skills that their students lack or are weak in are also very helpful.

The format given for teaching social skills is very helpful and based on research in the field.

SCIENCE MATERIALS

BIOLOGY, AN EVERYDAY EXPERIENCE

Kaskel, Hummer, and Daniel
Glencoe/McGraw-Hill
936 Eastwind Drive
Westerville, OH 43081
(800)334-7344
FAX: 614-860-1877
www.glencoe.com

Description.   Glencoe describes this book as "designed for students who've had little success with science in the past."

Each chapter of this textbook is divided into sections, which make it easy to break down into smaller portions and enables students to process the information better. Review questions are provided at the end of each section to reinforce the concepts covered. This book is well illustrated with color photographs and diagrams that are appropriate to each topic. In addition to the above noted items laboratory manuals, videodiscs, study guides, computer test banks, transparencies and evaluation materials are also available. The text provides "mini-labs" that can be completed in 10–15 minutes. These can introduce or reinforce the objective of the lesson. More extensive lab work is also available.

Each lab reinforces the use of the scientific method to solve problems. Idea maps are provided throughout the book for students with a visual learning style. Each chapter ends with a chapter review that summarizes the key points of the chapter. A number of questions assist students in preparing for the chapter test.

In the teacher wraparound edition, each chapter begins with a planning guide, technology resources, a list of necessary materials, and objectives for the chapter. This is very helpful in planning for the presentation of the upcoming chapter. The Science and Society sections are placed throughout the book. These sections include information about a science-related topic. This encourages students to form their own opinions and discuss these issues.

Age and Readability.   This book is written for high school students whose reading ability is closer to that of the low-to-average middle school student. The readability for this textbook is grade 5, based on the Fry Readability Graph.

Durability.   This textbook is very durable. It has a hard cover and is well made. Its useability is average. A lot of information is contained in this text, and it may be difficult for some students who are easily distracted. The book is also large and heavy.

Adaptability.   *Biology, An Everyday Experience* has been adapted for students with special needs: it is written to interest high school students but the readability is significantly lower than an average high school textbook. This book can be further adapted for students with special needs. For example, the teacher can use the instructional conversation strategy to guide the students through the material. Focus pictures, study guide workbooks, and reinforcement worksheets allow the teacher to further concentrate on the most basic concepts presented in each chapter.

Teacher/Student Directed.   This textbook is best used under the direction of the classroom teacher. The teacher should provide direct instruction, discussion, concept review, opportunities for cooperative learning, and lab experiences. Student involvement with lab work and discussion is important for skill assessment. Because some students do not have adequate written language skills, they are unable to demonstrate their knowledge on written assessments. Classroom discussion affords the auditory learner an opportunity to learn the information being presented and discussed. Students with good verbal communication skills have an opportunity to demonstrate their knowledge in this portion of the class. A student could use this text, as well as the study guide workbook, reinforcement worksheets, chapter reviews, and tests as an independent study course.

Critique.   This textbook and the resource materials assist teachers in providing a structured biology course for students with emotional and behavioral disorders. The readability is also appropriate for this group of students. Because each chapter is divided into sections and the vocabulary is controlled, students are able to achieve greater success. The reteaching worksheets assist teachers in directing review sessions. The colored pictures and diagrams provide interest in the textbook and spark discussions. Students are able to relate much of the material to their everyday lives and the world around us. [Critiqued by Judith Walsh]

BIOLOGY PRINCIPLES & EXPLORATIONS

George B. Johnson, and Peter H. Raven, 2001
Holt, Rinehart, and Winston
1120 South Capital of Texas Highway
Austin, Texas 78746-6487

Description.   This book is a broad-based biology text that offers in-depth coverage on several biological phenomena, procedures, laboratories, and discussions. Each chapter is designed in a way that explains the smaller components first, which lead into the larger concepts. Science literacy is an important aspect in new pedagogical strategies and *Biology Principles & Explorations* has begun the process of encouraging learners to think critically and relate science to their own life and to world issues currently in the news. It stimulates students to reflect on the history of science to understand present-day ideals and to visualize future endeavors.

Age and Readability.   Written for introductory biology educators and their students at the high school level, this text is appropriate for the beginning biology student. This material should not be used without extra support with students who have limited reading abilities because some of the language is science specific. Additional supplementary readings are provided from varying science journals, including *Science News,* with which students may also need help understanding the language used to fully comprehend the messages stressed in each of the complementary articles.

Durability and Useability.   An overwhelmingly large text, this book has a secure bind and feel to it. The students are only allowed to check it out when necessary, so its life is prolonged in the classroom rather than destroyed in lockers, backpacks, and on the bus.

The text offers more than 143 experimental labs as well as outside resources to support certain concepts and topics within the curriculum; integrates history; and challenges students to solve problems both in the classroom and outside school. It is very useable and has proved to be the book of choice at my high school.

Adaptability.   Students with special needs are currently using *Biology Principles & Explorations* and are successful when they are given extra support from lead teachers and special educational assistants. It is helpful to prepare an outline of the most important concepts to grasp for students with special needs before class discussions, labs, and lectures commence.

Teacher/Student Directed.   The direction of involvement shifts from being teacher centered to student centered, depending on the content and what phase is being discussed. For example, when talking about global warming, the educator may begin by presenting information on basic chemical reactions, but then turn discussion over to students when looking at possible solutions.

Critique.   *Biology Principles & Explorations* is a great tool to use with secondary students in introductory science courses. As a tool, however, it should not be used alone. It works better as a resource to use to structure and design a class but needs other support to teach the elements of biology. It begins the process of teaching the nature of science in each chapter by including aspects of history, science content, lab experiments, and thinking and reasoning skills of science. The book lags in explaining the nature of science and technology as it pertains to new standards that stress science literacy. This book needs to expand on personal use of science and technology, social impact of science and technology, and attitudes or habits of mind (*Constructing Science in Middle and Secondary School Classrooms,* 1997).[1] However, the book does a great job of guiding learners in conducting investigations, helping to interpret meaning, and begins the process of applying that knowledge to current issues. [Critiqued by Ann Bahnson]

[1]D. K. Baker and M. D. Piburn, *Constructing Science in Middle and Secondary School Classrooms* (Boston: Allyn and Bacon, 1997).

THE PACEMAKER CURRICULUM, FEARON'S HEALTH, 2nd edition (1994)

Globe Fearon
240 Frisch Court
Paramus, New Jersey 07652
www. pearsonlearning.com

Description.   This textbook is specifically made for students with learning and behavioral problems. It is a health book and covers the basic units of a health class. (Students are commonly required to take health classes to graduate from high school.) It is a great text to use with this population because it is a comprehensive collection of related information that is laid out in an easy-to-read and -understand format. Each chapter has key words that are defined on the first page, within the chapter, and also in the glossary. The pictures are simple and easy to understand and appealing to different types of learners. The text is large print and easy to read and notes appear in the margin. At the end of each chapter are chapter summaries that cover the key points, along with chapter quizzes, health checks, and health issues, to stimulate thinking or discussion. Health Practice questions also appear throughout each chapter to make sure that the students understand the material. Four appendices and an index are included.

Age and Readability.   This text is intended for grades 6–12; it is high-interest, low-readability material. It can be used with students with a lower-level reading ability. It was specifically designed for use with students with special educational needs.

Durability.   The textbook is very easy to use, and the chapters flow in an easy-to-follow format. It is durable but will need to be updated when new information becomes available in the health field.

Adaptability.   Because *The Pacemaker Curriculum, Fearon's Health* was intended for use with students with disabilities, the required health material has already been adapted for use with a different population.

Teacher/Student Directed.   The teacher does not need to be present to teach the entire lesson unless the student's disability requires someone to read to them. The book can also be taped so that even these students can use it independently. Most students with disabilities should be able to read and synthesize the materials with minimal teacher assistance. However, the ability to read, at low levels, is required.

Critique.   I am currently using this textbook with my students in special education. (One student reads at the second-grade level and is able to read and understand the material.) The pictures are clear and descriptive and the highlighted terms are very helpful. It is very useful for giving students in special education a less stressful and more understandable alternative to the traditional health texts used in most schools. The text moves at a good pace, the readings are simple, and the questions are worded to be easily understood. The Note to the Student feature is useful for motivating students because it tells them how to use the book and why they need to learn about health. This text does a great job of making health material relatable, useful, and interesting to students with special needs. [Critiqued by Katherine Lovenberg]

SOCIAL STUDIES MATERIALS

CURRENT ISSUES 2002

Close Up Publishing
44 Canal Center Plaza
Alexandria, VA 22314-1592
(800)765-3131

Description.   *Current Issues 2002* is a soft-covered, 350-page book that discusses current issues, government, international relations, history, and economics. The book is divided into three main sections: The Federal Government, Domestic Policy Issues, and Foreign Policy Issues. Each individual section is devoted to a specific topic. At the end of each section are three questions, which are debatable.

Age and Readability.   The intended age group for this book is most likely 16 years old and up. However, the preface of the book states that the material is for people of all ages. However, some of the issues presented in this book are meant for mature audiences; topics such as health care, immigration, federal budget, and so on could be taught to younger readers but would probably be more engaging for older readers. The book can also be used for older students with lower skills.

Durability and Useability.   The answer to the question of durability is yes and no. I could say yes because the topics and information are quite new. In fact, the information was just printed and is hot off the presses. I could also say no because *Current Issues* is published every year, and every year something else is added or changed.

The answer to the question of useability is yes. The book is quite user friendly and I have already used it quite extensively in my classroom. The topics are important and need to be discussed. I am very pleased with the book in regard to all its features.

Adaptability.   As stated earlier, *Current Issues* can be adapted easily for students with special needs. For example, I recently taught the section Constitutional Rights in my class. I started out asking students the questions presented at the beginning of the chapter. Next, I outlined the information from the book and adapted it for a PowerPoint presentation. I also included my own presentation of the Bill of Rights, in PowerPoint format. I like to present the book from various angles. On certain occasions, we read the chapters together; other times I have the students read the material by themselves. Sometimes, I extract the important information and present it in lecture format, either through straight note taking or PowerPoint presentation.

Teacher/Student Directed.   *Current Issues* is the type of material that can teach itself. It would be beneficial to have the teacher as a guide while students engage with the material in the book. However, students could probably complete the lessons on their own if they had to. Some sections in the book are more difficult than others because the topics discussed are more complicated than others, for example, immigration and human rights and health care.

For students to gain knowledge from this book, their involvement must be extremely high. They should go over certain vocabulary prior to reading certain sections, stop and discuss certain points through the readings, and discuss the questions at the end of each reading.

Critique.   As I have stated before, I am extremely happy with *Current Issues.* I was first introduced to it last year. Another special education teacher with endorsements in the social sciences gave me her copy to look through. Once I picked it up and started to skim through it, I knew that I wanted to use it for my class. I then ordered this year's version and have been using it since. Some parts of the book are better received than others, depending on what is important and relevant to the students. However, all sections of the book are equally important and I would like to explore them all. One feature that is especially helpful is the workbook that accompanies the text. In it are quizzes and tests, as well as true/false sections and fill-in-the-blank and multiple-choice questions. Overall, I feel that *Current Issues* is a good choice. I plan to continue using it in the future. [Critiqued by Mike Lovenberg]

TRIBES, A NEW WAY OF LEARNING AND BEING TOGETHER

Joanne Gibbs
Center Source Systems LLC
412 Aviation Blvd., Suite F
Santa Rosa, CA 95403
(707)573-8737
FAX: 707-573-8311
Web www.tribes.com

Description.   This program is most effective when the whole school is involved and trained in *Tribes*. The tenets of the program are that all children should be honored for their uniqueness and should feel safe at all times. Caring and involved adults, meaningful participation, and positive high expectations are components of the program. The concept of tribes, or a learning community, is beneficial to all students. This program gives students a way to feel pride and success. Through the process, all students are looked at for their gifts and positive qualities, not their deficits and wrong choices.

   This material is also a great resource for information on the development of children and on how children learn. The program is flexible and includes activities for large groups and small groups. The materials help the facilitator design an interactive learning experience that works well for all learners in the community.

Age and Readability.   The book is for educators and administrators. The activities are designed for students in grades K–12. Some activities can easily be used at all grade levels. They are coded for specific age groups. Activities can easily be modified to make them easier or more difficult. Activities range from critical thinking to simple relay games.

Durability.   The Tribes program will stand the test of time. Districts all over the United States are using this program to help build schoolwide community. In an age when guns, knives, and an overabundance of violence occupy our thoughts, there needs to be a way to bring together all students and adults. Kids who are involved in this program learn self-worth and the ability to appreciate everyone regardless of differences.

   The only drawback to the program is the fact that you must be trained. If you are interested, talk to your school about individual training for yourself or, even better, for the school as a whole.

Adaptability.   The Tribes program is a good way to teach social skills because it emphasizes a caring, accepting environment, and children feel safe and included. It is especially helpful that the Tribes program uses all three learning styles: auditory, visual, and kinesthetic. In this way, teaching styles are made effective for many types of learners. (For example, in the program the teacher models proper responses, giving students a clear understanding of teacher expectations.) It is also a very positive program in expressing "appreciations" after every turn.

Teacher/Student Directed.   The Tribes program needs one person to be the facilitator. (It doesn't need to be a teacher, but it needs to be someone knowledgeable in Tribes.) All students need to play an active role for the community to be successful. Tribes allows for a wide range of abilities—there are lessons for all abilities and age levels. Students are also expected to lead the group in discussions. This should be easy for them because they are being taught to be comfortable in their community.

Critique.   I strongly recommend this program. I have used it successfully in the second and fifth grades. The climate of the whole classroom changes once the community circle begins. Any child can be successful in this program because it entails lots of verbal interactions and group work. There is something for everyone. Appreciations are expressed sincerely, and children come away from the experience with a sense of pride and self-worth. Discipline problems and detentions in my class, and in the school overall, declined when the program was used. Children who have positive self-esteem are more likely to interact more positively with each other. Students learn to talk out their issues in a constructive way.

Especially encouraging about the Tribes program is the transformation of the children. These transformations don't happen overnight. It takes a lot of hard work and dedication. The program gives you more knowledge than you ever imagined. You will also be able to enjoy your students more because a bond of mutual respect is created. I was amazed at the positive results I had in just a few weeks. Every teacher should at least read *Tribes* to see whether it can be of value to your classroom. Your whole attitude about discipline and your role as a teacher could change overnight! [Critiqued by Sara Goetsch]

OTHER MATERIALS

THE TOUGH KID TOOL BOX

William B. Jenson, Ph.D., Ginger Rhode, Ph.D., and H. Kenton Reavis, Ed.D.
Sopris West
1140 Boston Ave.
Longmont, CO 80501
(303)-651-2829

Description.   *The Tough Kid Tool Box* is a supplement to *The Tough Kid Book*. It is a tool book that provides techniques that can be used in the classroom to facilitate learning. The book provides different interventions to motivate students who have behavior concerns. Each section of the book gives a definition of an intervention, a description of the intervention, as well as complete steps for implementing the intervention. The seven interventions can be used to monitor progress, provide an incentive for the student, and provide information and data for the IEP team.

The book also discusses making contracts with the student. A contract gives students the opportunity to be a part of the decision-making process. Another section of the book discusses ways to motivate a child using charts. Charting can be used as an incentive system. Students are able to watch their chart, thus monitoring their own behaviors. If students are successful on their chart, they may receive rewards for their appropriate behavior.

The authors of the book encourage teachers to make copies of their tools in the book to use in their classroom. This helps with discipline, and behavior concerns, and saves teachers time as the charts are already available in the book.

Age and Readability.   The charts and intervention strategies that are given can be used with students in first through eighth grade. The manual is written clearly and gives excellent examples to assist any teacher.

Durability and Useability.   *The Tough Kid Tool Box* and *The Tough Kid Book* have durability because each tool can be copied, which is encouraged by the authors. It has many ideas and tools for charts that can help in the classroom and with individual students.

Adaptability.   This book can be used to assist teachers with any student who has behavioral issues. It can be adapted to the present level of the student. One section has "mystery motivators." An empty box is set for each day of the week. On the top of the page is a neat picture. The teacher can put stickers in the boxes if the student is complying with the specified criteria. Or an invisible marker indicates an "r" in each square. Each day the student uses a marker to uncover the "mystery." If an "r" is in the box, a reward is received by the student who meets the criteria.

Teacher/Student Directed. In developing the tools for each student, the teacher may be the one defining the behavior and the reward system. Many of the tools can be created together by the teacher and student. Some tools are very simplified for younger students as well as for students with special needs. The tools can also be used with a higher-skilled student with or without special needs. The teacher and the student can be involved in the decision-making process to determine whether the goal was achieved.

Critique. The teacher that introduced me to the book stated that she used the book every day in her first year of teaching. The book has great examples and ideas. There are so many ideas and different types of tools that it is valuable for many different students. Students and teachers can work together to develop the tool and the reward if the criteria are met. If the student is involved in the process, the tool will undoubtedly be more effective. It is impressive that the book encourages this option of working together.

For the book to be most successful, it is important to gear each tool to each student's ability. Some students may need minimal goals on their tool to receive their reward. In this way the student can grow, as the tools get more difficult. The tools and goals can be stepping stones that keep going up. A student needs to start at the lowest step they can achieve.

Students can monitor their progress because the tools are concrete and visible tools, which assists them in visualizing their progress. If they are not doing as well as hoped, the tools can be a guide and a marker for them to work harder. The incentive or reward should be linked to something the student enjoys or likes. The student should feel proud and their self-esteem should improve. Having confidence and self-esteem is a big part of learning. [Critiqued by Thada Pourier]

Appendix A
Icebreakers

SIGNATURE HUNT

Ask the members in the group to match each person with at least one descriptor.

1. _____ I am an oldest child.

2. _____ I am left-handed.

3. _____ I live above the fourth floor.

4. _____ I believe in ghosts.

5. _____ I *love* chocolate.

6. _____ Summer is my favorite season.

7. _____ I celebrated my birthday this month.

8. _____ I play a musical instrument.

9. _____ I am a youngest child.

10. _____ I write poetry.

11. _____ I play team sports.

12. _____ I have been in a dramatic production.

13. _____ My bedroom is a disaster area.

14. _____ I have traveled to a foreign country.

15. _____ I read the comics first.

16. _____ I am artistic.

17. _____ I am a middle child.

18. _____ Math is my favorite subject.

19. _____ I am always moving around.

20. _____ I am planning to go to college.

21. _____ I have a cat.

22. _____ I am a picky eater.

23. _____ I love dogs.

24. _____ I am a couch potato.

25. _____ I have broken a bone.

CONCENTRATION AND FOCUS

David Puls

Objective
The purpose of this exercise is to demonstrate concentration while having a little fun. It is important to be able to follow directions and keep a clear mind. This exercise tests the participants on how well they can continue without becoming flustered.

Activity
The participants all stand in a circle, shoulder to shoulder. The facilitator gives one person a word (such as *choo, yo, ribbit*, or some other sound) and tells that person to say that word to the person to his/her right. The person to the right then says that word to the person to his/her right, and so on around the circle. Next the facilitator tells a participant another word or phrase (such as *all aboard, what's your name boogie woogie,* or some other goofy expression) and tells that person to say the word to the person to his/her left. That person then says the words to the person to his/her left, and the word continues around from person to person to the left. Then the facilitator tells one person to start the first word back to the right while continuing to say the word to the left. To make it more interesting, the facilitator can have the participants start handing two different balls or beanbags to the left and right while continuing to say the words or phrases to the left and right. To really shake things up, introduce a code word that reverses all the sequences. The facilitator can yell the code word, or the person with a certain colored ball can reverse it. The game continues until everyone is completely flustered.

Goal
To show the importance of listening, concentrating, and doing more than one thing at a time. It also demonstrates the importance of making a mistake, refocusing, and getting back on track.

COMMUNICATION EXERCISE

David Puls

Objective
Communication is part of everyone's life. Effective communication is important to success in the workplace. Oftentimes, messages, directions, and information are misinterpreted in the workplace. This exercise is an example of how information can be misinterpreted. This exercise can be somewhat humorous, but serves to show the benefits of clearly stating one's intentions to guarantee successful communication.

Materials
People, a couple of blank pieces of paper, and a drawing utensil

Activity
Three to 10 people sit cross-legged in a line facing forward. The person at the front of the line is given a piece of paper and a marker. The facilitators of the activity draw a simple object or picture on another piece of paper (such as a stop sign, sailboat, an animal, a tic-tac-toe board, or a word spelled out). The person at the end of the line is then shown the picture. Then, in complete silence (yeah, right), the person at the end of the line draws that object on the back of the person in front of him/her with his/her finger. That person attempts to interpret the object and then draw the object on the person in front of him/her. The person at the front of the line then attempts to draw the object that was drawn with a finger on everyone's back on the piece of paper that was given to him/her at the beginning of the exercise. The outcome is somewhat unpredictable depending on the difficulty of the object.

Goal
To demonstrate how information can be misinterpreted if effective communication is not used.

GET ACQUAINTED GAME

Linda Volk

Materials

3 different colored bean bags or soft foam balls

Directions

Everyone stands in a circle. Make sure name tags can be seen. One person starts by calling out another person's name (preferably someone not already known) and tossing the ball to that person. The key is to remember to whom you are throwing the ball. The person who catches the ball then calls out another name and throws the ball to that person. This is repeated until everyone has had a turn. Once everyone has the idea of the game, start over. The person who starts the ball should wait until three or four other people toss the ball and then throw a different colored ball following the same name-calling pattern. Each time you throw a ball, you throw to the same person *after* you have called his/her name. Eventually, all three colored balls are being tossed. This makes for lots of noise and ball throwing, so make sure people understand two safety concerns: not throwing too hard and not throwing until you have the person's attention.

SILENT SPEEDBALL

Janis Needham

Goal
To enhance nonverbal communication through eye contact and body language.

Materials
Participants, koosh ball

Estimated Time
5–15 minutes

Object
The object of the game is to get the other people in the group to sit down and be the last one standing. The game starts with participants standing in a good-sized circle. The lead person begins tossing the koosh ball to someone in the group. If a person drops the koosh ball he/she sits down outside the circle. If the person tossing the koosh ball throws it too high or too low, it is considered a poor toss, and the tosser sits down outside the circle. Participants may also sit out if they talk. This is the fun part of the game, which usually becomes so funny that everyone is trying not to laugh or talk out loud. The game is over when one person is left standing. If time is allotted, another game can be started.

NAME GAME

Janis Needham

Goal
To learn everyone's name

Materials
Participants

Estimated Time
5–10 minutes

Object
The object of the game is to get all the participants in a circle and learn everyone's name. The game can get a bit difficult so a little help from a friend in the group won't hurt. The Name Game starts with the lead person introducing himself/herself using his/her first name only. The game continues with the second person saying the first person's name and then his/her own name. The third person continues by stating the first person's name, the second person's name, and then his/her own name. The Name Game ends once everyone has had a turn and one final person volunteers to go one more time. However, before the person starts, everyone switches places to make the game a little more difficult. When the volunteer is finished, the game is over.

CIRCLE TALK ACTIVITY

Alice Paul

Objective
The purpose of this activity is to build and maintain self-esteem. It is believed that giving students an opportunity to express their feelings in a safe setting helps them communicate and cope with these feelings each day.

Materials
A space to form a circle and open-minded students

Introduction
We are going to do an activity to improve our listening skills. To listen well, we need to

- Stop talking
- Concentrate on what the speaker is saying
- Empathize with the speaker
- Refrain from mentally arguing with the speaker
- Eliminate distractions
- Try to understand the main point

Instructions

1. Only the person holding the bear may talk; everyone else is to listen attentively.
2. Pass the bear to the left. The bear is never to be dropped or thrown.
3. Anyone has the right to "pass"; the bear continues around the circle.
4. Talk only about what you think or feel on the subject, not on what someone else has said.
5. No put-downs are accepted, and no talking unless you have the bear in your hand.
6. Keep confidentiality within your group.

Possible Topics

1. What is your favorite movie, TV show, or song?
2. What would you do with a million dollars?
3. Where would you move if you could live anywhere in the world?
4. What are you good at doing?
5. What do you like about yourself?
6. What do you wish you could do better?
7. Name something you have always wanted to do.
8. Name a success you recently had.
9. What would you like to achieve in the next 5 years?
10. What would you like to achieve in the next 10 years?

Conclusion

- Was this activity easy or difficult?
- What did you learn from this activity?
- How did it feel to really listen to someone and to have others really listen to you?

Teacher Summary

It is important to keep the time frame open. Make sure each student has a chance to share what is on his/her mind. Instruct the other students to observe good listening strategies.

Supplemental Activities

You may use circle talks to discuss a problem that the class is having, or use a suggestion box in which the students put topics for discussion.

PLACING VALUE

Alice Paul

Objective
This is a cooperative and risk-taking activity that can be played by a small group of students in a classroom.

Materials
Die, paper, pencils

Introduction
The purpose of this activity is to allow students to work together in a game that encourages risk taking. It also reinforces basic mathematics skills, such as knowledge of math facts, addition, subtraction, and multiplication.

Instructions

1. Each student draws a tic-tac-toe grid on his/her paper.
2. Explain that you are going to roll the die and they are to place the number you roll in any of the boxes in the top two rows. The bottom row is where the sums of the numbers are placed. Tell the students to predict where to put each number to get the greatest sum. The object of the game is get the highest possible sum from the numbers rolled. (Do the first activity with them to demonstrate the game.)
3. The teacher rolls the die until the boxes in the top two rows are filled.
4. Students add up the top two rows, if you are using addition.
5. Compare answers. Did anyone get the highest possible sum?
6. Have the students take turns rolling the die.

Conclusion

- What made this activity easy or difficult?
- Was it difficult to predict where to put the number?
- What happens if you put a number in the wrong box (make a mistake)?
- What is the relationship between taking a risk and reaching a goal?
- How does this game compare to life?

Teacher Summary
This exercise reinforces math skills that are needed in everyday life. It also encourages us to take a risk to achieve a goal. If we never take a chance, we can never achieve our goals. Mistakes are okay. We can learn from them so that each time we get better at analyzing the risks and reaching our goal.

NURSERY RHYMES HAVE NEW MEANING

Each student recites his or her favorite nursery rhyme and tells why it is his/her favorite.

For older children, have the students each describe a character in the nursery rhyme that they identify with and describe why.

MY FAVORITE ENDING

If you have a large number of students and you want them to work in groups, put students in small groups of four to six. Each group is given a nursery rhyme or fairy tale and must supply a new ending.

TV NEWS STORY

Have students imagine they are TV news anchors who

a. tell a nursery rhyme or fairy tale in a modern way as if it were breaking news
b. report on interviews with the main characters in a nursery rhyme or fairy tale
c. report on the death of a character from a fairy tale or nursery rhyme as if he or she had just died and give their obituary

Examples: Jack Be Nimble Jack Be Quick, Little Miss Muffett, Old King Cole, Sing a Song of Sixpence; Mary, Mary Quite Contrary, Mary Had a Little Lamb, Simple Simon, Hey Diddle Diddle, Jack and Jill, and Hickory Dickory Dock.

IF I WON THE LOTTERY I WOULD

Students describe what they would do if they had a million dollars to spend. After the students talk about this, have a discussion about values and making a difference in the world.

GUESS WHO CAME TO MY DOOR?

Going around the room, each student tells who they would like to knock on their door and why. This can be expanded by having each student think of a good question to ask this person. The person can be dead or alive, famous, or unknown.

LEARN FAIR

Each student must answer all of these questions. After they answer them, anyone in the class can ask them about their answers.

a. If I could learn more about anything in the world I would like to learn more about _____.
b. The reason I would like to learn this is _____.

A MEMORY FOR DETAIL

Take a group of students into a room they have never been in before. Let them stay a total of 2 minutes, no more or less. Take them back out again and ask the boys in the group to write down what they remember; then ask the girls to write down what they remember. Compare the descriptions of the room done by the different groups.

MY FAMILY ROLE

Different roles get played out in every family. As family members, we each find our position in the family, and with that position there is a job. How do you relate to the other members of your family? Are there certain ways of behaving that seem to be yours alone? Perhaps it is your job to entertain, so you are the one who comes up with a joke or has a game for everyone to play. Or are you the one who is always responsible? Think about your role in comparison to the other roles in your family. How are they alike and different?

Now think about your role when you are with a group of friends. How is that alike or different? What is your role like in school? Why might this be?

Here are some possible roles you might play:

Problem solver
Victim
Rescuer
Comedian
Mediator
Comforter
Confronter
Healer
Protector
Secret keeper

Appendix B

TEACHER RESOURCES

TEACHER RESOURCE 1.1   Requesting Letters of Recommendation

Dear _____,

As we discussed, I need letters of recommendation for my teaching file

at _____. Thank you for agreeing

to write this letter for me. I am very excited and hopeful about getting a teach-

ing job in the area of _____. I believe my strengths lie

in the area of _____. Enclosed is a prestamped and

addressed envelope for your convenience.

Thank you again for all you have done for me,

TEACHER RESOURCE 1.2   Classroom Behavior

What behavior do I want?

_____

_____

_____

_____

_____

What behavior must I have from every student?

_____

_____

_____

_____

_____

_____

What behavior can I *not* accept?

_____

_____

_____

_____

_____

_____

_____

TEACHER RESOURCE 1.3   District Office Letter

Dear _____,

As a new teacher beginning on your staff this fall, I am eagerly preparing for the school year. Could you please send me a copy of your district handbook, student handbook, and any other useful information that would help me as a teacher in your district?

Thank you for your assistance.

Sincerely,

TEACHER RESOURCE 1.4   Classroom Evaluation Form

Material	Problems Detected
_____ Student desks	
_____ Teacher(s) desk	
_____ Student chairs	
_____ Teacher(s) chairs	
_____ Tables	
_____ Cupboards	
_____ Bookshelves	
_____ Clock	
_____ Pencil sharpener	
_____ Sink	
_____ Drinking fountain	
_____ Waste baskets	
_____ Carpet needed	
_____ Carpet needs cleaning	
_____ Lighting	
_____ Heating	
_____ Air conditioning/fans	
_____ Television	
_____ VCR	
_____ Computers	
_____ Printers	
_____ Other:	

TEACHER RESOURCE 1.5   Curricular Materials

Material Name	Grade/ Reading Level	Publishers & Address	Cost

TEACHER RESOURCE 1.6   Student File Review

Name: Parent(s) name:
DOB: Address:

Home telephone:

Work telephone:

Medical Information
List pertinent information found in each area:

Vision

Hearing

Allergies

Chronic illnesses

Other

Special needs:

Accommodations:

Special parent requests:

Any unusual circumstances that need to be considered:

TEACHER RESOURCE 1.7   Handling Medication in the Classroom

Teachers need to ask these questions:

1. How does the child's medication affect his or her behavior?

2. What might I see if the child has an allergic reaction to this medication?

3. What are some potential side effects of the medication?

4. At what times of day does the child take the medication during school days?

5. What procedure should be followed if the child arrives at school without having taken medication that morning?

6. If the child forgets to take the medication until the time for the next dosage, should twice the dosage be taken?

7. What kind of adult supervision is necessary when the child takes medication at school?

8. When will the child be reevaluated for a change or discontinuation of the medication?

TEACHER RESOURCE 1.8   Introductory Letter Home

Dear _____,

I would like to introduce myself to you as the teacher of your child _____. It will be my pleasure to serve as your child's classroom teacher this year and I am very hopeful that we will have an interesting and productive year together.

If at any time you have questions concerning your child, please feel free to call me at school at _____, or at home at _____, or email me at _____. I am very interested in meeting you and getting to know you as well as your child and would like you to feel free to visit at any time.

I am including my classroom rules, which were developed by all the students in the class and me. I am also sending you my grading form so that you will be able to understand the monthly progress reports that I will mail you at the end of each month.

Please know that your child's welfare and education are of the utmost importance to me. Together I feel we can make this a wonderful year.

Sincerely,

TEACHER RESOURCE 1.9   Classroom Organization

_____ Desks for each student

_____ Area for detailed work/independent work

_____ Cubby area for individual student materials

_____ Class rules posted

_____ Procedures for leaving the room posted

_____ Emergency/medical procedures posted

_____ Class schedule posted

_____ Room number clearly visible on door

_____ My name clearly visible on door

_____ Class name clearly delineated on the door

Who do I contact regarding:

Allocation of existing and new furniture? _____

_____

Heating or air conditioning issues? _____

_____

Keys and locks? _____

_____

Light bulbs changed? _____

_____

Office/classrooms cleaned or vacuumed? _____

_____

Painting of offices/hallways/classrooms? _____

_____

Plumbing, electrical, or elevator concerns? _____

_____

Trash cans emptied? _____

_____

Windows washed? _____

_____

TEACHER RESOURCE 1.10   Things I Must Do

Do Today

1. _____
2. _____
3. _____
4. _____
5. _____

Do This Week

1. _____
2. _____
3. _____
4. _____
5. _____

Do This Year

1. _____
2. _____
3. _____
4. _____
5. _____

Do Next Year

1. _____
2. _____
3. _____
4. _____
5. _____

TEACHER RESOURCE 1.11   Classroom Clipboard Data Collection System

Students' names _____

_____

_____

_____

_____

_____

_____

_____

_____

_____

_____

_____

_____

_____

_____

_____

_____

_____

TEACHER RESOURCE 1.11   Classroom Clipboard Data Collection System

TEACHER RESOURCE 1.12   First Day of School

_____   Classroom areas are delineated

_____   Classroom rules are on the wall

_____   Classroom procedures are on the wall:

    _____   Emergency evacuation

    _____   Medical emergency procedures

    _____   Attendance, absence and tardy procedure

    _____   Classroom jobs

    _____   Procedures for leaving the room for the bathroom, library, or help

Homework procedures:

_____   When homework is due

_____   Where it should be turned in

_____   How it will be graded

_____   Where and how the work will be recorded

_____   How and when it will be returned to students

_____   What happens to corrected work that contains mistakes

_____   How late homework is treated

_____   Rewards for students who are ready

_____   Classroom schedule is on the wall

_____   Student seating is ready

_____   Clipboard with students' names, seating chart, etc. is ready

TEACHER RESOURCE 1.13   Student Orientation

I have covered these topics...

_____   How to enter school

_____   How to enter the classroom

_____   Where students' lockers are and how they work

_____   Main office, nurse's office, principal's office

_____   Attendance secretary

_____   Recess/study hall area

_____   Parking lot where students should be picked up

_____   Area where students catch the bus

_____   Bathroom rules

_____   Going to the library

_____   Lunchroom procedures:

   _____   How to get to lunch

   _____   How to get your lunch

   _____   Paying for your lunch

   _____   Getting milk

   _____   Where to sit

   _____   How to clean up after eating

TEACHER RESOURCE 1.14   The School's Social Environment

- Where do I go before school starts?
- Am I allowed to enter the school as soon as I get there?
- Where am I not supposed to go?
- Where could I go but better not because I would probably not be welcome?
- Is an adult supervising?
- Why is the adult there?
- Do different groups of kids always play together before school?
- Can I join them?
- How would I join them?
- What do I do when the bell rings?
- Do I have to line up?
- Where and how do I line up?
- How do I know whether it is recess or time to go home?
- Where do I go for recess?
- What do I do during recess?
- Are there places where I should not go during recess because it is not safe for students my age?
- Are there rules about where and how to play?
- Can anybody join in the games that kids are playing?
- If I have to ask, how do I do that?
- Can I go home for lunch?
- Is there a special door I must use?
- Where do I go for lunch if I am eating at school?
- Where do I sit to eat in the lunchroom?
- For a special school program or assembly, where do I go and how do I get there?
- Are the seats assigned?
- Do I have to stay with my class?
- After school, where do I go?
- When can I go?
- Do I have to leave school right away?
- Do kids play at school after school?
- Are there areas around the school I should avoid?
- Are there kids or adults I can ask for help if I need it?

TEACHER RESOURCES

139

TEACHER RESOURCE 1.15 Homework Information Sheet

Homework: _____

Is due _____

_____

Should be turned in _____

_____

Will be graded _____

_____

Will be recorded_____

_____

Will be returned to students_____

_____

That is corrected and contains mistakes _____

_____

That is late is treated _____

_____

TEACHER RESOURCE 1.16   Family/Community Resource Form

Student's name: _____

Date: _____   Grade: _____

Parent(s)/guardian(s) name(s): _____

Address of student: _____

If you or any member of your family is willing to talk to the class about your work or hobbies, we would be very grateful. Our classroom is interested in what people do for their occupation and for leisure. If you could fill out the form below with information about yourself and others you feel could help us, you would certainly enrich our classroom with your assistance and your input.

With thanks and appreciation,

Your name:_____

Phone number: (home) _____   (work) _____

Address:_____

Possible contribution: _____

_____

Community person's name and title if applicable: _____

_____   Phone: _____

Address:_____

Possible areas of contribution: _____

Other suggestions for speakers or topics for our class: _____

_____

_____

_____

Thank you in advance for your help,

TEACHER RESOURCE 1.17   Students and Their Special Needs

Student's name: _____

Reading level: _____   Math level: _____

Writing level: _____

Special needs: _____

_____

_____

_____

IEP goals: _____

_____

_____

_____

_____

_____

_____

_____

Special modifications: _____

_____

_____

_____

_____

_____

_____

_____

TEACHER RESOURCE 1.18   Teacher's Countdown Calendar

Twelve Months before School Starts

Eight Months before School Starts

Six Months before School Starts

Four Months before School Starts

Three Months before School Starts

Two Months before School Starts

One Month before School Starts

Two Weeks before School Starts

Two Days before School Starts

One Day before School Starts

Day 1!

Day 2

Day 3

TEACHER RESOURCE 2.1   Classroom Skill Evaluation Sheet

Subject: _____

Date: _____

Student's Name _____

_____

_____

_____

_____

_____

_____

_____

_____

_____

_____

_____

_____

_____

_____

_____

_____

_____

_____

_____

TEACHER RESOURCE 2.2   Lesson Plan

Unit: Anatomy

Topic: Circulatory system

Goals:

Students will observe circulatory system of fetal pig.

Students will identify and label parts of the circulatory system.

Materials

Fetal pig

Dissection equipment

Dissection manual

Procedures

Introduction (5 min.)

Give directions for today's activity (tying down the pig, etc.)

Remind students to finish dissections from Monday

Remind dissectors to slow down and work with the group

Suggest taking apart the dissection packet

Body (40–45 min.)

Student lab groups will dissect the fetal pig's circulatory system.

They will take OUI and view the heart and major blood vessels.

Assessment

Student

Students will be evaluated on their participation and appropriate behavior during the lab.

Students will need to complete the appropriate pages in their dissection packets.

Teacher

Did students participate and enjoy the lab?

Did the lab run smoothly? What would I change next time?

Were students able to relate topics previously discussed in class to this hands-on lab activity?

TEACHER RESOURCE 2.3   Lesson Plan 1

Unit:

Topic:

Goals:

Students will

Materials

Procedures

Introduction

Body

Assessment

Student

Teacher

TEACHER RESOURCE 2.4   Lesson Plan 2

Subject Area: Date:

Goals: Skills:

Content: Warm up/intro

                                        Closing:

Materials needed: Adaptations:

Evaluation of students: Evaluation of teacher:

TEACHER RESOURCE 2.5   Lesson Plan 3

Lesson plans for _____

Goal: _____

_____

Objectives: _____

_____

Purpose: _____

_____

Ability levels: _____

Materials: _____

_____

Activities: _____

_____

Set/introduction: _____

_____

Information to be learned: _____

_____

_____

Modeling: _____

_____

Guided practice: _____

_____

Independent evaluation of students meeting goals: _____

_____

Teacher evaluation: _____

_____

_____

TEACHER RESOURCE 2.6   Lesson Plan 4

Date: _____

Time required: _____

Objectives

_____

_____

_____

_____

Materials

_____

_____

_____

_____

Step-by-Step Procedure

_____

_____

_____

_____

Evaluation

_____

_____

_____

_____

TEACHER RESOURCE 2.7   Good Teaching Checklist

Name: _____

Date: _____

- Signal to the class when you are about to begin.
- Begin teaching only after you have gained the students' attention.
- Present information clearly and in the simplest way possible.
- Teach information in short sessions.
- Allow students to apply what you have taught them to make it their own.
- Provide students with constant feedback.
- Check students' understanding constantly.
- Acknowledge and elaborate students' responses.
- Teach and reteach students until the information or skill is implanted.
- Review skills often, emphasizing what is most important.
- Inform students when a time of transition is coming.

TEACHER RESOURCE 2.8   Brain Research on Learning and Memory

- Memory is the process by which we learn information, so use initial rehearsal and secondary rehearsal strategies to help your students learn.

- Give students ample time to go from initial rehearsal to secondary rehearsal and vary methods of practice.

- Help students make connections between what they already know and what they need to learn.

- Help students use information so they can see how it has relevance to their life. Using what they learn helps students remember it.

- Use seatwork effectively, not just for rote learning. Effective seatwork is having students review, apply, and manipulate the information or skills you have taught them.

- Provide assistance and ample time for students to make important associations; do not leave this important stage of learning up to chance.

- Use relevant tasks and varied materials to give students reasons to spend enough time with new information to integrate it into their own understanding of the world.

TEACHER RESOURCE 2.9 Effective Teaching Checklist

Name: _____   Date: _____

1 = Poor   2 = Fair   3 = Average   4 = Good   5 = Superior

_____ Prepares and organizes lessons well; lessons are clear and appropriate to age and ability of students

_____ Motivates students to participate actively in learning

_____ Gains students' attention

_____ Has good knowledge of curriculum content; selects and uses appropriate curricular materials

_____ Evaluates pupils' learning and effectiveness of instruction

_____ Is flexible and creative

_____ Adapts instruction to classroom situations and individuals' needs

_____ Is dedicated to teaching

_____ Is dependable in meeting responsibilities

_____ Has neat appearance; possesses poise and self-confidence

_____ Speaks with clarity, good projection, inflection, and correct speech

_____ Honestly self-appraises teaching effectiveness

_____ Accepts and uses constructive criticism

_____ Accepts all students as individuals

_____ Is able to work with students of different groups (students from minority backgrounds, with disabilities, or from low income families)

_____ Communicates with and develops rapport with students of various groups

_____ Effectively relates with school staff; has respect and consideration for colleagues

_____ Displays concern for total school program

_____ Constructively participates in the school community

_____ Is well integrated in the school community

_____ Volunteers to do things and works cooperatively to solve
all school problems

_____ Knows all school personnel (cooks, secretaries, aides, etc.)

_____ Displays effective classroom discipline procedures

_____ Participates in faculty meetings, school assemblies, and department
meetings

_____ Evaluates and adjusts to individual learning styles

_____ Effectively puts research-supported educational theories
into practice

   _____ cooperative groups

   _____ critical thinking

   _____ phonics

   _____ paired instruction

   _____ problem-solving strategies

   _____ interdisciplinary units

   _____ learning styles

   _____ achievement motivation

   _____ emerging technologies

_____ Total Points Earned

TEACHER RESOURCE 2.10   Motivating Factors

Every time you teach check how many motivating factors you are using. Hopefully you use at least one factor each time you teach.

_____   Appropriate level of work for each student.

_____   Real-life work (this work matters to the student and will be useful in 5, 10, or 15 years)

_____   Imagination

_____   Surprising facts

_____   Community speaker (parents, grandparents, community expert)

_____   Empowerment (giving students choices about what they do or how they do it)

_____   Positive reinforcement system

_____   Other

TEACHER RESOURCE 2.11   Field Trip Planning

_____ Parents and the community have been contacted for help and input.

_____ Transportation arrangements have been made.

_____ Insurance and liability regulations for transportation (whether walking, taking buses, or using private cars) have been checked.

_____ Proper arrangements have been made regarding the facilities at the destination: restrooms, cafeteria, picnic tables, parking areas.

_____ Proper arrangements have been made regarding students who do not wish to participate in the field trip.

_____ Transportation or lunch money and other fees have been collected (if applicable).

_____ Financial assistance has been secured for students who cannot pay for trip.

_____ Parental permission notes have been sent home.

_____ Parental permission notes have been returned.

_____ Students have been informed on how to behave, and what to wear in the event that restrictions on clothing apply in place of visit.

_____ Students have developed a list of tasks and behaviors for which each student has been assigned a responsibility.

_____ Students have been told what to expect and have been given adequate background knowledge to understand what they will see.

_____ A student-generated list of questions has been prepared from which students may ask questions of individuals at the site.

_____ Cameras, camcorders, tape recorders and note pads are available for recording specific information.

_____ Safety hazards (if any) have been noted and appropriate precautions taken.

_____ A first-aid kit is available for emergencies.

_____ Students have been paired and assigned buddies (or groups of interest before arriving at destinations).

_____ Teacher has reviewed school policies on field trips.

TEACHER RESOURCE 2.12   Goal Sheet

My goals for the month of _____

Goal 1: _____

_____

_____

Goal 2: _____

_____

_____

Goal 3: _____

_____

_____

Goal 4: _____

_____

_____

My goals for the month of _____

Goal 1: _____

_____

_____

Goal 2: _____

_____

_____

Goal 3: _____

_____

_____

Goal 4: _____

_____

_____

My goals for the month of_____

Goal 1: _____

_____

Goal 2: _____

_____

Goal 3: _____

_____

Goal 4: _____

_____

_____

My goals for the month of_____

Goal 1: _____

_____

_____

Goal 2: _____

_____

_____

Goal 3: _____

_____

_____

Goal 4: _____

_____

_____

TEACHER RESOURCE 2.13   My goals for the year of _____

Goal 1: _____

_____

_____

Goal 2: _____

_____

_____

Goal 3: _____

_____

_____

Goal 4: _____

_____

_____

Goal 5: _____

_____

_____

Goal 6: _____

_____

_____

Goal 7: _____

_____

_____

Goal 8: _____

_____

_____

TEACHER RESOURCE 3.1   Student Inquiry

Student's name: _____

Help me get to know you. Please finish these sentences for me...

1. What I like to do best of all is... _____

_____

_____

_____

2. The most important person in my life is... _____

_____

_____

_____

This person is important because... _____

_____

_____

_____

3. What I'm really good at is... _____

_____

_____

_____

4. What I need to improve on is... _____

_____

_____

_____

5. When learning something new, I like to (circle)

     hear it   see it   read about it   touch it

TEACHER RESOURCE 3.2   Classroom Communication Rules

1. Respect everyone in the class and be a good listener.

2. Only one person in a group talks at a time.

3. Look at the person who is speaking and watch the speaker's body language to better understand the speaker's meaning.

4. When students tell you personal information about themselves or their family, this information is not to be shared with anyone else.

5. Treat others the way you would like to be treated.

TEACHER RESOURCE 3.3   STOP—A Body-Positioning Exercise

1. Find a large space (perhaps outside).

2. Have the class count off by 2s.

3. Students form two lines about 5 feet apart facing each other.

4. The teacher says go and the 1s walk, one step at a time, toward the 2s.

5. The 2s say stop when the 1s feel close enough for comfort but not too close.

6. The game ends when all the 2s have stopped the 1s.

7. Students look at the varying distances for comfort.

8. Repeat the procedures switching the roles for the 1s and the 2s.

   STOP

   Stay

   Three feet

   Outside of other

   People's space

TEACHER RESOURCE 3.4   A Sample of Robert's Rules of Order

The *chair* is the main person in charge.

The *floor* is given to the person who has permission to speak.

1. *General Method*

Anything that needs to be talked about is brought to the floor. This is often a motion or an action to be taken if no one disagrees.

2. *Obtaining the Floor*

To get permission to speak the person must be the first to stand up when no one else is speaking. With permission they can then address the chair and speak.

3. *Motions*

    a. First, a motion is made (which means someone suggests something).
    b. Next, the motion is seconded; if someone else agrees, they can also stand up and say *second.*
    c. The chair then repeats the motion.

4. *Opening Debates*

After a motion has been made, the class is asked whether they are ready for the motion. They can say *yes* or *no.*

5. Voting

If a motion (suggestion) does not need any discussion, the chair can immediately put it to a vote. To vote, each individual can say *aye* to vote yes or say *no* to vote in opposition. For example, the chair would ask the class to vote by saying, "The question is on the motion to _____. Those in favor say *aye.* The chair then listens to how many say *aye.* Then the chair says, "Those opposed say *no,*" and the chair listens to those votes. If the aye's win, the chair says, "The motion is adopted." If not, the chair says, "The motion is lost."

TEACHER RESOURCE 3.5   Positive Examples of Role Models

1. The people I want most to be like are

   _____

   _____

   _____

2. Their best qualities are

   _____

   _____

   _____

   _____

3. They are good role models because they do

   _____

   _____

   _____ that helps others.

4. They display their integrity by

   _____

   _____

   _____

TEACHER RESOURCE 3.6   Developing a Teacher Consultation Team

1. Volunteers are gathered who have the time and interest to serve on a consultation team.

2. A coordinator for the teacher consultation team is identified. This person can facilitate meetings, take notes, complete the paperwork, and serves as the contact person for other teachers in the school who need assistance.

3. A regular meeting time is set. These teams are only effective when they meet regularly.

4. The team, or coordinator, sets an agenda for each meeting and uses a team problem-solving process.

TEACHER RESOURCE 3.7   Collaboration Checklist

_____   **1.** We agree that we would like to collaborate.

_____   **2.** Our teaching styles and skills will complement each other.

_____   **3.** We are open to trying new ways of doing things and experiment-
ing with innovative teaching styles.

_____   **4.** Each of us has written out our own teaching style preference and
educational values.

_____   **5.** We have jointly developed a teaching mode; we know who is
responsible for what.

_____   **6.** We have a plan to evaluate our successes and areas in which we
want to improve.

_____   **7.** When we have a difference of opinion, we agree to

_____

_____ .

Signatures

_____

_____

_____

_____

_____

TEACHER RESOURCE 3.8 Why I Chose to Be a Teacher

1. Each member of the team, starting with the individual who has been in the school the longest, gives five reasons why they wanted to be a teacher/ social worker/administrator, etc.

2. As they give each reason, the other members of the team raise their hands if they share that reason.

3. After one person finishes, the next person, moving clockwise, gives their reasons.

4. The first person makes a list of the reasons on the board or on a piece of paper. When everyone is finished, the first person ranks the reasons and reports the top 10 reasons.

5. These reasons are saved and a copy is given to each person.

6. When things are not moving well on the team and people seem to be stuck or frustrated at a meeting, someone should pull out these reasons and read one or two to change the focus to a more positive one.

Good luck!

TEACHER RESOURCE 3.9   Information about My Child

Student's name: _____

Parent's names: _____

Dear Parents,

In an effort to facilitate the best education possible for your son or daughter, I am asking you to share what you know about your child's learning habits and preferences. Would you please fill out this information and send it back to me at school? I appreciate your help in getting to know your child.

1. What are your child's greatest strengths?

2. In what areas could your child use more help?

3. How does your child like to be rewarded?

4. What works well to motivate your child?

5. Place a 1 next to how your child learns best. Place a 2 next to how your child learns next best.

   _____ Hearing about it

   _____ Seeing it

   _____ Reading about it

   _____ Doing it

   _____ Other

6. Please list your long-term goals for your child.

7. Please provide any other information about your child or things going on in his or her life that could help me work with him or her.

Thank you so much for your time and information.

Sincerely,

TEACHER RESOURCE 3.10   Assignment Sheet

Name: _____

Today's date: _____

Subject	Assignment	Check if completed
Reading		
Language arts		
Math		
Social studies		
Science		
Health		
Applied arts		

TEACHER RESOURCE 3.11   Tips to Improve Cross-Cultural Communication

- Respect yourself and everyone you meet unless they mistreat you (then stay away from them).
- Stay open to new ideas and new ways of doing things.
- Always remain flexible.
- Look at other people's point of view.
- Don't make assumptions.

TEACHER RESOURCE 3.12 Cultural Considerations for Working with Children from Traditional Hmong Families

1. Parents of children from traditional Hmong families may have had little or no formal education in their home country.

2. These families often place great respect and trust in professionals, assuming teachers know what is best for their child.

3. When individuals from this culture come to the school and meet school officials and teachers, they may bow slightly or bend over to signify respect for individuals they perceive as possessing higher status.

4. Many individuals in this culture believe that direct eye contact indicates disrespect, distrust, anger, or confrontation.

5. They may also feel that a display of negative emotion or aggression is bad, so they will not argue.

6. To people of the United States, Hmong individuals appear to be nonassertive and overly polite. They may automatically say yes to questions or give socially desirable or expected answers just to be polite or to avoid embarrassment. They believe their opinion is not as important as living in harmony.

7. Time as we perceive it in the United States is not part of the traditional Hmong way of life. Watches, appointment books, and even calendars are not routine possessions.

**TEACHER RESOURCE 3.13   Cultural Considerations for Working with
Children from Native American Families**

1. The traditional Native American family has as much diversity across tribes as across all other cultures.

2. Often the clan or family in Native American cultures is first in importance, individual needs are second.

3. Individual wants and desires are expected not to overcome the good of the entire group. However, each person is viewed as unique.

4. Elders and extended kinship are respected and valued in almost all Native American cultures.

5. Children are taught to listen without asking questions. In many tribes asking questions of an elder may be considered rude, and the offending individual is ignored as punishment for the question.

6. Children are expected to learn by example rather than by verbal directions. Directions may also be considered rude because they are viewed as too forceful and bossy.

**TEACHER RESOURCE 3.14   Cultural Considerations for Working with
                          Children from Hispanic Families**

1. Many traditional Hispanic families have a very diverse, yet closely tied, extended family network.

2. In this framework children are often viewed as family members first and as individuals second.

3. The closeness of the family unit creates a common hesitancy to use "outsiders" for help.

4. Typically, the father is the head of the household, and the mother is expected to be devoted to him and to the children, placing her needs last.

5. In traditional Hispanic families older children, especially females, are expected to care for younger children and older grandparents and eventually parents when the need arises.

6. Children are often given a lot of love and affection and are taught good manners and acceptable "public" behavior at an early age.

TEACHER RESOURCE 3.15   Cultural Considerations for Working with Children from African American Families

1. African American families' long experience of institutional racism, prejudice, and economic oppression has resulted in their distrust of many public systems, including the public school system.

2. Fathers in African American culture often have a peripheral place in their children's lives.

3. Many African American families have very strong family/kinship bonds.

4. Children often grow up in multifamily, multigenerational households.

5. Children from this culture may develop a learning style based on emotions, body language, and social nuance, making them especially adept at understanding social situations and reading the emotions and moods of the individuals around them.

TEACHER RESOURCE 3.16 Cultural Considerations for Working with Children from Traditional Asian Families

1. In traditional Asian culture individuals value the larger social good over individual needs.

2. Often, hierarchical roles and status govern behavior and subordination. Rules are very important and need to be followed.

3. Children may be strictly controlled, and parents often have high expectations for them.

4. Education is often highly valued. Teachers are highly regarded and are not questioned or contradicted.

5. The interdependence of individuals is valued, especially in the family.

6. Many traditional Asian families are extended and multigenerational.

TEACHER RESOURCE 3.17   Testing Your Communication Skills

1. Give a short example of how you could control a situation that might escalate.

2. What are your keys to effective two-way communication in the classroom environment?

3. On a scale of 1–10 how would you rate your communication skills?

4. What steps could be taken to improve your communication skills?

5. What is one good way to get to know your students' parents?

6. What are some ways you can get to know your fellow teachers?

TEACHER RESOURCE 4.1   Assessing the Classroom

Students who come to class early and want to stay late looking for work	
Students who come to class early and want to stay late to talk	
Students who arrive late for everything academic (or who stall for things they seem to dislike)	
Students who arrive late for everything, even things they like (recess, lunch, art, etc.)	
Students who seem to avoid adults	
Student who seem to cling to adults	
Students who seem to avoid their peers	
Students who cling to their peers and seem to be unable to do things independently	
Students who like to lead a group of their peers in a positive way	
Students who want to take over the class and lead their peers in revolt	
Students who try to help others and seem to enjoy taking care of their friends	
Students who seem to bully or lash out at other students	

TEACHER RESOURCE 4.2   Behavior Parameters for Different Situations

Lectures

_____

Group time

_____

Assignments

_____

Skill development and practice time

TEACHER RESOURCE 4.3   **Behavior Notes**

You were listening really well in class today.

Thanks,

_____

It would help us both if you got to work a little faster. You can get a lot done when you do.

Thanks,

_____

You did a really nice job in class today.

Thanks,

_____

Could you help me by keeping your hands to yourself? Your neighbors and I would appreciate it.

Thanks,

_____

Every time I looked at you today you were working hard.

Thanks,

_____

TEACHER RESOURCE 4.4   Simple Steps to Handling Misbehavior

1. Describe the offending behavior and the behavior you want.

2. Give a warning quietly and in a nondisruptive manner.

3. Give the student a choice of two options, or discuss alternatives later.

4. Follow through with a punishment that you can back up and deliver.

TEACHER RESOURCE 4.5   Consistent Handling of an Angry Student

1. Separate the student from the confrontation and provide a slowing-down, cooling-down activity.

2. Assure the student that the time to talk to him or her will come. (Then be sure that it does.)

3. Stay calm and detached using only descriptive words.

4. Save your own anger or frustration for important times, and try to listen to the hurt under the student's anger. You can accomplish two things: becoming more sensitive and effective and calming yourself down if you also are angry.

5. Avoid a power struggle because power struggles rarely produce a resolution, especially in the long run.

TEACHER RESOURCE 4.6   Steps to Evaluating an Argument with a Student

1. Why did the problem occur?

   — Did I send inconsistent messages?

   — Does this child have family problems that cause them to try to gain control of all situations?

   — Was I losing site of classroom activities?

2. Do I have a system for management?

   — Such as points, privileges, grades, coveted activities?

3. Do I present clear and consistent consequences?

   — Am I ready with, and clear about, what happens when students choose to misbehave?

   — Am I prepared for the worst (at which point it won't be as bad)?

4. Do I give my students clear choices?

   — Do I teach students about making choices so they can learn *internal* (not *external*) locus of control

   — Do I teach students that what they do matters?

   — Do the students understand the concept of play and pay?

   — Are they mentally capable of seeing the relationships between what they do and the consequence for that behavior?

5. Do I make rules simple for my students by teaching them which ones are not debatable?

   — Am I clear that many rules are schoolwide or societal and not just mine?

TEACHER RESOURCE 4.7   Responding to Misbehavior

Acceptable Misbehaviors	Unacceptable Misbehaviors	My Response (Possible Alternatives)
Arguing with each other Arguing with teacher	Swearing Leaving the room without permission Fighting	Time-out

TEACHER RESOURCE 4.8   Procedures to Use When a Student Appears Ready to Become Violent

1. Stay calm and consider who can assist you.

   (Stay near your source of help whether it is a phone or office button, or a teacher next door.)

2. Make sure you and your classes are safe.

   (Have everyone leave the room if necessary.)

3. Don't
   a. Touch the student
   b. Talk about the student's punishment
   c. Make threats to the student
   d. Argue with the student

4. Instead, try to gain the student's cooperation.
   a. Reflect the student's feelings in a calming way. Say something like, "It seems like you are feeling frustrated and angry."
   b. Offer to help the student talk out the problem.
   c. Ask the student for a *little* request, for example, "Come closer to me so we can talk a minute. I need to know what upset you."
   d. Commence with your prepackaged plan and follow it with as little deviation as possible depending on the situation.
   e. After the cooling-off period, talk about the incident with the student.

TEACHER RESOURCE 4.9   Thinking Through Problems

Name: _____   Date: _____   Time: _____

What I did: _____

_____

Why that did not work: _____

_____

_____

Instead, to get what I want I could try to: _____

_____

I should stop doing this: _____

_____

_____

What I wanted to happen: _____

_____

_____

What an observer would say happened: _____

_____

_____

What I will do in the future: _____

_____

_____

What I need from my teacher to help my plan: _____

_____

_____

TEACHER RESOURCE 4.10   Normal Reactions to a Crisis Situation

Anger	Irritability
Denial	Loneliness
Depression	Loss of appetite
Disbelief	Restlessness
Distractibility	Sadness
Emotional numbing	Shock
Fear	Sleep disturbance
Feeling vulnerable	Tearfulness

TEACHER RESOURCE 4.11   In Case of a Disaster or Crisis

Adults need to find ways to help children and adolescents manage their uncertainty, fear, and grief.

- Talk with students about their thoughts and feelings.
- Make sure your class takes a break from the media.
- Encourage students to become involved in recreational activities that give them a break from the crisis: going for a walk, enjoying nature, playing a game, reading a book, watching a video, or taking part in any other activity that they find refreshing.
- It may be helpful for students to gather with their own community faith group.
- Encourage students to become involved in volunteer programs such as food drives or car washes to help victims of the disaster or crisis.
- Encourage students to eat regularly and get sufficient sleep.

TEACHER RESOURCE 4.12   Dealing with Bullies

1. Arm your entire class with behaviors that will keep every student safe.

2. Counteract the bully's two weapons:
   a. Fear of intimidation
   b. Shame of losing face for breaking the unspoken rule of not telling an adult.

3. Teach students about their own power in numbers.
   a. Students stand with each other, face up to what is right, and refuse to accept the bully's harassing behavior.
   b. Teach a unit on how to be good citizens and protect and support each other.
   c. Students practice what to do in a harassment situation.

4. The code of not telling an adult must be broken if children are to obtain the support of open and understanding adults who can help when a bullying situation occurs.

5. Enlist the help of parents to eliminate retributions in the community for students who stand up to a harassing child.

TEACHER RESOURCE 4.13 **Checklist for Emergency Classroom Evacuation**

1. How fast can you get your students out the door?

2. Can the children in your class pass through the doorway quickly and at least two at a time from any place in the room? _____

3. Have you discussed with your class the easiest way to exit the classroom?

4. Have you practiced exiting the classroom with your students? _____

5. Is your desk near enough to the door so you can block, lock, or barricade your door to keep out the danger of potential violence in the hall? _____

6. Does your school have a warning system to warn you of impending dangers or violence in the building? _____

TEACHER RESOURCE 4.14   Behaviors That May Be Exhibited by Students Prone to Violence

- Increased use of alcohol or drugs
- Constant discussion about alcohol or drugs and drug paraphernalia
- Recurrent sadness, negativism, or depression
- Suicidal comments
- Verbal outbursts
- Unstable emotional responses
- Increased mood swings
- Fascination with violence
- Increased isolation (other students tend to stay away)
- Unexplained increase in absences
- Withdrawal of large amounts of money

TEACHER RESOURCE 4.15   Crisis Management

- First assure your own safety.
- If you think you are facing a crisis, chances are you are! Listen to that tickling feeling in your stomach and take the necessary precautions.
- Stabilize the situation by getting other students away.
- Resolve the situation by calming student down or getting help from someone that can contain him or her.
- Help the student get the assistance they need to feel better.

TEACHER RESOURCE 4.16   Breaking Through to Individuals in Crisis

1. Slowly and quietly repeat yourself if your instructions are not followed.

2. Break the individual's emotional level.

3. Get the individual to refocus on you.

4. Continue to talk very softly and slowly.

5. Model what you want the individual to do.

6. Keep in control of yourself.

7. Remove all emotions from the situation. Keep your personal emotions at bay so that you don't get tripped into the student's anger.

8. Slow things down.

TEACHER RESOURCE 4.17   Classroom Emergency Safety

- Get everyone onto the floor with their heads covered.
- Barricade the door if the individual is not in the room.
- If the individual is in your room, find areas you can control.
- Keep students in another part of the room away from the violent individual.
- Get everyone out of the room if possible.
- Send a student for help.
- Most importantly, have a preset plan that you run through with your students before the emergency.

TEACHER RESOURCE 4.18   Suggestions for Helping Children Deal with Separation and Loss

- Be open with the individual and encourage him or her to talk about the person.

- Ask the student what they are experiencing or how they are dealing with the loss

- It may help children to bring to school pictures of the individual so they can tell you about this person and the feelings the students has for him or her.

- Children may need to have some form of physical contact while talking about their loss, or they may need to be physically active while they talk to help them express themselves.

- Give the child something meaningful to do, such as building some form of memory box. This box could contain items of special significance to both of them.

- Some children feel a need to keep a journal to share with the person they are separated from or unable to contact.

- If the individual is going away, such as for military duty or because of divorce, the child can make a memory box to give to the individual to remind him or her of the many things they shared together.

TEACHER RESOURCE 5.1   Do's and Don'ts of Using Positive Reinforcement

Do

- Use positive reinforcement mindfully.

- Change reinforcers often because students get tired of any reinforcer given too often.

- Reinforce constantly when teaching new behaviors.

- Slowly demand more learning from students each time you teach and reinforce new behaviors. (Up the ante.)

Do Not

- Continue tangible reinforcers indefinitely. Students should be weaned from primary reinforcers, such as food and objects, and move on to secondary reinforcers, such as praise and high fives.

- Reinforce a child to produce perfect work only, especially if he or she is a perfectionist. Teach children to enjoy the process, not just a perfect product.

TEACHER RESOURCE 5.2   Ideas for Reinforcers

Provide a list of homework alternatives from which students may choose

Have a free period

Choose a student to work with for the day

Take the class outdoors

Design a class web site with your students

Select a "Student of the Day"

Choose a student to run errands for the day

Choose a student to lead the line to recess, special classes, lunch, etc.

Allow students to tutor one another

Reserve a period to read a book

Excuse students from a homework assignment

Allow a student to supervise an activity

Select a student to have lunch in the teacher's lounge

Allow students to write on the board

Make a bulletin board with your students

Allow a student to take home a class animal

Choose a student to take a message to another teacher

Select a student to distribute and collect materials

Extend recess

Play favorite music for the class

Choose a student to help decorate the classroom for a holiday

Allow a student to conduct a class discussion on topic

Excuse a student from a quiz

Allow a student to listen to music with headphones during class

TEACHER RESOURCE 5.3 Do's and Don'ts of Using
Negative Reinforcement

Do

- Use negative reinforcement in a positive way to increase behaviors that help your students learn.
- Use negative reinforcement and positive reinforcement together.

Do Not

- Bring negative things into your classroom only to remove them for reinforcement.
- Use negative reinforcement too often because students might begin to associate you and your classroom with bad things happening or try to avoid you to rid themselves of the negative association.

TEACHER RESOURCE 5.4   How to Set Up a Token Reward System

1. Describe each behavior to be performed and what is acceptable.

2. Post rules of behavior where all students can see them.

3. Reward students systematically with tokens, such as plastic chips, when they comply with the rules.

4. Encourage students to accumulate tokens that later can be exchanged for tangible rewards, such as toys, books, or school supplies, or for privileges, such as extra computer time, free time to work on homework for another class, or the opportunity to be a helper in another room.

5. Always have an assortment of edible back-up reinforcers, such as candy, cookies, gum, etc. Students may also be allowed to exchange their tokens for these edibles.

6. Set up a store or treasure chest with items clearly priced so students know the cost, in tokens, of each back-up reinforcer.

7. Inform students when and how they can exchange their tokens for back-up reinforcers. The end of each day may be appropriate for younger children. Once a week should be sufficient for older children. You may choose to let them exchange tokens more frequently in the beginning, and decreasing as time goes on.

8. Decide whether you will ignore other infractions of rules or have students pay back tokens for broken rules before you set up a token program.

9. Always award tokens fairly and consistently.

TEACHER RESOURCE 5.5   Do's and Don'ts of Token Reinforcement

Do

- Have a fair and consistent method of giving tokens.
- Have an adequate supply of tokens and items or privileges for which they can be exchanged.
- Develop a manageable way for students to store their tokens that is safe and nonintrusive.
- Set aside specific times for students to exchange tokens for rewards.
- Set up a store, treasure chest, or exchange box in which to keep desirable objects that students can exchange for their tokens.

Do Not

- Use everyday objects for tokens that can easily be counterfeited, such as marbles or paper clips.
- Use tokens that are so valuable to a particular student that he or she will not enjoy exchanging them for the reward.
- Permit students to stockpile so many tokens that they do not need or want to work or behave anymore.

TEACHER RESOURCE 5.6   Sample Contract for Modified
                           Course Requirements

Dear _____ and _____
           (parents)   (student)

This is to notify you that _____ is having difficulty meeting
the present course requirements of _____ for the following
reasons:

We will make the following modifications, and he/she will be graded according
to how well he/she achieves his/her individual objectives rather than in
comparison to the other students in the course. The semester course
grade will be computed using only the scores obtained after the modifications
have been made. They will reflect the amount of effort and achievement on
_____'s part.

Objectives, Modifications, and Materials

I understand the conditions of this contract and agree to fulfill these objectives
as well as I can

_____ (Student's signature)

I (we) understand the conditions of this contract and grading policies, and
agree to _____'s participation.

_____ (Parent(s) signature)

I (we) agree to help this student reach **these** course objectives by providing
the modifications in materials and techniques listed above. He/She **will be**
graded **on** how **well he/she achieves these** objectives, from this day forward,
and not in comparison **to other students' achievements.**

_____ (Teacher(s) signature)

_____ (Administrator(s) signature)

TEACHER RESOURCE 5.7   Sample Contingency Contract

I, _____ , agree to

_____

_____

_____

_____

_____ .

My teacher, _____ , agrees to _____

_____

_____

_____ .

If I am able to complete this correctly, I will receive _____

_____

_____ .

Teachers _____

_____

_____

Student _____

Parent(s) _____

Administrator _____

Date _____

This contract will be reviewed on _____

TEACHER RESOURCE 5.8   Certificate of Excellence

CERTIFICATE OF EXCELLENCE

PLEASE DEPOSIT _____ POINTS INTO THE ACCOUNT OF

_____

FOR THE WEEK OF _____.

SIGNED BY _____

TEACHER RESOURCE 5.9   Do's and Don'ts of Contingency Contracts

Do

- Indicate the target achievement in detail so everyone clearly knows whether and when it has been achieved.

- Make the contract fair and clear.

- Make the reward come as soon as possible after the task/behavior has been achieved.

- Decide in advance on the date of review and renegotiation of the contract and include this in the written contract.

- Provide each participant with a copy of the contract.

- Have all parties sign the contract.

Do Not

- Allow contracting to become a power struggle.

- Ever initiate a contract when one person is being pushed or forced to comply.

- Begin a contract by giving large rewards; otherwise there is little incentive to work harder.

- Make contracts your entire discipline system.

- Change contracts that are already signed. Instead, draw up a new contract so that it is valid.

- Overuse contracting. Having too many contracts becomes confusing.

TEACHER RESOURCE 5.10 Sample Contract for Modified
Course Requirements

Dear Mr. and Mrs. Holstein and Justin,

This is to notify you that Justin is having difficulty meeting the present course requirements of English literature for the following reasons:

1. He has not turned in his chapter outlines for our first book "Cold Mountain."
2. He did not get a passing grade on the test on "Cold Mountain."
3. He has not yet contributed in our daily class discussions about the book we are reading, which is 25% of the grade.

We will make the following modifications, and he will be graded according to how well he achieves his individual objectives rather than in comparison to the other students in the course. The semester course grade will be computed using only the scores obtained after the modifications have been made. They will reflect the amount of effort and achievement on Justin's part.

Objectives, Modifications, and Materials

1. Justin will be given a study guide to use as he reads with four questions to answer for each chapter. The paragraphs that contain the answers will be highlighted in green in his book. The answers to these study guide questions will take the place of the chapter outlines.
2. Each week Justin will be given a quiz with questions from the chapter that will take the place of the end-of-the-book test.
3. Before each class discussion Justin will submit three questions or statements that relate to the section of the book to be discussed. He will be graded on this instead of class participation.

I understand the conditions of this contract and agree to fulfill these objectives as well as I can

_____ (Student's signature)

We understand the conditions of this contract and grading policies, and agree to Justin's participation.

_____ (Parent(s) signature)

We agree to help Justin reach these course objectives by providing the modifications in materials and techniques listed above. He will be graded on how well he achieves these objectives, from this day forward, and not in comparison to other students' achievements.

_____ (Teacher(s) signature)

_____ (Administrator(s) signature)

TEACHER RESOURCE 5.11   Guidelines for the Use of Punishment

1. Use punishment sparingly. Save it as a last resort.

2. Use punishment only in combination with positive procedures.

3. Be sure that the student dislikes the punishment more than he or she likes the positive consequences of the behavior you are trying to change.

4. Always tell students precisely why they are being punished.

5. Always tell students how they will be punished, how long, and under what circumstances.

6. Describe to students the alternative behaviors that are to replace the punished ones.

7. Describe the reinforcement procedures you will use to help students learn and use the new appropriate behavior.

8. Present maximum intensity of the aversive event from the beginning; otherwise students may slowly become adapted to the aversive consequence.

9. Be sure that punishing a student does not attract the attention of other students. A student's misbehavior is much more difficult to change when he or she has an audience.

10. Discontinue any punishment that is not readily effective and try something else.

11. Phase out the punishment program as soon as you are able to continue teaching.

TEACHER RESOURCE 5.12   Definitions of Time-Out Procedures

Nonexclusionary Time-Out

1. The first level of time-out is removing materials being used inappropriately by a student.

2. A child's chair can be pulled away from a group in which he or she was not behaving well.

3. For mild misbehaviors a child may be required to put down his or her head for a designated period of time.

Observation Time-Out

1. Students are excluded from being involved in the group.

2. Students may, however, still see and hear the activity.

3. Students are allowed access to the information that the other students are receiving.

Exclusionary Time-Out

1. Student is denied access to reinforcement.

2. Student is removed to a screened-off corner of the classroom.

3. Student is not allowed to be a part of the activity for a designated period of time.

4. Students have additional incentive to practice self-control because they are not allowed to participate in the classroom until they do.

Seclusionary Time-Out

1. Misbehaving student is moved completely out of the area.

2. This is often a time-out area.

3. Space must be supervised by a staff member

4. Only used for serious, out-of-control behaviors, such as physical harm to self or others, trashing the room, etc.

TEACHER RESOURCE 5.13   Location for Seclusionary Time-Out

- The room should have appropriate lighting and ventilation, and not be locked.

- The room should be of adequate size and shape (at least 6 × 6 feet in size) to provide comfortable access by the student and staff.

- The room should not be left unmonitored.

- The room should be free of objects that may be potentially hazardous to an aggressive student.

- The floor and walls should be padded or carpeted if the student is likely to be highly aggressive or physically threatening to self and/or others.

- The doorway should be sufficiently large and unobstructed to allow for safe physical passage of the student.

- The time-out room should be

    — away from high-traffic areas
    — away from doors and windows
    — out of other children's view and where the child cannot easily see the rest of the class
    — within the view of the teacher or staff member observing the child during time-out

TEACHER RESOURCE 5.14   What Logs for Time-Out Rooms Should Include

1. The date the student is put into time-out

2. The time the student goes into time-out

3. The behavior that precipitated the time-out

4. The child's behavior during time-out

5. The time the student leaves time-out

6. The staff person responsible for the child during time-out

TEACHER RESOURCE 5.15 **Time-Out Log**

Student _____

Supervisor _____

Date	Time In	Time Out	Behavior Before t-out	Behavior During t-out

TEACHER RESOURCE 5.16   Do's and Don'ts of the Time-Out Procedure

Do

- Begin by selecting a specific misbehavior and explain to the student the behavior you would like to see instead.

- Gather information on how often and under what circumstances this misbehavior is occurring.

- Choose the type of time-out that works best for the student.

- Obtain parents' informed consent before placing their child in a time-out room.

- Clearly define time-out procedures to the child before implementing.

- Explain expectations and post them for readers in the time-out areas.

- Do "practice" sessions when the child is not in crisis.

- Reinforce positive behaviors that occur after a time-out.

- Use time-out consistently for effectiveness.

- Time-out is most effective when used throughout the school.

- Use time-out before student loses control.

Do Not

- Use time-out sporadically or without first thinking it out carefully.

- Permit the student to talk or interact with others during time-out. This interferes with the punishment.

- Comment on or discuss the offender's inappropriate behavior when he or she returns from completing a time-out. This would be doubling the punishment.

- Use time-out with a student if it is ineffective. Some children are not able to accept the conditioning.

- Slowly increase the amount of time the student must serve in time-out; otherwise the student becomes acclimated to the time-out, and it loses its punishing power.

- Time-out is contraindicated if it frightens the student. Educators are not in the business of terrorizing children.

- Overuse time-out. Any procedure used too often loses its effectiveness.

TEACHER RESOURCE 6.1   Modification Suggestions

Student _____

Grade

Date

Class Assignments

_____   Allow extended time, as needed

_____   Allow use of highlighted textbooks

_____   Reduce amount of written work

_____   Give written instructions on paper

_____   Give written instructions on the board

_____   Give alternatives to written work (e.g., oral or taped answers, drawings, projects)

_____   Encourage computer word processing

_____   Provide peer tutor

Tests

_____   Allow unlimited number of retakes

_____   Permit use of self-prepared notes during tests

_____   Require test to be completed as much as possible from memory, then allow student to use sources to go over the test again in another color pen *for effort credit*

_____   Provide tape recorder for oral answers

_____   Allow answers to be written on test (instead of using bubble sheet or punch check)

_____   Allow tests to be taken in quiet room with no distractions, or in special education room

_____   Provide individualized test that is rewritten and modified (simplified language, etc.)

_____   Arrange a study session with the student at an agreed-upon time

_____   Design an extra-credit option: student shares information learned that is not on the test

_____   Allow extended time

_____   Provide test read-alouds

_____   Offer the services of a scribe to record student responses

_____   Provide a vocabulary list for fill-in-blank or essay tests

_____   Shorten lists for matching choices

_____   Permit the use of review guides directly related to test questions

Lesson Presentations

_____   Provide note taker

_____   Provide visual aids to supplement lecture

_____   Write notes on the board

_____   Provide written, along with oral, instructions

_____   Check student's comprehension regularly

_____   Ask student to review key points orally

_____   Provide incentives for attentiveness (such as seating choice, passes, privileges, points)

_____   Allow in-class assistance from special services

_____   Reduce distractions; seat student at front of class

_____   Increase incentives to work on assignments during work time

_____   Seat student near positive role model

_____   Provide student with extra set of books for home

_____   Allow student to turn in assignments to teacher's mailbox

_____   Provide extra work sheets for in-class folder

_____   Assign peer tutor

_____   Provide a written weekly schedule of lesson plans and assignments

_____   Make eye contact prior to directions/instructions

_____   Implement behavioral contracts

_____   Use cues to keep student on task

_____   Look for signs of stress; provide encouragement or reduced work-load

_____   Send notes home to parents

_____   Provide alternative work space

_____   Look for signs of agitation; use strategies to avoid anger-related problems

_____   Praise specific behaviors

Special Considerations

_____   Make accommodations for special dietary needs

_____   Allow extra time between classes

_____   Adapt physical education requirements

_____   Allow student to move about or stand as appropriate when necessary

TEACHER RESOURCE 6.2 Learning How to Learn

Student's Name: _____

Strategy	Knows	Emerging	Not Yet
Can organize own learning environment			
Uses good time-management skills			
Previews content before reading/studying			
Attends to important information			
Has adequate test-taking skills			
Predicts important consequences			
Takes notes in a useful manner			
Summarizes what was learned			
Understands and remembers vocabulary			
Remembers what was learned			
Uses various forms of reference materials			
Finds relationships between old and new			
Transfers learning to other situations			
Works and learns independently			
Evaluates own performance			
Asks for help when needed			

TEACHER RESOURCE 6.3   Routine Attention-Getters for Use in the Classroom

- Flick the lights or just turn them off until all students are listening
- Stand in the directions/teaching part of the room
- Stand directly in front of students who need cueing that it's time to listen
- Place a stop sign or picture of an ear on the overhead projector
- Place one finger in front of your lips and wait until all students do the same
- Raise your hand when you need a turn to speak and have other students do the same
- Clap your hands three times
- Ring a bell
- Begin singing or chanting a choral response
- Use the time-out symbol from sports

TEACHER RESOURCE 6.4   Classroom Behavior Checklist

Teacher: _____

School:_____   Student _____

Class/Grade: _____   Date: _____

_____ 1. Complies with simple directions

_____ 2. Works without disrupting or bothering peers

_____ 3. Engages in social/recreational activities at appropriate time

_____ 4. Modifies behavior when given verbal feedback

_____ 5. Reacts appropriately to changes in routine

_____ 6. Uses time appropriately between activities

_____ 7. Locates personal possessions and returns them to appropriate location.

_____ 8. Locates class materials and puts them away when finished

_____ 9. Goes to various areas in the room when asked

_____ 10. Makes transition from one activity to the next

_____ 11. Follows general rules and routines established in classroom

Key

I = Independent
P = Needs prompting
0 = Cannot do

TEACHER RESOURCE 6.5   ABC Observation Form

Student: _____   Grade: _____

Year in school: _____

Date of observation: _____

Task or activity: _____

Behavior of interest: _____

Antecedent	Behavior	Consequence

TEACHER RESOURCE 6.6   Intervention Strategies Checklist

_____ 1. Observe behavior carefully. Define the behavior so that others can also know what behavior you are concerned about.

_____ 2. Use the ABC Observation Form to record the antecedents and consequences of the problem behavior.

_____ 3. Choose a behavioral technique to modify the problem and intervene early. (Is the curriculum, schedule, or reinforcements to blame?)

_____ 4. Set consequences to help the student behave positively; set consequences to help the student not behave negatively.

_____ 5. Involve others as needed:

   _____ Call in other teachers

   _____ Call in the parents

   _____ Call in school psychologists

   _____ Call in social workers

   _____ Call in the principal

   _____ Call in community support services

TEACHER RESOURCE 6.7   School Phobic Treatment Must Be Progressive

- When refusal is recent and sudden—Return student *immediately* to school.

- When absences are long—Practice *gradual desensitization*.

- When school refusal is chronic—Seek high level of home–school cooperation.

TEACHER RESOURCE 6.8   Gifted and Talented Programming

- Continual skill assessment

- Self-paced, mastery-based curriculum

- Talent assessment

- Parent involvement

- Instructional strategies that teach and challenge higher-level thinking

- Radical acceleration of coursework

- Mentorships

- Independent research and discovery

- Cross grade-level grouping

- Individualized educational planning

TEACHER RESOURCE 6.9   Functional Reading Vocabulary Words for Children with Cognitive Disabilities

Stop	Go	Enter	Girls
Up	Dynamite	School	Boys
Slow down	Down	Explosives	School bus
Flood area	Men	Fire	No trespassing
Off	Women	Fire escape	Private property
On	Exit	Poison	Men working
Cold	Entrance	Wet paint	Yield
Hot	Danger	Police	Railroad crossing
In	Be careful	Keep off	Telephone
Out	Caution	Watch for children	Slippery
PG13	Bus stop	Danger	Exit only
Restaurant	High voltage	Food	Water
Under 17 not admitted		Caution	Blind driveway

TEACHER RESOURCE 6.10 Tips to Help Students Who Are Poor or Homeless

- Find places in the classroom where it is safe to store special items that the student may want for school but does not need immediately.

- Be sure that the student has access to a good quiet study area at school where he or she can do assignments.

- Collaborate with parents or guardians, shelter workers, social service agencies, etc.

- Give the student some control over his or her learning, such as allowing the student to make some choices about what he or she wants to learn and how and when the learning will proceed.

- Make learning meaningful and fun!

TEACHER RESOURCE 6.11　　Interventions for Students at Risk for School Failure

- Develop tasks with the child that pique his or her interest.
- Use students' natural curiosity to motivate them.
- Give students more control over what they learn and how they learn it.
- Have students work collaboratively with other students.
- Establish peers as teaching partners so students can teach and learn from each other's experiences.
- Seek collaboration with other helping professionals while working closely with parents or other caregivers.
- Refer student who presents symptoms and signs of alcohol or drug abuse to an AODA Wellness program.

TEACHER RESOURCE 6.12   Signs of Possible Neglect or Abuse

Possible Indicators of Physical Neglect

- Underfed or constantly hungry
- Begging or stealing food
- Slow growth rate
- Frequent or constant uncleanliness
- Frequent or constant fatigue
- Unattended medical needs
- Lack of supervision
- Poor school attendance
- Drug or alcohol problems

Possible Indicators of Physical Abuse

- Unexplained bruises or welts
- Unexplained burns
- Unexplained fractures
- Unexplained cuts or scrapes
- Unexplained stomach injuries
- Unexplained visual or hearing defects
- Human bite marks
- Fear of adults
- Overly aggressive or withdrawn
- Frightened of parents
- Afraid to go home
- School problems

Possible Indicators of Sexual Abuse

- Difficulty in walking or sitting
- Pain or itching around genitals
- Stomachaches
- Bed-wetting
- Sleep problems
- Depression or withdrawn behavior
- Poor peer relationships
- Sudden onset of behavior problems
- Unusual knowledge of or interest in sex

TEACHER RESOURCE 6.13   Signs of Possible Alcohol or Drug Abuse

Overall School Performance:

- Changes in school attendance
- Decrease in schoolwork production
- Falling grades
- Detachment from other students
- Disinterest in anything at school, especially former involvement with clubs, sports, or groups

Physical Signs of Drug or Alcohol Abuse

- Poor grooming
- Red and/or wet eyes
- Sleepiness or overactivity
- Dilation or contraction of pupils
- Disorientation

Behaviors in Students Heavily Involved in Drugs or Alcohol

- Change of friends
- Increased paranoia
- Secreting of possessions
- Ambiguous information about activities and whereabouts
- Association with new friends known to be drug or alcohol users
- Stealing and theft
- Borrowing money constantly
- Possession or obsession with drug paraphernalia

TEACHER RESOURCE 7.1 SHOT Test of Multisensory Teaching

To administer the SHOT test, take any lesson you have planned and evaluate whether it uses all three senses:

1. **S**eeing or visual modality

2. **H**earing or auditory modality

3. **T**ouching or manipulative modality

TEACHER RESOURCE 7.2   Skill Graph

Subject _____   Class _____

Date _____   Teacher _____

Skill _____

Student's Name	Yes	No	Student's Name	Yes	No

TEACHER RESOURCE 7.3   Marking and Scoring an Informal Reading Inventory

Example reading passage: If you find him, let him go.

Marking the Inventory

0 = omitted a word   (If you find ____, let him go.)

S.C. = self-corrected   (Don't count a self-correction as wrong.)

N.R. = not read   (Name the word after 5 seconds)

~ = transposed words   (If you find him, let <u>go him</u>.)

^ = added a word: (If you find him, <u>then</u> let him go.)

Scoring the Inventory

Independent reading level = word recognition of 96%–99% correct and comprehension of 75%–90% correct

Instructional reading level = word recognition of 92%–95% correct and comprehension of 60%–65% correct

Frustration reading level = word recognition of 90% or less correct and comprehension of less than 60% correct

TEACHER RESOURCE 7.4   Reading Comprehension Questions

Student's name _____

Date tested_____

Tested by _____

1. Please explain the title of the story. _____

_____

_____

2. What was the topic of the story?

_____

_____

3. Can you order the story in detail?

_____

_____

4. Can you draw any conclusions about the story?

_____

_____

5. Can you think of examples of explain cause and effect in the story?

_____

_____

6. Did the story have a moral?

_____

_____

TEACHER RESOURCE 7.5   Writing Assessment

Student's name _____ –

Date tested _____

Tested by _____

Scoring scale: N = Not yet, D = Developing, A = Achieved

Handwriting

_____ Legible in manuscript

_____ Legible in cursive

_____ Correctly copies sentences from board

_____ Correctly copies sentences from book

Spelling

_____ Correctly spells phonetically regular words

_____ Correctly spells phonetically irregular words

Punctuation

_____ Capitalizes at beginning of sentences

_____ Capitalizes proper nouns

_____ Period, question mark, exclamation used correctly

Vocabulary

_____ Effective word choice

_____ Usage

_____ Mechanics

Content

_____ Organization

_____ Purpose

_____ Development of idea

_____ Communicates with audience

Sentence structure

_____   Complete sentences

_____   Constructed effectively

Paragraph structure

_____   Topic sentence

_____   Ideas developed

_____   Well organized

Creativity

_____   Novelty of ideas

_____   Captivates

_____   Unusual plot

Functional writing

_____   Meaning is clear

TEACHER RESOURCE 7.6   Problem-Solving Steps

1. *Read and understand.*   The student studies the problem to ascertain what is sought.

2. *Use correct operation.*   The student develops an action strategy for solving the problem.

3. *Organize facts.*   The student organizes the information given in the problem.

4. *Compute answer.*   The student selects and applies the correct computational operation.

5. *Check answer.*   The teacher evaluates the answer for correctness and reasonableness.

TEACHER RESOURCE 7.7   Clustering Mathematical Errors

1. *Guessing error.* These errors often lack logical quality, indicating a lack of basic understanding of the processes or skills being assessed.

2. *Place value error.* This cluster of errors shows that the student has little understanding of place value or of the arithmetic steps to show it.

3. *Wrong operation error.* These errors result when the student either performs the wrong operation by ignoring the sign or changes the process of one or more of the computation steps, and creating a different algorithm that results in an incorrect answer.

4. *Omission error.* This cluster of errors is indicated when a student leaves out a step in the process or leaves out a part of the answer. An omission error differs from a process substitution error in that it results in an incomplete rather than different algorithm.

5. *Directional error.* These errors result when the steps of the computation are performed in the wrong direction and/or order even though the operations are performed correctly.

6. *Placement error.* These errors result in wrong answers because the numbers are written in the wrong place even though the computations are often correct.

TEACHER RESOURCE 7.8   Portfolios

To be filled out by the student:

Name: _____

Date: _____

Name/title of product: _____

_____

Description of product:_____

_____

_____

_____

_____

Why did you choose to include this product in your portfolio? _____

_____

_____

_____

_____

How does this product demonstrate that your schoolwork is improving? ____

_____

_____

_____

_____

To be filled out by the parent/guardian/caregiver:

How did your child share information about this product with you? _____

_____

_____

How did you acknowledge/celebrate your child's progress? _____

_____

_____

Student's signature: _____

Parent's/Guardian's signature: _____

Please give this form to your child to return to school. Thank you!

TEACHER RESOURCE 7.9 Individualized Student English Contract

This contract will coordinate the articulation agreements that have been made between Mrs. Miller, instructor, and Josh Harding, the student, for the 2002 fall quarter grade.

Minimum requirements to earn a C:
(You may choose, and are encouraged, to earn more than a C.)

- Attendance: no more than 3 unexcused absences a quarter.
- Complete all assignments before November 10th.
- Earn a passing grade of 75% on all grammar quizzes and make all corrections.

		Quiz Scores	
_____	2 pen pal letters	_____	Quiz 1
_____	2 group writing projects	_____	Quiz 2
_____	4 short stories written successfully according to rubric	_____	Quiz 3

Minimum requirements to earn a B:

- Assume a group leadership role 3 times during writing lab.
- Attendance: no more than 2 unexcused absences a quarter.
- Complete all assignments before November 10th.
- Earn a grade of at least 85% on all grammar quizzes and make all corrections.

		Quiz Scores	
_____	2 pen pal Letters	_____	Quiz 1
_____	3 group writing projects	_____	Quiz 2
_____	5 short stories written successfully according to rubric	_____	Quiz 3

Minimum requirements to earn an A:

- Assume a group leadership role regularly during writing lab.
- Coordinate group materials/units and assist another student with project.
- Attendance: no unexcused absences.
- Complete all assignments on time, with an above-average group evaluation.
- Earn a grade of at least 95% on all grammar quizzes and make all corrections.

Quiz Scores

_____ 　2 pen pal Letters　　　　　　　_____ Quiz 1

_____ 　4 group writing projects　　　　_____ Quiz 2

_____ 　6 short stories written　　　　　_____ Quiz 3
　　　　　successfully according to rubric

Student's signature: _____　Date: _____

Grade contracted for: _____ 　Signature of teacher: _____

TEACHER RESOURCE 8.1   Tips to Help Teachers Find Their Way Politically

- Find spaces in the school where you can feel relaxed and safe to talk without having individuals overhear your conversation and misconstrue your meaning out of context.

- Find people you can trust and talk to. You may want to talk to one person about personal issues, to another person about political issues, and to yet another person about curricular information.

- Find out which people are good with kids and see whether you can enlist their support for your students. You may know a custodian who is great with a certain type of student and who will help, or a coach or art teacher who might befriend a student whose needs you cannot meet.

- Encourage your school to encourage and be supportive of its staff and the need for all to collaborate.

- Make sure the staff at your school knows who you are. Be visible.

TEACHER RESOURCE 8.2   Testing Your Political Awareness of the Educational System

1. How does the Secretary of Education get his or her job? _____

    _____

2. What three contentious issues face your school and your district in the next year? _____

    _____

3. Do you have an approach for handling sensitive issues that come up in your classroom? _____

    _____

4. Are you aware of the political issues in your school district? What are they? Have you ever gone to a school district meeting? _____

    _____

5. Who is your school district superintendent? How is he or she regarded?

    _____

6. How do you handle yourself in teachers' meetings? How would other teachers describe you? Outspoken? Quiet? Nonparticipatory? _____

    _____

7. Do you know your principal? What is his or her management style? ___

    _____

8. How active is your local PTO or PTA? _____

    _____

9. What are the political issues important to your teachers' union? _____

    _____

10. Are you presently paying for union membership through your paycheck? What benefits do you receive?

    _____

Bibliography

Airasian, P. W. (2001). *Classroom assessment concepts and applications.* Boston: McGraw-Hill.

Alberta, P. A., & Troutman, A. C. (1999). *Applied behavior analysis.* Upper Saddle River, NJ: Prentice Hall.

Algozzine, B., & Kay, P. (2002). *Preventing problem behaviors.* Thousand Oaks, CA: Corwin Press.

Bender, M., & Valletutti, P. C. (1990). *Teaching functional academics.* Austin, TX: Pro-Ed.

Bernsteen, D., & Farber, E. (1997). *Language and communication disorders in children.* Boston: Allyn & Bacon.

Bigge, J. L., & Stump, C. S. (1999). *Curriculum, assessment and instruction for students with disabilities.* Belmont, CA: Wadsworth Publishing.

Bodine, R., Crawford, D., & Schrumpf, F. (1994). *Creating the peaceable school: A comprehensive program for teaching conflict resolution.* Champaign, IL: Research Press.

Bos, C. S., & Vaughn, S. (2002). *Strategies for teaching students with learning and behavior problems.* Boston: Allyn & Bacon.

Brophy, J. F. (1997). *Motivating students to learn.* New York: McGraw-Hill.

Canfield, J. (2000). *101 ways to improve self-esteem.* Boston: Allyn & Bacon.

Campbell, D. (1993). *100 ways to use sound in learning.* Tucson, AZ: Zephyr Press.

Campbell, D., & Brewer, C. (1992). *Rhythms for Learning.* Tucsan, AZ: Zephyr Press.

Carnine, O., Silbert, J., & Kameenui, E. J. (1990). *Direct instruction reading.* Columbus, OH: Merrill/Macmillan.

Cavey, D. W. (2000). *Dysgraphia: Why Johnny can't write.* Austin, TX: Pro-Ed.

Charles, C. M. (1996). *Building classroom discipline.* White Plains, NY: Longman.

Clark, B. (1992). *Growing up gifted: Developing the potential of children at home and school* (4th ed.). New York: Merrill/Macmillan.

Coleman, M. C., & Webber, J. (2002). *Emotional and behavioral disorders: Theory and practice* (pp. 189–192, 243–244). Boston: Allyn & Bacon.

Cox, J., & Daniel, N. (1985). *Educating able learners.* Austin, TX: University of Texas Press.

Cunningham, C. (1996). *Understanding Down syndrome: An introduction for parents.* Cambridge, MA: Brookline Books.

Daniel, N., & Cox, J. (1988). *Flexible pacing for able learners.* Reston, VA: Council for Exceptional Children.

Davis, G. A., & Rimm, S. B. (1998). *Education of the gifted and talented* (4th ed.). Boston: Allyn & Bacon.

Diamond, M., & Hopson, J. (1998). *Magic trees of the mind: How to nurture your child's intelligence, creativity, and healthy emotions from birth through adolescence.* New York: Dutton.

Dixon, B., & Engelmann, S. (1979). *Corrective spelling through morographs.* Chicago: Science Research Associates.

Dowdy, C. A., Patton, J. R., Smith, T. E. C., & Polloway, F. (1997). *Attention-deficit! hyperactivity disorder in the classroom: A practical guide for teachers.* Austin, TX: Pro-Ed.

Doyle, T. (1991). *Why is everybody always picking on me? A guide to handling bullies.* Middlebury, VT: Atrium Society Publications.

ERIC Clearinghouse on Disabilities and Gifted Education. (1996, spring). Beginning reading and phonological awareness for students with learning disabilities. *Teaching Exceptional Children, 28*(3), 78–79.

Fowler, C. L., & Davis, M. (1985). The storyframe approach: A tool for improving reading comprehension. *Teaching Exceptional Children, 17,* 296–298.

Fowler, M. (1992). *CH.A.D.D. educators manual: Attention deficit disorders.* Plantation, FL: Children and Adults with Attention Deficit Disorders.

Fowler, M. (1999). *Maybe you know my kid: A parent's guide to identifying, understanding, and helping your child with ADHD* (3rd ed.). New York: Birch Lane Press.

Frost, J. A., & Emery, M. J. (1995, August). Academic interventions for children with dyslexia who have phonological core deficits (*ERIC Digest* E539). Reston, VA: ERIC Clearinghouse on Disabilities and Gifted Education. (ERIC Document Reproduction Service No. ED 385 095).

Gable, R. A., & Warren, S. F. (Eds.). (1993). *Strategies for teaching students with mild to severe mental retardation.* Baltimore: Paul H. Brookes.

Garrity, C., Jens, K., Porter, W, Sager, N., & Short-Cammilli, C. (1994). *Bully-proofing your school: A comprehensive approach for elementary schools.* Longmont, CO: Sopris West.

Goldstein, A., & Conoley, J. C. (1997). *School violence intervention: A practical handbook.* New York: The Guilford Press.

Gordon, S. B., & Asher, M. J. (1994). *Meeting the ADD challenge: A practical guide for teachers.* Champaign, IL: Research Press.

Goswami, U., & Bryant, P. (1990). *Phonological skills and learning to read.* Mahwah, NJ: Lawrence Erlbaum.

Grandin, T. (1996). *Thinking in pictures: And other reports from my life with autism.* New York: Vintage Books.

Grapes, B. J. (2000). *School violence.* San Diego, CA: Greenhaven Press.

Graves, M. (1989). *The teacher's idea book: Planning around key experiences.* Ypsylanti, MI: High Scope.

Greene, R. W. (1995). Students with ADHD in school classrooms: Teacher factors related to compatibility, assessment and intervention. *School Psychology Review, 24,* 81–93.

Griffith, P. L., & Olson, M. W. (1992). Phonemic awareness helps beginning readers break the code. *Reading Teacher, 45(7),* 516–523.

Hallahan, D. P., & Kauffman, J. M. (2000). *Exceptional learners.* Boston: Allyn & Bacon.

Halsted, J. W. (1994). *Some of my best friends are books: Guiding gifted readers.* Scottsdale, AZ: Gifted Psychology Press.

Harrington, K. (1998). *For parents and professionals: Autism.* East Moline, IL: Lingui Systems.

Harrington, K. (2000). *For parents and professionals: Autism in adolescents and adults.* East Moline, IL: Lingui Systems.

Hartman, D. (1987). *Motivating the unmotivated: A practical guide for parents and teachers to help them help teenagers through the tough years.* Lakeland, FL: Valley Hill.

Humphries, T. (1992). Learning American sign language. Englewood Cliffs, NJ: Prentice Hall.

Jenson, W. R., Sloane, H. N., & Young, K. R. (1988). *Applied behavior analysis in education: A structured teaching approach.* Englewood Cliffs, NJ: Prentice Hall.

Kids of survival: Real-life lessons in resilience. (1998). *Reaching Today's Youth: The Community Circle of Caring Journal, 2(3).*

Kremer, B., & Farnum, M. (1985). Dropouts, Absentee and Illinois Education Policy. *Illinois Association for Counseling and Development Quarterly, 97,* 19–26.

Levine, M. (1993). *All kinds of minds.* Cambridge, MA: Educators Publishing.

Lieberman, A. (1998). *Active learning.* New York: The Brain Shop; Longmont, CO: Sopris West.

Long, N. J., & Morse, W. C. (1996). *Conflict in the classroom.* Austin, TX: Pro-Ed.

Lovitt, T. C. (1995). *Tactics for teaching.* Englewood Cliffs, NJ: Prentice Hall.

Maheady, L., Harper, G. F., & Sacca, M. K. (1988). Peer-mediated instruction: A promising approach to meeting the diverse needs of LD adolescents. *Learning Disability Quarterly, 11,* 108–113.

Mandel, H. P., & Marcus, S. L. (1996). *Could do better: Why children underachieve and what to do about it.* New York: John Wiley & Sons.

Matson, J. L. (Ed.). (1990). *Handbook of behavior modification with the mentally retarded* (2nd ed.). New York: Plenum.

McBride-Chang, C. (1995). What is phonological awareness? *Journal of Educational Psychology, 87(2),* 179–192.

McCarney, S. B., & Bauer, A. M. (1995). *The learning disability intervention manual.* Columbia, MO: Hawthorne.

McCormick, L., Loeb, D. F., & Schiefelbusch, R. L. (1997). *Supporting children with communication difficulties in inclusive settings.* Boston: Allyn & Bacon.

McDonnell, J., Wilcox, B., & Hardman, M. L. (1991). *Secondary programs for students with developmental disabilities.* Boston: Allyn & Bacon.

Molnar, A., & Lindquist, B. (1989). *Changing problem behavior in schools.* San Francisco: Jossey-Bass.

Nadeau, K. (1998). *Help4ADD@high school.* New York: Advantage Press.

National School Safety Center. (1989). *Set straight on bullies.* Westlake Village, CA: Author.

Nowicki, S., & Duke, M. P. (1992). *Helping the child who doesn't fit in.* Atlanta, GA: Peachtree Publishing.

Obiakor, F. E. (2001). *It happens in "good" schools.* Thousand Oaks, CA: Corwin Press.

O'Connor, R., Jenkins, J., Slocum, K., & Leicester, N. (1993). Teaching phonemic manipulation skills to children with learning handicaps: Rhyming, blending, and segmenting. *Exceptional Children, 59,* 532–546.

Oelwein, P. (1995). *Teaching reading to children with down syndrome: A guide for parents and teachers.* Rockville, MD: Woodbine House.

Oldrieve, R. N. (1997). Success with reading and spelling: Students internalize words through structured lessons. *Teaching Exceptional Children, 29(4),* 57–64.

Quill, K. (1995). *Teaching children with autism: Strategies to enhance communication and socialization.* Albany, NY: Delmar Publishing.

Raffini, J. P. (1994). *Winners without losers: Structures and strategies for increasing student motivation to learn.* Boston: Allyn & Bacon.

Rankin, L. (1991). The handmade alphabet. Pittsburgh, PA: Dial.

Reeve, R. E. (1990). ADHD: Facts and fallacies. *Intervention in School and Clinic, 26,* 70–76.

Repp, A. C., & Horner, R. H. (1999). *Functional analysis problem behavior.* Belmont, CA: Wadsworth.

Rhodes, W. C. (1967). The disturbing child: A problem of ecological management. *Exceptional Children, 33,* 449–455.

Rhodes, W. C. (1970). *Exceptional Children, 36,* 309–314.

Rice, M. L., Wilcox, K., & Bruce, B. (1996). *Building a language—Focused curriculum for the preschool classroom.* Baltimore: Paul H. Brookes.

Richard, G. J. (1997). *The Source for Autism.* East Moline, IL: Lingui Systems.

Richards, R. G. (1998). *The writing dilemma: Understanding dysgraphia.* Riverside, CA: RET Center Press.

Rief, S. (1993). *How to reach and teach ADD/ADHD children.* West Nyack, NY: Center for Applied Research in Education.

Rief, S. F. (1998). *The ADD/ADHD checklist: An easy reference for parents and teachers.* New York: Prentice Hall.

Robinson, G. A., & Polloway, E. A. (Eds.). (1987). *Best practices in mental disabilities* (Vol. 1). Des Moines, IA: Iowa State Department of Education, Bureau of Special Education.

Ross-Flanagan, N. (1995, June 14). *Learning to live—and succeed—with attention deficit disorder.* Saint Paul Pioneer Press, p. E8.

Rutherford, R., Nelson, C. M., & Wolford, B. (1986). Special education programming in juvenile corrections. *Remedial and Special Education, 7,* 27–33.

Salend, S. J. (1998). *Creating inclusive classrooms.* Upper Saddle River, NJ: Prentice Hall.

Sanders, M. G. (2000). *Schooling students placed at risk.* Mahwah, NJ: Lawrence Erlbaum.

Schloss, P. J., & Sedlak, R. A. (1982). Behavioral features of the mentally retarded adolescent: Implications for mainstreamed educators. *Psychology in the Schools, 19,* 98–105.

Schmitz, C. C., & Galbraith, J. (1985). *Managing the social and emotional needs of the gifted: A teacher's survival guide.* Minneapolis, MN: Free Spirit.

Schmuck, R. A., & Schmuck, P. A. (2001). *Group process in the classroom.* Boston: McGraw-Hill.

Schultz, J. B., Carpenter, C. D., & Turnbull, A. C. (1991). *Main-streaming exceptional students: A guide for classroom teachers* (3rd ed.). Boston: Allyn & Bacon.

Schulze, C. B. (1993). *When snow turns to rain.* Bethesda, MD: Woodbine House.

Schwartz, S., & Miller, J. E. (1996). *New language of toys: Teaching communication skills to children with special needs.* Bethesda, MD: Woodbine House.

Shalom, D. B. (1984). *Special kids make special friends.* Bellmore, NY: Association for Children with Down Syndrome.

Shore, K. (1998). *Special kids problem solver.* Paramus, NJ: Prentice Hall.

Silver, L. (1998). *The misunderstood child: Understanding and coping with your child's learning disabilities* (3rd ed.). New York: Time Books.

Smith, R. (Ed.). (1993). *Children with mental retardation: A parents' guide.* Bethesda, MD: Woodbine House.

Sousa, D. A. (2001). *How the special needs brain learns* (2nd ed.). Thousand Oaks, CA: Corwin Press.

Stone, P. (1988). *Blueprint for developing conversational competence.* Washington, DC: Alexander Graham Bell.

Swanson, H. L. (1999). *Interventions for students with learning disabilities: A meta-analysis of treatment outcomes.* New York: The Guilford Press.

Tabors, P. O. (1997). *One child, two languages.* Baltimore: Paul H. Brookes.

Trainer, M. (1991). *Differences in common: Straight talk on mental retardation, down syndrome, and life.* Rockville, MD: Woodbine House.

Treffinger, D. (1986). *Blending gifted education with the total school program.* East Aurora, NY: D.O.K.

Walker, H. (1999). The present unwrapped: Change and challenge in the field of behavioral disorders. *Behavioral Disorders, 24*(4), 293–304.

Weber, K. (1982). *The teacher is the key.* Denver, CO: Love.

Wicks-Nelson, R., & Israel, A. C. (2000). *Behavior disorders of childhood.* Upper Saddle River, NJ: Prentice Hall.

Winebrenner, S. (1996). *Teaching kids with learning difficulties in the regular classroom.* Minneapolis, MN: Free Spirit.

Wink, L. W. (2001). Have you helped a teacher today? *Parade Magazine,* 26 August, p. 4.

Wlodkowski, R. J., & Jaynes, J. H. (1990). *Eager to learn: Helping children become motivated and love learning.* San Francisco: Jossey-Bass.

Wunderlich, K. C. (1988). *The teacher's guide to behavioral interventions: Intervention strategies for behavior problems in the educational environment.* Columbia, MO: Hawthorne Educational Services.

Zeigler Dendy, C. A. (1995). *Teenagers with ADD: A parents' guide.* Bethesda, MD: Woodbine House.

Index